Border Crossings

With special thanks to

PUBALI BANK LIMITED
ঐতিহ্যের পথ বেয়ে অর্থনৈতিক অগ্রগতি
www.pubalibangla.com

Border Crossings

My Journey as a Western Muslim

Mohammad Tufael Chowdhury

unbound

First published in 2021

Unbound

TC Group, Level 1, Devonshire House,

One Mayfair Place, London W1J 8AJ

www.unbound.com

Text design by Ellipsis, Glasgow

A CIP record for this book is available from the British Library

ISBN 978-1-78352-969-8 (trade hbk)
ISBN 978-1-78352-970-4 (ebook)

Printed in Great Britain by CPI Group (UK)

1 3 5 7 9 8 6 4 2

For Rehana

Contents

Prologue

Heathrow Airport, London

'Good morning, Sir. Could you step aside please? I would like to ask you a few questions.'

'Sure,' I reply, rubbing the tiredness out of my eyes, putting up no resistance to the familiar drill.

My questioner is evidently a government official undertaking extra surveillance following yesterday's terrorist alerts. I found out about the elevated security at London's airports on BBC News before boarding the crowded British Airways flight fourteen hours ago.

'Where are you arriving from today, Sir?'

'Dhaka. Bangladesh,' I add, thinking that the sun must be setting there about now.

'And what were you doing in Bangladesh, Sir?' he says with a monotonous drone, leafing through my passport at the same time.

'I was there on holiday, visiting relatives.'

I look over the thin-framed, wispy-haired officer as he begins to examine my documents. His drab suit matches the grey, speckled carpet of Terminal 4's arrivals hall. Passengers silently weave through orderly queues, some speaking in muffled voices and others looking subdued from jet lag, a total contrast to the cacophony of loudspeaker announcements and disorganisation of Dhaka Airport. Where Heathrow's carpets snuffle out noise, the gritty wheels of roller bags and lopsided trolleys click-clack across Dhaka Airport's cracked-up tiles. Back in the first-world silence of the UK, I am missing the homely untidiness of Bangladesh: the vibrant colours, humid smells and incessant raising of voices. From his tired attire I cannot determine whether the officer is from the Metropolitan Police or British Intelligence. He has a kind, bedraggled-looking and spotty face. The thinning hair on his head is longer at the sides than on top.

The blemishes on the maroon cover of my British passport include a crease that runs all the way down it, like a white-water spring descending a craggy Alpine mountain. The officer turns the pages with care, separating the leaves with meticulously shaped fingernails. His professionalism and duty to care momentarily cushion me from the cold reality of my travel experiences today, littered as they are with an incessant amount of scrutiny and suspicion over who I am, and why I am travelling. He too asks me about my reasons for travelling so much, about my family origins and, in particular, about my frequent visits to the Middle East.

'I work for an international consulting firm and am involved in a number of assignments around the world, so I have to fly around frequently. Plus I travel a lot personally too, especially to the Middle East and Asia.'

'What about the trips to Syria, Sir, and to Lebanon, and Jordan? Were these for business also?'

As he poses the question, I catch him noticing the gold British Airways frequent-flyer identification tag dangling from the strap of my knapsack. He cannot tell that I went to the West Bank last year, since at the conclusion of a nine-hour ordeal at the border crossing, I'd requested the Israeli authorities not to put a stamp in my passport but to do so on a blank sheet of paper instead. Whilst his questioning is thorough, it is nowhere near as forensic as the Israelis', whose methods are purposeful and meticulous, full of mind games. I don't mention the West Bank trip.

'Mostly those were holiday trips. One trip to Jordan was for business.' I wince at the memory of that awful meeting in Amman some months ago when the executive we were negotiating with walked out of a heated session.

'Do you have any particular reason for spending so much time in the Middle East?'

'I am learning Arabic and like going to the region to practise. And I go to Saudi Arabia from time to time to perform the Muslim pilgrimage at Makkah.'

I feel a desire to get this questioning over with, and to get out of Heathrow and make my way into London.

'Where were your parents born?' the officer asks.

'My parents,' I repeat back, looking at the officer but mumbling the words under my breath.

Since childhood I have been forced to deal with such inquiries, a necessary evil these days for many Muslims who travel a lot, their privilege of anonymity in travel temporarily withdrawn. As time has gone on, I have developed my techniques to a point where I can confidently challenge, when needed.

'You don't really need to know where my parents were born, do you?' I reply, nodding my head gently in the direction of my passport, the Queen's coat of arms showing proudly on its cover.

I am employing the same tactic I used successfully when stopped in Milan's Linate Airport a few weeks ago, but that was with a smiling and casual Italian immigration officer who looked like he just wanted to practise his English. Today, I fear I've made an error of judgement by challenging this man barely a few weeks after the 7/7 terrorist attacks in London. The officer looks back at me, speechless, and as the seconds tick by, I wonder what will happen now.

'Have a good day, Sir,' he smiles back.

I wheel my suitcase up the ramp towards the Heathrow Express and wonder whether I can reach the canteen in South Bank before they stop serving lunch. It is 12:08. If the Bakerloo Line is running OK, I can just make it.

One

British, Not Western

I was born and raised in Britain but it wasn't till I was in my mid-thirties that I was referred to as a Westerner. Surprising you might say, given that as a child I spoke English with a perfectly formed middle-class accent, at Oxford University I wrote compelling essays on the values of liberal democracy, and I started my career at a blue-blooded consulting firm founded during the Victorian pomp of Imperialist Britain. Despite the racism of the 1980s and 90s, as a brown-skinned young person in Britain being accepted as British was already becoming possible. But acceptance as a Westerner wasn't as straightforward. This required being seen as someone who subscribed to the dominant culture of the white, English middle class – something which for me as an observant Muslim of Bangladeshi ancestry was optically impossible to do. The fact that I subscribed to the Western ideals of freedom, democracy and liberalism didn't count for much. In the early days, I wasn't even going to be accepted as 'one of us' even in terms of national identity.

Signs I exhibited of British patriotism would regularly be slapped back in my face by way of a taunt or often unintended slight which put me back in the box of the tryhard outsider. At the same time, my family community didn't see me as proper Bengali either, giving me the cold shoulder treatment and regarding me as an Englishman in brown skin. English people see me as brown, and Bangladeshi people see me as white. So, there I was, the subject of an at times unrewarding, no-win upbringing of coping with being the outsider a lot of the time, stuck between incompatible worlds. My cultural relevance was not appreciated. I was a migration rounding error.

It was an Oxford friend who described me as the Westerner, one drizzly afternoon as we both sat at a favourite café in Marylebone.

'Mohammad, your way of thinking and your ideals around freedom, social responsibility, equality and respect mean you are basically a Westerner.'

We had debated this point many times in the past, about the parallels between the philosophy of Plato, John Stuart Mill and Adam Smith and the social conscience and economic principles found within the teachings of Islam.

'The fundamentals of what you believe in are also better catered for by this country or America than by most Muslim nations, too. Most of them are further from Islamic ideals than the West. Face it, you are a Westerner more than anything else.'

Unused to the label, this last statement took me by surprise. Living my life as an outsider, I'd never thought about being accepted as a Westerner. My aspirations had been restricted to being seen as British, until this moment.

As we chatted, I was complaining that life for Muslims in Britain had become difficult post the 9/11 attacks in New York. The discussion simmered quickly to a heated debate and to put a stop to it, she abruptly told me that I need to accept Britain as an open-minded country underpinned by values that do more to protect the spirit of Islam than most Muslim nations do.

This was two years post 9/11, a time when suspicion over Muslims in the West had never been greater. Almost every month, one Western country or another would announce that an Islamic terrorist attack had been foiled or had taken place. Muslims in the West were experiencing a level of isolation and mistrust they had never felt before. Within just a few years from the early 1980s, the suspicion that Muslims could not be trusted as signed up members to the ideals of Western society escalated sharply. All of a sudden Muslims were being profiled as being different ideologically, singled out as a group as if they were the new Cold War protagonist, a new enemy but this time within our own borders. Anti-Muslim suspicion was cropping up everywhere, a shadowy and ill-defined phenomenon whose many examinations were generally impossible to counter. Life became a daily test littered with innocently formed questions that came up in conversation. When you fast, how can you possibly cope without water intake all day? Are children forced to fast? Why don't women drive in Saudi Arabia? Can you help us understand what the Muslim terrorists want? Why are Muslims so angry? People repeatedly asked you to explain your beliefs and justify your and others' (other Muslims, that is) actions.

The pillorying of Islam and its followers became all but legitimised in many Western countries, helped along by leading thinkers and writers and encouraged by influential leaders. Some commentators have even drawn parallels between how Muslims are being grouped now to how Germany classified Jews in the 1930s. Post 9/11 there sprouted a host of sometimes confusing activities that confirmed the new term of 'Islamophobia' really was taking hold. The United States began to take specific and often randomly targeted measures to monitor the movements and activities of Muslims, such as putting people (including myself) on no-fly lists. This escalation of security procedures for people arriving from overseas is something which remains a nervous subject for myself until today. Conversely, Britain began to recognize Muslims for their contributions to society, convening vacuous commissions to write patronising reports on the good things we are doing for the nation, rubber-stamped by hand-picked Muslims who were drawn into the lure of recognition, including titles such as OBEs and MBEs,* this might bring them. There was a slap of tokenism to this, as if the celebratory aspects of recognising Muslims' contributions were politically motivated and shallow. The falseness of these actions worried me, as though even the moderate political leaders of the left and the right

---

* Order of the British Empire, or Member of the British Empire.

were secretly wondering 'is there really something wrong with them?'

Things were not right for me. After the shattering events of 9/11, I had begun to feel foreign in my home town of London, where matters were to become significantly worse post the murderous 7/7 attacks of July 2005. I felt under scrutiny, sensing and sometimes imagining anonymous stares and stolen looks, accentuated when I was alone or carrying a bag. As a professional, the situation was gradually becoming harder and harder. I was working as a management consultant and travelling intensely, taking over one hundred flights per year. I remained keen to work in 'exotic' locations, see the world and apply myself to solving business problems in places where the challenges were unique and particularly difficult to address without solutions which had to be thought through with local context as well as a global worldview. Despite my family quizzing my desire to keep travelling so much in these tricky times, there was a stubborn side to me that insisted I continue and not curtail my movements just for fear of backlash. During the next few years I was to be questioned, detained, interrogated or physically searched by security police and border officials in London, New York, San Francisco, Milan, Jersey, Boston, Dubai, Madrid, Brussels, Dallas, Cairo (twice), Paris and near Jerusalem, and refused entry visas to Australia and India without attending special interviews at embassies and producing old, expired passports to provide historical proofs of travel. India only ever granted me a single-entry visa, until I went to live and work there in 2011.

My personal life was in turmoil, too. Following a decade of strained marriage to a fellow Muslim student I had met at Oxford, the day 9/11 happened I was waking up to a cataclysm of a more personal nature: divorce. Whilst we had felt matched to each other and were committed to making things work, over time it became evident to me that this union had little chance of being successful. The aftermath of a decade's struggle left me emotionally exhausted and damaged, lacking in my usual vitality and enthusiasm for life, and seeking solace in trusted friendships that were to see me through some dark days. It took a few years for me to recover from the trauma of divorce. During my difficult times of facing border crossings post 9/11, I was also dealing with dissolving the demons of my personal experiences.

Perhaps with not the best timing, I started learning Arabic at the time, to understand my faith better and give me a fresh challenge as I looked to rekindle my life. Over the years I had grown sick and tired of the idiocy of reciting prayers in Arabic but not understanding a word. By 2005, I was beginning to emerge from painful years of self-reflection into the beginnings of a new revival. Attending a wedding in Istanbul, and by now speaking reasonable Arabic, I decided to add to the trip a coastal journey across southern Turkey, Syria and Lebanon with the objective to immerse myself into the culture of the Levant. This was my first chance to 'go live' with Arabic. I was excited. I kept a daily journal through the trip, shared as a regular weblog with friends. Wherever I went in remote parts of southern Turkey and northern Syria, I was welcomed. These people gave me in an instant what the British and Bangladeshi sides in my life hadn't been able to give me ever: unconditional acceptance. I eagerly drafted out the first cut of *Border Crossings*, typing away during solitary evenings in hotels, after meals with my laptop on the table in noise-filled, atmospheric brasseries, and during overnight flights as I zigzagged across the world on an endless run of business trips.

The first drafts were somewhat cathartic, littered with weird dream sequences I was experiencing at the time and full of self-reflection. But from that perhaps necessary and personal process, I refined the narrative into reprising a more relatable story of how I was brought up in a crossover generation where our parents naively imparted the religious and social perspectives of their homeland to us. They left us to close out the gaps between what to expect and what happened, but real life was more brutal, littered with three-way clashes between the cultures of being British, Bengali and Muslim.

As I laboured through the narrative, I realised that even in my formative years, seeds were being sown that would later help me conquer my challenges and emerge as a more culturally settled person. In particular, I saw how learning to converse in multiple languages helped me bridge cultural gaps, and how my global perspective connected my modest and immaterial individual life to the unfurling of major world events. As political upheaval and Islamic fundamentalism spread across Asia, Europe, the Middle East and Africa, my career opportunities mesmerised me, taking me to the world's hot spots and exposing me with uncanny regularity to societies in flux. Regularly I got to look inside and, due to the nature of my work as a government adviser, here and there I got to apply a twist to the golden thread of political and social reform. I worked on topics which were pertinent to social trends that were resulting in political upheaval in Muslim countries. For example, in Egypt I headed government relations for a major telecommunications operator at a time when the military-backed government of President Hosni Mubarak was attempting to get mobile operators to open up their networks for more surveillance of potential uprising activity. A few years earlier, I had advised the Saudi Arabian government over liberalising access to the internet, having to consider carefully how to create competition in internet services provision whilst safeguarding against uncensored content in politics, religious topics and pornography.

Throughout my life and career, I have occupied the cultural no man's land I have been stuck in ever since school days. This extends to today, living and working in an Australia that is undergoing its own sometimes fractious evolution into becoming a genuinely multicultural society. But as time went on, I became aware that living with cultural ambiguities breeds advantages in communication and empathy. *Border Crossings* is my journey, but the narrative is my way to relate to yours. This is regardless of whether you happen to be a Muslim, of any faith or of no faith at all, whether you are man or woman and British or any other nationality, because we live in a world where we are exposed to some form of being the 'other' some of the time, and most of the time for many. My journey has been one of understanding, accepting and benefiting from being treated as an outsider. It has taken a few knocks to appreciate it, but I have discovered that the hardship of being the 'other' is also one of life's hidden privileges.

Two

Foreigner in My Own Country

EGH 218J. That was the registration plate on my parents' Sunbeam Arrow. Midnight Blue was the colour, according to the Owner's Manual which also explained in words and diagrams how to do such bizarre things such as check the gaps in spark plugs, or obvious ones such as opening the glove compartment. I recall Owner's Manuals as always being dog-eared and bent out of shape from being crammed into cubby holes that were barely large enough to hold a pair of gloves. Our glove box, like most, was laden with all sorts of rubbish, such as gooey ballpoint pens without tops, Little Chef restaurant guides, broken sunglasses, a Quranic* prayer to keep us safe in travel and a couple of random empty cassette boxes.

I was obsessed by automobile registration plates. I remembered so many of them. I am sure my father, or

---

* The Quran is the holy book for Muslims, and contains many short prayers for different needs and occasions.

Abba* as I called him, took interest in them too. I never got around to asking him about his view on number plates, as with so many topics, given that I lost him to a relatively early death when he was fifty-six and I was twenty-four. It is just that so many of our family picture albums feature photographs of his earlier cars, most with the number plates showing prominently. The number on his first car, a Ford Anglia, was DYN 655C. The 'C' at the end meant that it was a 1965 model. Number plates were exciting to me because there was so much information in the numbering and letter sequences that could be analysed. It helped you place those around you in terms of wealth, status and economic power. Abba bought that car with the five hundred pounds he won on the football pools, and used it for starting his third weekly job, to give driving lessons to his mates who had come to England to follow in his footsteps. The young Mashahid Ali Chowdhury arrived in England in 1957, in his early twenties and with not a penny to his name. Abba's first two jobs were with British Railways during the week and life insurance salesman during the weekends, a routine he maintained for eight years until he took his first big business gamble, which was to open the Curry Queen restaurant in Lewisham in 1965. I don't know how much his friends paid him for the driving lessons, if anything.

All that took place well before I was born. I never saw the Anglia and only came to know it from the countless photos Abba had taken of it. The snaps represented a 1960s genre,

---

* Bengali for father

11

captured in some picturesque spot or other, often with my father standing by the driver's door or doing something posey, such as peering out into the distance, or sporting a fashionable mix and match of jacket, trousers and sturdy English shoes. The albums were of the period too, with thick black leaves and slippery translucent paper that left a white line wherever it got creased, and diagonal slits into which to insert the photo corners. I used to remember my uncle Asyad Mama's* plates too, from his Hillman Imp. Asyad Mama was my mother's brother. In line with the tragic fortunes of nearly all of the men from my mother's distinguished lineage, he died young, from pneumonia, in 1974. The Imp had a rear window that doubled for an opening hatch. I don't remember the plates now.

Despite being perhaps the most significant financial asset that shaped our livelihoods, the Curry Queen doesn't feature in any of the hundreds of family pictures that date back to the mid-1960s. Established a year before I was born, the Curry Queen was to become an institution for the entire family, a landing pad in the UK for dozens of migrating Bangladeshis, responsible for employing men from the extended Chowdhury clan across three generations and providing a stream of wages and profits that fed scores of people in England, Dhaka and Sylhet. 'CQ' generated the cash that meant my sister and I were among the first Bangladeshi kids in our community to study at a private school, and that enabled my father to launch a string of

---

* Bengali for maternal uncle

business ventures once Bangladesh became independent in 1971. Like hundreds of 'Indian' restaurants across the UK that were primarily set up by Bangladeshis from Sylhet, the Curry Queen served as job centre, shelter, social club, laundry, canteen, language centre, confidence builder and lifeskills unit for dozens of immigrants, leaving most with a needed sense of purpose and identity, and cash, with which they were to move on, often to bigger and better things that they could do for themselves. In my mind, Curry Queen didn't feature in our albums because the photos were designed to relate a fiction, a collage that narrated a fanciful immigrant fantasy of new cars, sharp-suited young men and their attractive, sari-laden wives building a successful life in England, their new home. These albums were there to serve up a rose-tinted nostalgia, sampled by elders back home, of how their young offspring were pioneering a new seam of success in a foreign land. The Curry Queen, a small establishment with modest furnishings and replete with a bar serving liquor to customers who mocked bow-tied Bengali waiters with a racist disdain, didn't offer the sort of imagery that would embellish this narrative.

My mother Sabequa, or Amma,* used to drop me off at Riverston School in the Sunbeam every morning. Riverston was the junior school I attended all the way from kindergarten until moving to St Dunstan's College in Catford when I was almost eleven, a more established and storied institution. Driving down the Sidcup Road deep in South

---

* Bengali for mother

East London, most drivers would hardly guess that Riverston was a school at all. The anonymous row of buildings which made up the establishment resembled a row of Victorian residences, in communion only because their front gardens had been replaced by a gravelly car park. The only aspect of Riverston's façade that would catch the glimpse of a passing driver was the knee-high wooden fence that Mr Davies had erected along the front of the school. As one sped by, the corner of the eye would be caught by a white flash of wood-work running unbroken for several seconds against South East London's generally uninspiring backdrop of dull cement and masonry.

Mr Davies was our Headmaster. Mrs Davies, his wife, the Headmistress. Mr and Mrs Davies were both Welsh, and for reasons I never understood, their nationality was something they were always making a big fuss about. Mr Davies drove a dark brown, L-registration Daimler 4.2 which he parked outside the Upper School, the second of the school's four buildings. I knew it was a Daimler because it had one of those large, chromium Ds on the bonnet and two fuel-filler caps for its pre-oil-crisis twin petrol tanks. I would walk past it deliberately slowly, sneaking a look at the decadently appointed interior and admiring the stitched leather upholstery and rear seat central armrest. I felt sure Mr Davies knew we did this and that it probably gave him a sense of smug satisfaction.

Behind the red brick façade, Mr and Mrs Davies ran Riverston strictly, patrolling the corridors whenever they wished. Whilst in my mind Mrs Davies enforced the desired sense of public school decorum her husband had seemingly tried to create around us through Riverston's dress codes and timetabled rituals, she would sometimes walk around as though at home, wearing a denim skirt and Dr Scholl's sandals. She dressed formally during public sports days or open evenings, when both the Headmaster and his wife would behave immaculately. Our parents had been shielded from these contrasts in the Davieses' conduct, until the day they went in to tell them that I would not be staying at Riverston for secondary school but going to Eltham or St Dunstan's* instead, depending on which school offered me a better option. They wanted Mr Davies to share in their pride that one of his students would be graduating to a well-recognised establishment for further education. But instead the school focused on the risk of losing one of their best boys to another school, and tried to convince my parents to keep me at Riverston. The meeting got fiery, and I remember how surprised my parents were when they got home. Surprisingly, they told him he could do his worst, but there was no way they would change their minds about me going to Eltham or St Dunstan's.

My parents had to eke out their hard-earned income to spend it on sending my sister and myself to a school that aspired to be so much yet it seemed to me attained so little distinction. I recall Abba and Amma's frenzy just before the beginning of every term, scraping the cash together for yet another school fees instalment. But investing in education

---

* St Dunstan's College is situated in Catford in South East London.

was one of the struggles that gave my mum and dad their greatest pleasure, to feel that the fruits of their efforts were going into our futures. My father had to leave education with his Higher School Certificate (the equivalent to British A-levels) in the early 1950s to support his family, who had seen much better days but were now experiencing a period of terminal economic decline. In contrast, Amma grew up with her university education ransomed to continuously winning scholarships, since her widowed mother had lost her late husband's lands after the Partition of British India, and didn't have the financial resources to fund her four daughters and four sons through higher education. Maybe the satisfaction of giving us a good schooling was what gave Amma her contented look every morning when she dropped me off, given that they were investing whatever they could in giving us the best chance possible to integrate and be successful in this foreign land. Or perhaps it was just the relief that she had got me to school on time again, somehow, and could spend the rest of her day in peace before we got back home.

As the first generation of Bangladeshis born in Britain, we grew up with many stigmas. Most of these emanated from our immigrant status, underlined by relative poverty compared to our peers, a lack of recognised education in our parents, a lack of social and cultural context to our neighbours and a lack of professional status since my father was a businessman. Our stigma was accentuated by the fact that my parents chose to buy our first house in a predominantly white area and send us to a private school which had very few children of colour there. But because our school was also an emerging institution with many shortcomings, our stigmas extended beyond our immigrant status to one of a general underdog status. One of these stigmas arose from the fact that Riverston had no proper sports facilities of its own. The gymnasium was our assembly hall and dining room too, and the three-in-one combination meant that during physical education lessons one's plimsolls would occasionally slip on fragments of school dinner spilt earlier. Swimming lessons were taken at Eltham Public Baths, which we travelled to every Wednesday in the velour-seated Duple coach that Mr Davies hired from some local company. Relishing neither the swimming nor the changing, I most looked forward to the air-suspension ride to and from the baths. On the contrary, I dreaded communal showering after swimming and then having to change in shared facilities. In line with Islamic principles of decency, I found any form of public undressing to the point of taking all of one's clothes off a little embarrassing. Years later, as I grew from being a boy into a young man, to do so several times a week at St Dunstan's College was distressing. It was awkward for me because others wouldn't see this as inappropriate at all, to the extent that some boys would even discuss the state of each other's genitalia while standing under the steamy shower heads of the school's Victorian tiled bathroom. By contrast, I would shower quickly and change in a corner, tucked away or standing at angles so that my modesty would only be exposed for the briefest few seconds possible. The speed this required in threading my legs through my underpants meant that I would regularly lose balance while trying too hard, attracting even more attention from class-mates as I hopped about clumsily, while they believed I had something wrong with my private parts. Perhaps they thought this was linked to the fact that I was not white and not English.

I hated having to be different in the changing rooms and longed for the acceptance that comes with being seen as a 'normal' child and not someone who is for some reason different, or even weird. For a while I became known as 'brown Mo', anointed thus on a coach trip back from the baths, with the boys inspired by the unforgettable Boney M hit 'Brown Girl in the Ring'. They chanted the lyrics out loud with Mo in place of Girl. What I disliked most about this experience was that the teacher was too weak to do anything to stop the singing, and secondly, that Mo was, in my thoughts, a disrespectful shortening of the name of our Holy Prophet Mohammad PBUH.* Such were the early experiences I and many other Asians† like me grew up with. With these constant reminders of how we were different, and inferior for being so, came the lure of giving in and 'assimilating' to the common culture with the promise that the taunts would stop if you did, or on the other hand rejecting it completely and becoming an outsider. The feelings of loneliness and isolation created through experiences such

---

* Muslims wish peace upon any of their prophets (including Abraham, Moses, Jesus and Mohammad) whenever saying their name by reciting a short prayer in Arabic meaning 'May peace be upon him', and this is silently assumed for similar reference points throughout the remainder of the book.

† The term 'Asian' in this book refers to the British definition, which is people from the Indian subcontinent.

as being called 'brown Mo' would force us towards making that polarising choice, between assimilation or staying on the outside.

I never used to go to the prayers part of Assembly, thanks to special religious dispensation from the school, granted also to two Jewish friends, Daniel and Rachel. There were two Hindus and another Muslim girl from a Bangladeshi family but their parents did not make an issue out of attendance at prayers. One of the Hindus, Raj, was in my class, and I later found out that his parents *did* want him to miss prayers, but to not look more different than he had to, Raj attended prayers without his parents ever knowing about it. Daniel, Rachel and I would sit alone in our classroom whilst everyone else in school sang morning hymns and chanted the Lord's Prayer, in a unison which even for an outsider such as me was moving to observe. Miss Wyndham, the music teacher, would play the piano accompaniment, and Mrs Forth, the buxom lady who taught 4F, would lead the voices with her powerful, resonating shrill. Strangely united by our non-Christianness every morning, the three of us would wait until the end of the first hymn, walk down from 2W towards the hall so that we would reach it just as prayers ended. We three became friends by circumstance, visiting each other's houses for tea, while our parents made ridiculous small talk, such as the respective locations of synagogues and mosques in South London. The classroom was situated way over on the second floor of the furthest of Riverston's four buildings. To get to the hall we had to climb one flight of stairs, traverse a sloped melamine-floored corridor that connected us to the adjacent building, and then descend another three. The singing would resonate through the corridors as we walked, making it easy to identify the tune as well as to gauge when the performance was entering its final crescendo. The union of voices would magnify our feeling of exclusion, something that all three of us must have felt but never discussed.

Christianity was not just the religion observed at school; it was the defining platform for British culture as Britain had been for all intents and purposes a Christian land for many centuries. Even though many British had seen other religions and cultures through the duty and travails of Empire, experience on British (and most other Western countries') shores of other faiths was limited. With this backdrop, Daniel, Rachel and I each experienced our own versions of exclusion in junior and secondary schools. At this early age I began to learn to occupy cultural grey areas, thanks to the isolation I experienced growing up in South East London coupled with the rejection by relatives who regarded me as English (or 'Ingleesh', as they would pronounce it) and not Bengali. Despite being born in Britain and of Bangladeshi* parentage, both the English and the Bengali sides of my existence stressed how I was different and not how I fitted in. A move to adopt either a predominantly English or Bengali world view might have been so

---

* The terms Bengali and Bangladeshi are easily confused. The state of Bengal was partitioned in 1906 by the British to separate the mainly Hindu West Bengal from the principally Muslim East Bengal. East Bengal became East Pakistan in 1947, and then Bangladesh in 1971. West Bengal remained part of India. The language of Bengal is Bengali, or 'Bangla' to the locals.

much easier: it could have saved me a lifelong series of dilemmas and crossing borders. But neither side looked right. Middle ground occupation seemed the only course and adjusting to it became a matter of survival. But with the experiences of exclusion we all had to go through, many of my contemporaries struggled with adjustment, and this is partly why so many Muslims who grew up in the 1970s and 1980s in Britain today, feel disenchanted and bitter with the society around them.

By the time we reached the doors to the school hall, the second hymn would either just be finished or about to end. Then would come the Lord's Prayer, by the end of which we would have joined the bench where the rest of my class would be standing already. I felt as though some of the teachers were looking on disapprovingly as we took our places at the end of the row, as though our abstention from prayers was a slur on the school, something to be ashamed of. As soon as everyone sat down, there were the Head-master's announcements, and then the Head Prefect would call out other chores and news items.

In my years of school going I estimate I must have heard the Lord's Prayer well over a thousand times. But to this day I do not know the verses word for word. I consciously tuned out of morning prayers, focusing my senses instead on paintings, or furniture, or when at St Dunstan's, on the young Miss Brown, the only female teacher at the school and the most attractive woman known to me and my friends for some years. Shielded as we were from meeting girls, a number of my close friends at school had a crush on her all through middle school. I used to wonder why Christians called God 'hello' – until years later I realised that the line from the prayer was 'Hallowed be thy name', and not 'Hello be thy name'. I drew an odd satisfaction from being exposed to the prayer daily without recalling its words. More secure today in my identity as a Muslim, I take active interest in reading and understanding prayers recited in other faiths, and even in evoking them where the content of the prayers coincides with my own beliefs.

I do not suppose my parents empathised with what it felt like for my sister and me to be so different from our class-mates and friends. Amma and Abba were detached from our everyday challenges, having grown up in British India and then post-independence Pakistan at a time when reli-gion had not been an important differentiator of identity, since Muslims and Hindus were well integrated socially and culturally. And everyone in my parents' schools would have been brown, spoken the same language, dressed the same and eaten the same food. As far as apparent indifference to our school experiences was concerned, the same went for Maulvi Sahib* as it did for my folks. Maulvi Sahib would come to our house in Mottingham, South East London, on Wednesday evenings to discuss Islam and to teach us how to read the Quran. Only it wasn't strictly Islam, but life and what to do about it. Sometimes he would give us examples from history or from real situations, and at other times he would make us read chapters from books that recalled

---

* Religious teacher. Maulvi means cleric or minister, and Sahib (pronounced *saab*) lit-erally means sir or mister.

interesting stories from the time when Islam began. The stories always had a lesson or point to them, but I found them more interesting because of their romantic Middle Eastern setting, with camels and dates and nomadic tribes. Some of the stories reignited my own memories of the Hajj* which our parents had taken us on a few years earlier.

Hajj was a wonderful adventure which did a lot to establish Islam and its core principles in me. Dressed simply in two white sheets, one around the waist and the other around the torso, we ate and slept in cavernous tents with hundreds of people, and drove across miles and miles of baking Saudi Arabian desert in huge, gas-guzzling American cars with exotic names such as Chevrolet Impala and Cadillac Seville. We listened to racy Bedouin tunes played by drivers as we sped through acres of nothing between historic cities such as Medina and Makkah (often written as Mecca), and then swarmed on foot with tides of pilgrims flowing mile upon mile from one encampment to another. Some of the walking requirements for Hajj were so strenuous for us children that Abba would hire the services of someone to piggyback us through some of it.

Most of all, the stories in Maulvi Sahib's books would remind me of the one night we spent in Muzdalifah, in the open desert near Mount Arafat perched on the edge of Makkah.† I spent the entire evening on the slopes of the mountain, lying on my back, staring up at the deep blue-black

---

* pilgrimage to Makkah

† It is obligatory for pilgrims to spend one night in the open on Muzdalifah, a rocky mountain close to Arafat, to complete the ritual requirements of the Hajj.

sky, inhaling all the smells and listening to the sounds of pilgrims fidgeting and settling down for some hard-earned rest. Into the early hours, I could hear the diesel groans of trucks grinding the sand beneath their tyres and grumbling off into the desert to start another long voyage.

Maulvi Sahib recommended that we should never attend prayers at school, because if we listened to the Lord's Prayer too often, we might be taken in by its exhortations. Though he meant well for us, Maulvi Sahib's limited experience of school life in Britain left us with little more practical guidance than my parents could give on how to negotiate growing up as an outsider. One of the books, a thick one with a dark blue hard cover, we only read from when he came so that we might choose the best chapters every week. But I read it secretly and found stories about marriage, sex, divorce and other subjects that he had wanted to leave until later. Maulvi Sahib gave us homework every week, which usually included practising in advance the next section of the Quran so that we could read it more easily during our lesson. Neither my sister nor I ever did much and he never seemed to mind.

Until I began to appreciate the satisfaction of being able to recite the Quran with at least a little fluency, I disliked reading Arabic. Though beautiful to look at and melodic to the ear, Arabic was a foreign language with a strange script that was hard to read, and pointless since we did not understand what anything meant. The people who taught me didn't understand what it meant either, and neither did those who wanted me to learn it. Our method of learning was first to memorise the letters of the Arabic alphabet, then to understand how they were joined up by the basic vowels and variations, and finally to practise reading faster, and faster, and faster. To this day amongst non-Arab Muslims, the speed and lyricism of reading the Quran is emphasised more than its comprehension. The consequent lack of understanding of the Quran's contents is why few Muslims appreciate the meaning of any of it, let alone its interpretation or historical context. This ignorance leaves most Muslims ill-equipped to explain the Quran when challenged and, in today's world where the text is often criticised, pushes them into emotional and defensive acts of Quranic justification. Years later, when learning Arabic for myself, I found out that some of what we had learnt wasn't Arabic at all, but a bastardisation of Arabic, Persian and Urdu, through a curriculum created decades ago by Urdu-speaking scholars in the Indian subcontinent, to make it easier to learn Arabic from a base language of Farsi (Persian) or Urdu. I felt cheated to find this out thirty years later. Today, in countries as far-flung as India, South Africa, Tanzania, Zimbabwe, the US and Europe, the same methods of teaching the Quran still exist. Muslim teachers and imams, many from India and Pakistan, took the same books with them during their migrations to Africa in the early- and mid-20th century, and to the US and Europe later on.

Little did I appreciate it during childhood but learning how to communicate in additional languages made my border crossings easier. Versatility in pronunciation was a key benefit. The Bangla alphabet has 52 letters in place of English's

26, with as many as three versions of the English letter 'S', two of the letter 'J', and so on. Bangla has many softly-pronounced or nasal sounds, so that when it came to learning French when I was eight, I picked up the pronunciation far quicker than most of my English-only-speaking classmates. I had frustrations with learning to read Arabic but pronunciation of Arabic letters added to my vocal versatility. Arabic has sounds delivered with a glottal stop in the throat, and others made by the tongue touching the roof of the mouth or the back of the top row of teeth. By the time I was ten years old, I could pronounce perfectly in English, Arabic, Bangla and French. By the time I was fifteen, I had also acquired Latin and German and completed a year of Russian at school. My language skills provided me with a gateway to acquire fragments of other languages too with an ability to achieve localised pronunciation right from the start. These linguistic skills regularly started opening doors for me, when speaking Arabic with clients and officials all over the Middle East and North Africa, Hindi or Urdu in India or Pakistan, or fragments of Russian in the former Soviet republics, Burmese in Myanmar, Italian, Spanish and even a few phrases of Shona while working in Zimbabwe and Twi in Ghana. My native English meant I could connect immediately and culturally in countries such as the US or Australia as well, better than immigrants who hadn't learnt English to the same degree of fluency. Language skills reinforced my ability to instantly dissolve trust barriers and relate to others. Language widened my window to the world, to understand others more deeply and see their context.

I wasn't thinking of these benefits aged seven. Due to the attitude adopted by my parents and Maulvi Sahib that we must read the Quran even if we made little effort to understand it, I developed a resentment for the entire exercise. Completion of an entire reading of the Quran, which I did by the age of ten or so, was nothing short of a miserable chore.

'Tufael,' you must love the Quran and respect it.'

I was unimpressed as to how the murubbi[†] could read the text at great pace but not understand any of it. Maulvi Sahib knew substantial tracts of the Quran by heart, understood by way of having memorised Urdu translations alongside it, now relayed to us in English. Others would demonstrate how they could read at great speeds, intelligent adults who would drone on in Arabic for minutes on end without the foggiest idea whether they were reading about a goat, a fig leaf, how to take witnesses or the story of a historic battle. I concluded that the murubbi's claim to infinite wisdom to be false. How could they speak of Islam with such authority, when they were in effect so ignorant? Instead of respecting the elders, I started to find the tradition of such respect to be a shallow hypocrisy.

I was never shown the depths of the Quran, and did not appreciate that it had to be read in Arabic because it was the authentic word of God, because that is the language in which it was revealed. I knew that as a fact, but its import to me as a teenager was slight, disappointed as I was in the

---

* My middle name, an Arabic word meaning 'small boy'.

† Bengali for elders (sourced from the Arabic *murabbi*); the title implies that these are people to be treated with respect.

murubbi for not addressing the more fundamental questions I was asking of them. I kept up the lessons principally out of obligation and for fear of the embarrassment of being eclipsed by my younger sister. I was not alone in this – most Muslims who come to appreciate the depth of the Quran only do so in later life, when accumulation of wisdom and the availability of time (and perhaps the proximity of death) lead them to study it more closely. I am destined to a similar fate. On a societal scale, this is damaging for the Muslim community, as so much of the population is ignorant of the tenets of our religious teachings.

In our house, as in most others I knew of at the time, the Quran was a virtually untouchable book. The few copies we owned were wrapped in velvet casings which Amma sewed especially, and then stowed safely out of reach on the top shelf of the bookcase which Abba had built in our living room. Copies perused less frequently would gather dust which would need to be blown off when retrieved. Years later, travelling in the Levant, I would be amazed to see the Quran appear almost anywhere – in a shoeshiner's shirt pocket, strapped to taxi dashboards, and placed accessibly by shopkeeper's tills. Yet we were told about how it was not permitted to touch the Quran without performing wudhu* first. Even today, I respect the need to be clean before touching the sacred text, but the qualifying criteria to reach the Quran were made to feel like obstacles. As time went on, I grew to fear the Quran rather than love it or understand it, found the

---

* Ablutions, consisting of washing the hands, face, arms and feet, gargling and clearing one's nostrils.

ritual of coming into contact with it cumbersome and the inaccessibility of its meaning restrictive. What a tragedy that in our formative years our relationship with our holy book was moulded in such a tainted way.

While studying for my Master's at Cambridge University, I enlisted for Arabic classes at the Middle Eastern Institute. In the sessions, my Arabic reading was reasonably fluent and comprehension, as to be expected, non-existent. I looked at the task before me to focus on learning grammar and vocabulary, felt that it would take significant effort and commitment for my comprehension to develop and gave up. It was only another dozen years later, in my mid-thirties, that I would finally address this long-standing frustration by taking up Arabic classes and successfully learning the language to a point of conversational fluency.

'NO! Do not read the translation by yourself. You must sit with someone who will help you understand it properly,' would be a typical refrain offered by murubbi, who were there to instil within us their social hierarchy of access to religious wisdom.

'If you pronounce the ayats incorrectly, you may end up reading something with the opposite meaning to what you intend. If you do that, you will be punished on the Day of Judgement and sent to the hellfire,' one of my cousins once said to me, as I was sitting casually in his house, proudly reciting a verse I had memorised enthusiastically the week before.

With all of the challenges we faced, quite how I emerged from my teenage years with a strong belief in our religion, and a polite ability to accept but not adopt Christian cultural traditions, is beyond me. Of course, it hasn't been the case with many. Hundreds of my contemporary Muslims have polarised from this middle ground – by adopting Christian culture, or on the other hand, rejecting British mainstream culture altogether and becoming fanatic in their observance of Islamic religious fundamentals. Many of that earlier generation have lost out on the richness offered by a more integrated and culturally journeyed upbringing. Whether it is some sections of the population that struggle with integration more than others, perhaps systemically due to socio-economic circumstances, is an important question to consider.

The books we learnt from were mainly printed in India or Pakistan, with the inside cover bearing the magenta rubber stamp of the book supplier, such as 'Ferozesons, The Mall, Lahore', or 'Islamia Book Gallery, Khan Market, Delhi'. The price would usually be written in a corner, in pencil. 'Rs.* 20/-' would be the house style. The figures always converted to a humble consideration, such as 60p. Most of the books bore a generic South Asian smell (glue and paper smells, I guess) and style of book production and binding, the hallmark of which was the brittle hardboard cover that made a cracking sound every time the book was opened, demanding a two-handed effort to prise apart the pages. The pages themselves were bound together with white cotton string, threaded through the centre fold in batches of a dozen odd leaves at a time.

---

* rupees

Maulvi Sahib explained to us not to write in books since this was disrespectful. At the end of our weekly lesson, after stuttering through a few more pages of Quran, he would write the date in the margin of the page we had reached. I used to think part of the privilege of being a Maulvi Sahib was to be allowed to write in books. I can see the dates today and work out that it took us nearly two years to read the entire Arabic script of the Quran's thirty chapters, approximately one chapter every three to four lessons. Many volumes had pages where the print block had fallen at a slight angle, making me dizzy as I read, as though I was ship's captain reading events in a logbook during a stormy night at sea.

We had never even stopped to think he could ever be called anything but Maulvi Sahib. Kareem Khan was a tall and thin young man with a long, black beard. He seemed rather terrifying at first sight to many of my English friends, clothed as he was in his sherwani* and topped with a black topi.† His parents had migrated to England in 1960, when his father was recruited from Hyderabad, India as an imam at one of London's first mosques. In lyrical tones from the Deccan plains of India, Maulvi Sahib spoke in Urdu with Amma. It did not seem right for them to speak in English when a subcontinental alternative was available instead.

I once asked him if he wore the sherwani especially to teach us in.

---

* A long coat, buttoned up to the neck and worn traditionally by educated Muslim gentlemen from the Indian subcontinent.

† cap

'No, I wear it to work too.'*

In his soft Hyderabadi lilt, Maulvi Sahib spoke with kindness and calmness, gesturing with his large, expressive and well-manicured hands. He led more by example and less by prescription. Even on the unforgettable day at Oxford University a dozen years later, when Maulvi Sahib sprang a surprise visit one afternoon and found me in my room, chatting with an attractive girl, he was mercifully gentle and understanding. I couldn't imagine Maulvi Sahib working in an office. He worked for a company in Charlton, South London as a computer programmer and lived in Orpington, Kent with his parents and younger siblings. Later he migrated to Canada to continue a simple life of teaching while earning enough money to get by. In his London days he owned a purple Hillman Avenger which he drove fast. I always imagined he would look rather funny being stopped for speeding, wearing his topi and all the garb. Maulvi Sahib didn't wear pointy shoes though, just normal ones. I wondered for years whether under his topi he was bald or whether he had a full head of hair.

'But I don't wear it when I play cricket,' he once said, smiling.

Maulvi Sahib had a habit of responding to a serious question with a considered answer and then a frivolous comment. His jokes would always come with a grin and a sparkle in the eye. He taught us with a smile, though at times he did not explain things in a way that made complete sense. I'm sure he

---

* At a mosque

knew that I would ask him whether he really played cricket, and one afternoon when he came to teach, he saw my new cricket bat and took my sister and me outside for what turned out to be a long fielding session in the back garden. Coming in to bowl, he did frighten me a bit with the sight of his quick arm swinging out from his ranging figure. The years I spent seeing him every week provided me with a robust and enduring sense of what Islam was about – partly from the books and stories but mainly from observing the man himself.

Alongside Maulvi Sahib I learned about Islam from my mother and father. Their influence was strangely complementary. I learned most about Islamic principles of behaviour, fairness, tolerance and conduct from Abba. Ironically, Abba practised the rituals of prayer with the least regularity in my family, and not once in my life did he give me any direct instruction on matters of religious conduct. Meanwhile, I learned to pray regularly and observe religious traditions more from Amma, who read Quran and never missed a prayer.

Mr Gerrard was the teacher who would most often patrol the corridors at Riverston during prayer time. He was a tall, lean man of at least six foot, usually dressed in a moss-coloured Austin Reed blazer and brown trousers. Daniel and I liked to imagine that he was having a fling with another voluptuous, middle-aged teacher. Sometimes he would give her a lift in his H-registration Wolseley 1800. One morning he pounced just as Daniel, Rachel and I were walking down to the hall while the second hymn played itself out. As though nabbing a petty thief, he caught hold of me by the ear, his fingernails digging into my ear lobe, and bade the other two to follow. Of the three of us, I was perhaps the obvious outsider with my more foreign-sounding name and brown skin, as Daniel and Rachel were both white and English-looking, or it might be that I was standing nearest to him. As we reached the hall's swinging doors he shoved me inside, ensuring that all would hear the clatter as I entered, with three hundred worshippers turning around to greet me with a uniformly disdainful look. That evening, I told my parents. The surprising thing was that they believed me and even more so that they went to speak to the head teacher.

I would convince myself that other parents stared at us as we drove away from school because our left-hand drive Sunbeam Arrow was such an unusual car. It was brand new, a distinctive blue the same shade as Prime Minister Harold Wilson's Rover parked outside No 10 Downing Street, and had left-hand drive. But I knew that they really stared because they had seldom seen a woman in a sari and head-scarf driving a car before. Perhaps they wondered how Asians could afford a fancy-looking American car and send two kids to private school. But it was probably seeing this Asian woman chat with other parents in fluent English that surprised them the most. I am sure nobody even noticed the car was a left-hand drive.

Driving about in the Arrow was wonderful. It was one of those early 1970s cars with lots of gadgets, such as a parking lamp which you could connect up through the cigarette lighter and little windows in the front which could be tilted open for ventilation. Except for being left-hand driven, the car looked identical to the British-built Hillman Hunter. We collected it from a dealer on Piccadilly that also sold Rolls Royce cars. A sticker on the windscreen denoted it was an import branded under the Rootes label, one of the UK market trading names for the Chrysler Corporation. Abba hadn't told us why we were going up to town that day. We drove into the dealership in our clapped-out Ford Escort, and half an hour later, out we came in a brand new car. Abba probably didn't realise it, but the excitement he created that day was one of the best gifts he ever gave me. While he would watch reports on TV of the Iranian revolution in 1979, I devoted more interest to spotting the Hillman Hunters on the streets of Tehran than to the unfolding political drama.* Abba's influence on me was subtle. His religious views were as understated as he was clean-shaven. Abba led by example, lectured little and mor-alised even less.

For all its attractiveness, the poor Sunbeam suffered for being under our ownership too. Soon after I started at St Dunstan's, Amma drove me to school every morning. Virtually every day for the first few months, the car would be spat on by two boys on their way to school. They were from Sedgehill, known as one of the roughest state schools in England whose boys were rumoured to flick concen-trated sulphuric acid at innocent victims and throw hot light bulbs at passengers in trains. I still recall the repulsive

---

* Chrysler had an agreement to assemble Hillman cars in Iran during the Shah's regime.

sight of the saliva on our windows. Starting as effervescent blobs on our windscreen, the spit would merge into globules and begin a slow trickle downwards, weaving down the glass until it dried up, leaving a stain all along its route. The boys had mouths especially designed for achieving long-distance spitting, with lips jutting out and reddened from the regular practise of transmitting large volumes of saliva across many metres. The shapes of their mouths dramatised the violence of their words too, making it easy for me to lip-read them through the closed car windows:

'PAK – E – E . PAK – E – E .'

I hated how the words were pronounced in their specific way, the last vowel stretched out, reminiscent of the oft-heard Wembley Stadium football chant for 'England, England'. All this made me resent being British. Every morning the same words would be mimed out in slow motion, mimicking the easy pace of the gob as it dribbled down the Sunbeam's defiled glass. The boys were relaxed in their assurance that the congestion left them several minutes for lengthy and considered humiliation. I recall vividly the sound of the spitting act – thick, viscous and frothy. I remember also the strain of effort that rippled through the boys' faces as they tightened their jaws at the moment of release. There were boys who could spit like that at school too, such as Michael the 'Gobber.' Gobber's mouth was some sort of percolator, constantly replenishing reserves, so that as soon as one mouthful was despatched to a customer another would be almost ready. I never made eye contact with Gobber.

The boys on Chinbrook Road, the main street than continued from ours on the way to school, weren't playground scientists like Gobber but street-hardened yobs. These boys seemed fearless. Spitting at us every day wasn't a dare; it was easy enjoyment that became the morning drill. Their cocky confidence meant they had no restraint. Starting at a distance, when exhausted from the effort, they would come up close, picking their favourite spots on our windows to cover them properly. We were their morning sport, the early high that would make the otherwise tedious walk to school something to look forward to. I don't know why we would lock the car doors every morning, as though they would ever want to get into a car full of greasy-looking Pakis.

Amma started driving me to school when our morning ride-share with another boy in my class, Craig, had to be discontinued. I thought that perhaps Craig's dad could no longer tolerate the spitting on his car, a fantastic green Ford Zephyr with tailfins which evidently didn't deserve such treatment. It was as if he felt outraged, and it is certain that being English he might not expect to be subjected to such humiliation.

'I am so sorry that you have had to put up with this, Mr Duggan,' my mother apologised as she wiped the boys' spit off his car the day he came round to complain.

In the repeated public trial that ensued every day, I felt the embarrassment of being a spectacle for others, the hurt from the humiliating behaviour and the disgust from watching someone else's spit run down the windscreen of our car. Most of all I felt shame. Shame at being brown. It was like being in a glass cage, sentenced to public humiliation for committing the heinous crime of being different. I craved the comfort of acceptance by my white schoolmates and friends, since the love of my family and relatives at home just wasn't enough.

The boys would have spat with greater relish had they known I'd been stupid enough to win the form prize for my laboriously completed summer project on the Queen's Silver Jubilee. The effort had become an obsession of collecting, researching, cutting and pasting, all neatly written up in my Osmiroid italic pen. My interest in the topic had been ignited through admiration for the Queen's achievement of surviving office for a quarter of a century, a period equivalent to more than twice my age. With Union Jacks all over the front cover, this was a labour of love that glorified my pride in being British and my admiration for the Queen herself. This was the same Britain that the spitting boys and the singers in the school coach baited me to hate. The italic handwriting was important since it endowed the words with a definitively royal look and I had even made sure to use Quink Royal Blue washable ink.

The spitting stopped one morning when, without any obvious forethought, Amma pulled up the handbrake, got out of the car and approached the two culprits who were about to mete out our morning punishment. Genuine fear overcame all my other emotions at this time, knowing that if something serious were to happen, nobody would do anything but watch this Indian woman in a cumbersome-looking sari and headscarf engage in an unnecessarily risky confrontation. But Amma's fearless body language told them and me that she was going to have no more of it. To my shock and surprise, the boys' confidence dissolved as easily as I had expected it would grow through such a confrontation. They drifted off like lazy hyenas after a failed hunt, careful not to make it look as though they were retreating.

The delay to the traffic along the Chinbrook Road from our momentary halt created a gap between our car and the one in front of us. In a typically understated British show of solidarity, or plain embarrassment perhaps, not a single driver honked in impatience. Such gestures were a lifeline to me. With the backdrop of a sometimes unwelcoming environment, signals such as these reassured me that Britain was home and that its people were by and large principled, stoic and tolerant. I felt bad for Amma because she had to clean the spit off the car every day after she returned home from the school run. Little did I realise then that this was just the beginning of what would become a life of being on the outside. Nor could anyone in the mid-1970s have predicted that it wasn't just our skin colour that was going to be the challenge, but Western society's perceptions about our faith.

The boys never bothered us again and neither Amma nor I discussed the matter, as though the whole episode had never taken place. Shame was the victor.

Three

The Allenby Crossing

The specific nature of racial discrimination I experienced as a child has all but dissolved from my life, although it continues to hound millions of others. But scrutiny of my identity as a Muslim has become ever more sinister. In my border crossings today, the open racism that I encountered on the drive to school has been replaced by the more opaque veil of suspicion of Islam. This is exemplified by frequent questions over the reasonableness of Muslims' sacredly held beliefs, mistrust over the motives and free-doms of women in hijab,* the trustworthiness of Muslim-looking men with long beards, or even the dangers of admitting foreign travellers with unfamiliar entry stamps in their passports. I am no different to most other travellers, but I can put my problems down to three factors: I often wear a short beard, my passport bears the name Moham-mad in it, and it has stamps from several countries in the

---

* A headscarf worn by women, principally associated with Muslims.

Middle East and Asia which have large Muslim populations.

Whether being questioned in a US airport or receiving
an obtuse look from a passenger on the London Underground, the rules of engagement in crossing borders today
are murkier than the bruising realities of the 1970s school
playground. Indeed, the question of my Muslim identity
sometimes rises up to create moments of uncertainty and
fear, just as it did when I made my first ever trip to the West
Bank to visit the Holy Lands.

14:10

'Follow me,' says the Israeli security official.

I am munching on a sandwich, the one I bought a couple
of minutes ago from the snack bar tucked in the corner of
the vast Israeli immigration hall. I am hungry and tired
from hours of standing, refusing to sit and give the officials
any impression that they don't need to rush. I follow the
man but first decide to discard the remains of the greasy
contents of my sandwich into a nearby bin. He looks on
suspiciously, wondering what it is that I have just thrown
away.

'Bit late for that,' I say to myself, thinking of the Jordanian
business card I have ripped up and discarded fragments of
in the same bin a few minutes ago.

The officers had asked me this morning if I knew anyone
in Israel or in Jordan.

'No,' I had said confidently.

Hours later and still in the immigration hall, sensing this border passage was becoming trickier, I discovered a Jordanian business card inside my wallet. Seeing it reminded me that I had met a cousin's friend last night in Amman, a former pilot for Royal Jordanian Airlines. Discreetly I ripped the card into little pieces as I ate my sandwich, throwing it away with the remains of my lunch. I felt relief as the shreds dropped from my greasy fingers, and craftily did I flick one half of the remains into one wastebasket and the rest into another.

Thinking of my recent crossings in Syria, Jordan and Lebanon, I wonder why this one is taking so much longer, and looking so much more difficult. Unlike at those crossings I sense a degree of distrust from the Israeli officials.

'Go on! Walk!'

He raises his voice and disrespectfully pokes me in the shoulder blade with a rigid finger. I look back at him with a brief but steely stare, and whilst continuing to walk, I slow right down. He resumes a more civil tone of voice and indicates to me where to go.

It was six hours ago at 08:15 when I disembarked the bus from Amman and strode into the Israeli immigration hall, excited at the thought that I would soon be looking round the age-old city of Jerusalem. This is a city I have meant to visit for so long and one destination in the Middle East which remains a huge gap in my cultural, religious and geographic experience. To reach the border post, the bus crossed the famous Allenby Bridge that straddles the River

Jordan, and is named after the soldier who led British Forces in Palestine in World War I.

14:12

The Israeli security official is a young man perhaps in his late twenties. He seems inexperienced, bearing a countenance halfway between petrified and irritated. His smart, striking blue T-shirt contrasts well with his light hair and olive skin, making a perfect ensemble. Blue is the official colour for the staff here who are not dressed in military casuals. I can't work out what uniform denotes which department. He has a name tag but I can't make it out. I think it is Ben. He is the first Israeli man I have spoken to today. As if by design, all the others who questioned me this morning were attractive women, dressed in camouflage-design military pants and knee-high boots, speaking varying amounts of English.

We walk across the large expanse of the immigration hall. It is a voluminous space with a corrugated tin ceiling that must be at least twelve metres high. In some parts it is a little lower, where they have fitted a partition for housing lighting and air-conditioning outlets. The height of the ceilings relieves feelings of being enclosed. Powerful gusts of conditioned, cooled air provide freshness and comfort. We pass through a number of barricades and swinging gates, and walk into a short and narrow corridor. There is a bench.

'Wait here,' Ben says.

The ceiling here is low, less than three metres high. In the passage there is just enough space for a long seat but with little room for anyone to walk past. Two other travellers occupy places along the bench. One is a middle-aged woman shrouded in a black hijab and with a pale, worried face. The other is a younger man, dressed shabbily in khaki pants and sandals and with a three-day scrub of greying stubble on his face. They are separate. Both look Arab. The man clutches a Jordanian passport with its distinctive black cover and silver lettering, the most tastefully designed passport I have seen. I can't see any of the woman's papers. She whispers sayings on a prayer bead whose pearls click-clack through her fingers. They both look harassed and tired. I speak to neither and avoid eye contact. I have already told the passport officials three times that I don't speak Arabic and want to avoid getting into conversation.

I feel sorry for these two, in the knowledge that as a UK citizen the officials are likely to accord me greater respect.

14:40

A few minutes later Ben calls me in to join him and another of his blue-shirted colleagues in a small room.

'Stand over there,' he points across the floor to the right from where we enter, stern and with a suspicious tone in his voice.

I step across as directed. The space is divided by a hanging rail and curtain which presumably can be pulled across as required.

'What is in your bag?'

'Books, papers, my camera . . . And I have another bag outside.'

'Do you have anything electronic in here?'

'Yes.'

'What do you have?' One of Ben's colleagues takes over.

The colleague doesn't wear a name tag. He is of a similar age to Ben but with black hair and more experienced-looking eyes.

'My camera, my computer and my mobile phone.'

'Take them out.'

I take out the items one by one, slowly and methodically. I am so prone to losing things that I want to know exactly what comes out and ensure that it goes back in again. In the last few months of travel, I have lost a pen, a couple of books and a favourite pair of trousers left hanging in a hotel closet in Texas.

'Is the computer on?'

'It is on standby.'

'Could you switch it off, please?'

'Sure.'

I am happy to switch off the computer. This entry business is taking longer than I expected, and I feel it is better my computer is rendered less accessible. I think of my name being on the US Department of Homeland Security 'no-fly list', entered by the overzealous US officials who naively quizzed me in Dallas on a recent trip, and feel perhaps the Israelis have picked up my name on their database. Post 9/11 there has been a marked increase in collaboration by security authorities, and all sorts of Mohammads put on the US list who have no association with terrorism. I flip open the laptop and start the process of booting it up to then power it down.

'What about the camera battery? Can you remove that, please?'

'Sure,' I reply.

Though it has been a long wait, I sense a need to slow things down now.

'Would you like me to do that right now, or shall I finish the computer first?'

I stop my activities to ask the question, mimicking their method of introducing layer upon layer of process into this exercise.

'Finish the computer first.' Ben's colleague is mildly irritated. 'One at a time is better.'

I slow it down some more. I want to control the pace of this. I want control over something at least, as I feel the situation slip away from my powerless grasp. I have been at the border six hours already, and most of the dozen or so travellers who were with me on the bus this morning have long gone. I have no idea where this is headed and now we enter yet another stage to this process of gaining, or not gaining, entry. I can tell that this security search is a sideshow, and that it is unlikely to play a positive role in gaining approval to let me in. As I comply with the requests to switch off the electronics from my bag, I wonder what else is in store.

Across the room at the desk, the Arab woman is being questioned about something. I look at the curtain. It is half drawn now. I don't like the look of it as it swishes and sways gently with passing gusts of air. I haven't seen out of a window for hours now, and begin to feel boxed in. I don't know whether it is light or dark outside. I continue and complete the process of disabling all of my electronic appliances including removing the battery from my phone, which in any case was already switched off. Once this is done Ben's colleague offers me water.

'No, thanks.'

Somewhat defiantly I show him the bottle I am drinking from already. He asks me to place it on the table, next to my phone and the other items. As the minutes tick by, the table-top fills with personal items taken one by one from my bag, my wallet and my person. My Waterman pen, my trouser belt, credit cards and travel papers, cash in various currencies, a diary and some books. Leaving the things aside, now Ben and his colleague turn to me. Ben draws the curtain shut. The rings whisk quietly along the cylindrical steel rail as the now impatient-sounding Arab woman and her questioner disappear from sight behind the partition.

14:50

'Stand here, please,' they signal to the centre of the small space created by the partitioning via the curtain.

This enclosed cubicle now gives me the impression that I am in a hospital, about to be examined.

'And remove your jacket first.'

I show them that I'd like to put the jacket on the bench behind me, and ask whether that's OK.

'Yes, yes.'

I stand upright, and on their signal stretch out my arms to either side.

'We will now ask you to remove some items of clothing,' Ben says as he unfurls a pair of surgical gloves fresh from a cardboard container on the table in front of us.

Noticing the container for the first time, I think of hospitals again. I feel the pumping of my heart as I watch the gloves make chewy noises as he stretches the translucent plastic over his palms. Whilst I undo the top button of my jeans, Ben wrestles with the gloves until they settle into position with a curt slap against the olive skin of his wrists. As I notice Ben's muscular arms I realise that whatever element of control I had in this skewed power balance is ebbing away.

Ben stands to attention. He is tense and holding his stomach in, as if in the early stages of a fitness programme or perhaps wanting to impress a girlfriend. The cream-coloured gloves are a sheath over his hands, revealing the profile of his bones and highlighting the sharpness of his fingernails. His tension unsettles me. I don't know what is going to happen, but I would rather it happens at the hands of someone who knows what they are doing. When Ben tells me to unzip and loosen my trousers further, my concern rises significantly. I search for diffusion tactics, and at the same time loosen the muscles in my shoulders and thighs, as if preparing for an injection.

'So, what is this questioning about? Is this immigration, or security?'

'No. This is just routine questioning. It is not part of the immigration process. Loosen your shirt buttons and lean your arms against the wall.'

Standing astride now, I consider cracking a joke but decide it would not be in good taste, present circumstances considered.

The wall he wants me to lean my hands against has a large Star of David flag pinned onto it. It is so large that there is no way I can lean without placing my hands on the flag. For a second I am unsure as to whether it will appear disrespectful to place my sandwich-greased palms all over it. I don't know the etiquette for leaning on Star of David flags. I look at it and feel the onset of frustration and anger. I remember gazing at Israel's serene-looking hills from a war-torn and broken Southern Lebanon last summer. I experienced feelings of frustration that day as I walked around the city of Tyre's shanty streets of rubble and bomb-smashed buildings, just a few kilometres from the tranquil-seeming hills of Israel, home to a bustling, affluent and fiercely protected economy.

The flag is bait. I decide not to ask too many questions. I lean on my fingertips and feel my body weight pressing against the ends. Forced against the hardness of the wall through the flag's thin fabric, the ends of my fingers blanch as the blood is pushed back from near the surface of the skin.

14:55

As his gloved hands work their way down from my shoulders towards my midriff, my usual propensity to sudden and violent spasms of ticklishness vanishes. It is the first time this has happened and I wonder whether I can learn some new technique from today for combating this problem. The affliction for me is more psychological than sensational. During childhood Amma could tickle me from eight paces by merely signalling that she was about to.

The search consists of Ben placing his hands side by side on a selected part of my body, holding still, and then pumping suddenly as if he is looking for embedded items buried away under my skin. I cannot work out what else might be the rationale for such a search method. He works his way down from my arms, shoulders and upper chest. As he reaches my waist, the position of his hands changes to encircle me.

'Pull your trousers down to your knees.'

I stare ahead at the Star of David just inches before me, and feel ill thinking of what might happen next.

'Down to your knees, I said!'

I comply, pulling my trousers down gradually and turning to look Ben in the eye as I do so. Unnecessary and degrading, Ben shows no compulsion to offer an explanation, nor does he register any concern for what he is about to put me through. With my eyes closed I turn back to face the wall, grit my teeth and loosen the muscles around my buttocks.

15:02

Afterwards, they return to my things. One by one, I show them each credit card, my UK driving licence and frequent-flyer cards, and all the other items which are in my wallet.

'How much money do you have?'

'About two hundred Jordanian Dinars, eighty US dollars, two hundred British pounds, five Euros and a small amount in some other currencies.'

'Not much then.'

'No, not much.'

But the question is out of place. So far this has been a physical search of my person and my belongings as though there is some security concern. This question has gone out of these bounds. Suddenly the two officers seem unsure of exactly what they are looking for, yet they continue a thorough search. They must be almost done with me. Or perhaps it means they are trying to kill time before some-one important arrives. Someone more important. I sit and wait. The flag on the wall stares back at me. Its size and closeness, and the thick blue lines that run above and below the star, make it look extra wide. Dominating this little cubicle, the flag conveys a feeling of intimidation and menace, no doubt intentionally.

Ben decides to take a picture of me with his digital camera. It is a small, rather basic-looking gadget. Now thinking that these two are merely a warm-up act, I am on the brink of giving him a cheesy smile as he gets ready. He takes a few seconds to adjust the camera and as the flash flickers in preparation for the shot, my eyes start to blink. By the time Ben clicks, my eyes are shut and the photo is of no use.

'Keep your eyes open.'

Irritated, Ben erases the picture and resets the camera. Something seems to be wrong with it. Ben is impatient, and paces around the room as he fidgets with the dials and buttons. My blinking is another one of those afflictions, like the ticklishness. But unlike the ticklishness this is one I have normally conquered. Only today the blinking seems to have come back. It takes Ben at least two minutes to reset everything to take one more picture. He tuts. His fingers look brittle as they wrap around the camera body, his knuckles are bony and rigid. The more Ben tenses up the more I relax, watching him relinquish his grip of the situation. On the second attempt, and on the third, my eyes are shut. Ben is really irritated now.

'I am not doing it on purpose,' I smirk.

Though unsuccessful in controlling my blinking, I relax more and more. The curtain swishes open. It is Ben's colleague. Ben puts the camera down for a moment and the two talk animatedly. I can see the room in full again now. As though we are viewing a new act in a long play, the Arab woman who was being questioned has gone. Another two officials walk in, one of them yet another attractive young woman, in a blue T-shirt that is two sizes too tight for her. She offers water to everyone in the room. Everyone except me.

I wait.

15:15

Another man arrives, looking like he has rushed to reach here. He doesn't wear any uniform, but instead is in a smart polo shirt, casual shoes and chinos. He is short, thin-haired and stocky, and looks confident and authoritative. Evidently he has been outside. He sweats and his bearded face is tinged with the ruddy complexion of someone who has just stepped in from strong sunshine. The others busy themselves briefing him. Clearly he is the senior guy around here.

'Good afternoon, Mohammad. T-hki arabi?'* He booms as he walks over and shakes my hand.

'I understand a few words.' I feel it is better to say this than a straight no as Shalev introduces himself to me with an unsettling air of self-confidence.

I have said all day that I don't speak Arabic, but saying to this man that I don't understand it at all would be foolish. Shalev is clearly some sort of intelligence officer. At his behest I go with him to another office, down a small corridor out through the back of the cubicle I was searched in. Politely he offers me water. I accept. He offers me tea

---

* Colloquial for 'Do you speak Arabic?'

or coffee. Realising this discussion will take time, I opt for coffee. I think of Ramallah where Leila, my Arabic teacher from London, is waiting for me, and then I think of Jerusalem.

Shalev's office has no windows, a few posters of tourist sites in Israel, a large desk and a computer. He speaks fluent Arabic in the Cham* dialect, as well as fluent English and his native Hebrew. He is friendly, relaxed, easy-paced, evidently of superior intelligence and unsettlingly calm.

15:20

I relax a bit more. At least now I am in the hands of someone who knows what he is doing. Like a concert pianist about to start a performance, Shalev readies his hands on his keyboard, looks up at the screen of his computer, and begins.

'So, the first name is . . . . . .' He looks again at my passport, '. . . Mohammad, right?'

'Yes.'

'wa baden?'

'After that?' I ask to check, alert not to make out that I understand the Arabic too readily.

The game is on.

'Tufael is the middle name. And Chowdhury the surname,' I continue.

---

* Cham refers to what was Greater Syria, or what is now largely Syria, Palestine and Lebanon.

'Do you know anybody in Israel?' His eyes are a clear and piercing blue. He doesn't flinch.

'No.'

I have already said 'no' to this question several times that morning during the first few questionings I have had from passport and immigration officials and feel comfortable that I have adopted a consistent approach. Leila's advice, when I spoke to her last night, was not to complicate matters by saying I know any Palestinians or speak any Arabic, since both will definitely raise suspicions. The advice was to stick to basics and say that I am here to visit Jerusalem, and not mention my intention to visit her family in Ramallah, the principal city in the Palestinian-controlled West Bank.

'Nobody at all?'

'No.' I think about Leila, waiting.

'Are you travelling alone?'

'Yes.'

Shalev asks me about my trip, where I have been and what I have done so far.

'What do you want to do in Israel?'

'I want to visit Jerusalem, the holy sites there. I am performing Umrah next week in Makkah, and this is a great opportunity for me to spend a couple of days here first to complete my tour of the holy places.'

'And what else?'

'That's it.' I think about my plans to visit Ramallah, and indeed to stay there instead of Jerusalem. I say nothing.

'And where will you be staying?'

'At the Dan Panorama Hotel.' I feel relief at having called

them from the Marriott Hotel in Amman early this morning and confirmed that they have a room available.

'And how did you know of the Dan Panorama?'

'I called the King David, and they put me through to the Dan when I decided the King David was too expensive for me.'

'And how did you know about the King David Hotel?'

'Everyone knows the King David. I called them about a room and they said it would be three hundred and six dollars. So I decided on the Dan Panorama, their sister hotel, which is one hundred and fifty-seven.'

'Thult.'

Thult means a third in Arabic and Shalev nearly catches me out as I am about to reply 'la, la nus', which means 'no, no a half'. Always ready to dive into anything that merits quantitative analysis, I just stop myself in time. I look back at him blankly, unsettled by how he has already read my character, my instincts and my nature.

'Thult. One third,' he repeats.

I wonder whether he realises that I am fluent in these types of conversations.

'La, la, nus,' I say now. 'It is a half of the King David rate, not a third.'

'Yes, yes. Of course it is.'

15:30

I replay in my mind the exercise I undertook in Amman last night, to clear out from my wallet and papers all evidence of knowing anyone in Israel or the Palestinian territories. When I spoke to Leila yesterday, I had jotted down a few notes on scraps of paper. Notes like 'Damascus Gate' to denote where to get a bus from to come to Ramallah, or 'Best Eastern Hotel' which is the place she suggested I stay at. Thankfully all that evidence was discarded last night. But sitting here in Shalev's office, I have a rotten, dishonest feeling.

'And where did you stay in Jordan?'

'Last night I was at the Marriott in Amman.'

'And do you know anybody in Jordan?'

'No.'

I feel terrible to be lying, but relieved at how I just discarded the business card of the retired airline pilot in the immigration hall more than an hour ago. Self-satisfaction momentarily gets the better of me.

Shalev asks my address. We are on safe ground again. As I call out the first line of my address, my mind races forward, looking for other topics where I may fall down. Leila.

'27 Berkeley . . .'

'Wait. Wait.'

Something seems to be stuck on the form into which Shalev is inputting information. He stops typing and depresses the backspace button on his keyboard several times. He is so calm and relaxed. There is no tension in his wrists as he types, no straining of his eyes or looks of irritation. Shalev knows so much more about leveraging control than Ben, about the relationships between pace, tension and composure.

'So, 27 . . .'

'Berkeley Mansions . . .'

'Hold on . . . hmm . . . what is the matter here.' He peers into his screen. 'Let me see . . . twenty-seven, wait, wait.'

There is something wrong with the form but it provides Shalev with an opportunity for playing a game too. He enjoys his work, and is evidently good at it. I lean back, try to relax my shoulders and sip some more of the thick, Arabic style coffee.

I too would be more relaxed had it not been for . . .

'Right. Now let's try.'

'27 Berkeley Mansions.'

'No . . . No . . . This is not going to work.'

. . . had it not been for those text messages I sent Leila from the immigration hall, just this morning.

'There are 464 tiles in the waiting room. 166 of them are blue, and 39 are cracked,' my second text to her had read, sent only a couple of hours ago.

The first one, in the circumstances, was worse:

'Hi. This is taking a lot longer than I expected. Don't call me just in case. I will call you when done. Ciao.'

A veil of tension begins to descend from the top of my head down towards my eyes. It feels as if it is about to blur my vision, like a thick winter mist. I am getting lost wondering how to play this. I need ideas and a plan, and I need them now.

15:45

'Let me write my address down for you on a piece of paper,' I say to Shalev.

'Yes, that is a good idea.'

This buys me some time. Thinking time.

Shalev hands me one small square piece of light green paper, plucked from a stack of them piled neatly on his desk. As I write down my address, slowly and methodically using block capitals, my mind buzzes.

I struggle over whether to confess that I know someone here or not. It is touch and go and I estimate that if they decide to trace my calls, I may have only a few minutes in which to spill the beans. Any longer and it is possible that the interview will be terminated, I miss the opportunity to confess altogether, and then get found out some time later.

I look at what I have written down on the piece of green paper: 'Regent's Park Road' instead of 'Regent's Park.' My mind is too distracted, clouded with uncertainty and in too many places at once. I decide not to cross anything out for now, afraid of looking less credible. I make doubly sure to write down the post code correctly.

'House telephone number?'

Make that five minutes. Shalev will obviously ask for my mobile number next. Presumably he has the ability to intercept any messages I have been sending while roaming on an Israeli cellular network. Perhaps from elsewhere too, since the intelligence and surveillance services here must be more capable than most.

'. . . 464 tiles in the waiting room . . . Don't call me . . . .'

The text messages flash before my eyes. I wonder how I can have the cleverness to tear up business cards and deal with all manner of other interrogations, yet have the idiocy of sending those texts. My face feigns calm but my mind races with options for how, not whether, to confess. I don't want Shalev to find out about my messages to Leila via his surveillance network. I want him to find out from me.

But I can't tell him now. It would be too abrupt and may raise more suspicions. I need a strategy to slip the information in without drama, confession or announcement. I don't want to contradict myself directly and make it look like I was lying. My objective now is to maintain credibility and not to undermine the short and invaluable relationship of trust that is developing with Shalev.

'Mobile number?' He looks up at me, his clear blue eyes innocent of my dilemma.

Whatever the strategy, the information needs to be imparted within two to three minutes now. Any moment this session might take a new turn which limits my possibilities for disclosure, for example if Shalev gets called away, leaving me in the novice hands of Ben and his accomplices.

Mobile number. The question rings in my mind.

'Plus four four . . .' I begin to call out the numbers.

I imagine my grey Nokia handset sitting on his desk. I imagine Shalev looking at it, switching it on and asking me for the PIN code, and then examining the numbers and details stored in the memory. I think of messages in Arabic text from friends, the language I have said I do not understand, and of Leila's phone number in the address book.

As another precaution last night, I had erased all recent call lists from my mobile. And then this morning I made several missed calls to a few UK and other numbers, not to make it look suspicious that my phone had no dialled numbers stored. I give myself some credit for this but realise that the steps I have taken are not enough.

'Plus four four ... seven ...' I repeat the numbers to Shalev, who still seems unaware of my anxiety.

One of his colleagues walks in. Shalev and the man speak in Hebrew. He has come in to ask if I need more tea or coffee. I see a lifeline, and jump in as soon as the man walks out.

'Hebrew sounds so similar in rhythm to Arabic,' I begin.

'They are cousins,' Shalev smiles.

Cousins. I wonder what this intelligent, seemingly balanced man thinks about Palestinian rights to their own, independent state.

'Yes, they are both derived from Aramaic and other languages. But Hebrew is much older than Arabic.' I am obsequious.

'Correct.' Shalev continues to type.

'I have an old Arabic teacher here in Ramallah.'

Shalev stops. He looks up from his keyboard and over to me, gazing inquisitively into my eyes. He has a slightly raised eyebrow.

'Oh?' he says.

'Yes. She was my teacher last year in London, and now lives here in Ramallah.'

'Ramallah?'

'Yes. Ramallah.' I pronounce the name clearly, spelling out each syllable, not wanting to look sheepish or confessional.

There is just the hint of a smug smile on the corner of Shalev's mouth. He does well to conceal it. He knows he has broken me down just a little bit, and he has enough experience to realise that he needs to help me come forward, not make me feel small and retreat behind my defences and fears.

'So, when was she your teacher? This lady from, er . . . Ramallah.'

'In 2005,' I pause for a second to take a breath. 'I called her a couple of times in the last week, saying I might come to Jerusalem and if so then perhaps we could meet.'

It is out. It is important I continue at a gentle, steady pace.

'Does she have Israeli ID? Is she allowed to come to Jerusalem?'

'I don't know. If she can come I could meet her.' I shrug my shoulders. 'It would be nice,' I throw in with faux nonchalance.

'What is her name?'

'Leila. Leila Sa'ed.'

'L . . . E . . . I . . . L . . . A,' he types slowly, muttering to himself in Arabic.

'And what is her phone number?'

I imagine a scene where some two hours later Shalev's assistant walks into the room with a computer printout of a text message that says there are 464 tiles in the waiting hall, and Shalev asks me:

'So, Mohammad, you don't know anybody in Israel?'

The instant relief of disclosure outweighs the possible disadvantages and consequences of my confession. Shalev asks me more about Leila, how much I know about her, what she was doing in London, what she does here, her age, her family, and so on. I think of Leila, of the brilliant future that awaits her as one of Palestine's finest young lawyers and of how much difficulty this incident might cause her now. Shalev finds her on his database, the one that apparently has a file on every adult Palestinian in the West Bank and Gaza.

'Yes. I have her here,' he says, smiling at his screen. 'S A E D. Do you have her numbers?' He smiles now at me.

'Not in my head. They are in my phone.'

Immediately Shalev grabs the handset on his desk phone and makes a call. His pace quickens and in an instant he appears purposeful and determined. He has a long conversation with someone about the release of my mobile phone. It fails. I feel guilty to be dragging my friend into this, but know this was the only safe option.

'Procedures, procedures,' Shalev sighs.

16:10

Shalev starts to look through my wallet. Methodically he flips it open, and initially just stares at it. He is scanning its layout, deciding how it is that he will work his way through it. He must check wallets all the time, and since they come in many shapes and sizes, I guess he has a technique which is attuned to accounting for each design. For mine, he seems to have partitioned it into the outside, the deep inside, the wings and the pockets. One by one, Shalev starts to work through each.

I am nervous again, and decide on a biscuit. Like the Star of David flag, the biscuits have been staring at me for the past half hour. I consider it might be a bad move to take a biscuit since it will make my mouth dry, but decide to go for it.

I think again of the Jordanian business card which I destroyed two hours ago. It would have been a setback for my credibility if Shalev had found it after I said I knew nobody in Jordan. It would mean more questions, more phone calls and more entries into the database. Knowing the business card is currently buried under a smelly kebab sauce, my nervousness abates.

Just as I relax something goes wrong. Shalev is looking at me, dangling a piece of paper he has just fished from my wallet.

'What's this then?'

'Oh shit. Oh shit,' I say to myself.

Shalev holds up a receipt, from Budgen supermarket in Kilburn, North London. Surely this innocent-looking sales chit is irrelevant, but no, there is Arabic handwriting on the back.

'Oh shit,' I think, 'it's the list of phone numbers Sabiha (my current Arabic teacher in London) had written down for me of her family in Damascus.'

I have been looking for this list for days, including while in Damascus earlier this week. It is not a disaster for the numbers to have been found, except for one issue. The names and numbers are all written in Arabic and according to what I have led these officials to understand I don't read Arabic very well.

'A B O U M U . . . What does this say?' Shalev hands me the receipt.

The game is on again. I scan the paper and feign a cropped brow reading it. We are both playing now.

'It looks like it says Abu Mohammad,' I speak as though I am Shalev's research assistant and we are both deciphering some obscure parchment.

'Which must be right because I believe the lady's brother is called Mohammad. So that must be her father's number.

'S . . . A . . . B . . . I . . . H . . . A. What is her family name?' Shalev stares into his screen.

'Suleymani.'

'SabihA, SAAbiha?' He plays with the name, pronouncing it several ways and looking for the right one.

I don't help him. He types and mutters more in Arabic, something about Suleymani. I feel awful that now another person's name is dragged into this, and her whole family along with it. All these names and numbers enter the database, one by one. It takes several painfully slow minutes to go through the contents of the Budgen receipt.

16:25

Shalev says something in Arabic which I genuinely do not understand. He explains it means 'they are all very qualified and intelligent people'. He refers to Sabiha's family, once he has found them on his database. His file notes say Sabiha's father is a dentist and Shalev already knows Sabiha is my Arabic teacher.

One thing leads to another and Shalev asks me if I know anyone else in Damascus. So I tell him about Rita, leaving out her well-known surname, and explain that she too was my teacher in Arabic, some two years ago.

'So many Arabic teachers?' Shalev craftily raises an eyebrow.

'Rita in Damascus was my conversational Arabic teacher,' I say, realising that my claim to speak 'only a few words' is wearing rather thin. I think about how Rita's grandfather was one of the Arab nobles who along with Lawrence of Arabia attacked Damascus during World War I.

But Shalev picks up on something else.

'Interesting,' he chuckles. 'One teacher here, one teacher in Syria, one teacher in London . . . and all women. All your teachers are women!'

'Yes, so they are,' I say, as if I have only just realised this.

'All single, I presume? Any of them nice?' he chuckles while casually glancing through more details on his screen.

'Look, Shalev, you have all my details now,' I laugh. 'Maybe you can find me a nice wife from your country, how about that?'

'Of course, for a certain fee . . .'

We laugh. I decide not to tell him about all the other people I know in Damascus, and say that I know nobody in Beirut when he asks me. Telling Shalev right now that the muezzin of one of Beirut's oldest mosques is a personal friend of mine would not be a good idea. Nor would it be helpful to mention my contact with a renowned Canadian journalist in Beirut who is one of the Western presses' fiercest critics of Israeli actions in Palestine, or that my father once met and donated funds to Yasser Arafat in Bangladesh at a fundraiser for the PLO.*

'I need the phone numbers of Rita in Damascus, and . . . Sabiha.' He still plays with the pronunciation, 'in London. She is in London. Right?' he doubts.

'Yes. That is right.'

Shalev needs access to my mobile handset now even more than before, and negotiates again down his phone line. Moments later another colleague walks in, holding my phone aloft. He puts out his hand, offering it back to me. My instinct is not to take it and I keep my arms close to my side. Shalev and the man speak. They come to an agreement. I take the phone and place it carefully on the desk.

'Let's finish these questions first and then I can take the numbers.' Shalev's game is sometimes predictable.

I guessed he would want to slow the pace as soon as we'd passed the crescendo of getting the phone back. I read it well and feel good that I didn't panic and switch the phone on as soon as I took it. I don't want anyone to think I am desperate to have my phone back, or anything else for that matter. I don't need my phone.

As Shalev types I keep looking at the handset, lying silently on the desk. And then I realise what it is. There is Arabic numbering on the keypad. It was a handset I bought

---

* Palestine Liberation Organisation

in Abu Dhabi a couple of years ago, to replace one I had lost during a trip out to Asia.

'It is so bloody hard to hide anything,' I think to myself. 'Everything real and true is interconnected in so many different ways.'

But the more I look at the phone the more relief I feel, replaying in my mind's eye the scene of his assistant walking in with a printout of my messages to Leila from their phone detection service.

Shalev asks me why Jerusalem interests me. I explain again I am Muslim and that I want to visit the holy sites there. For a moment he takes genuine interest in how seriously I take my religion and understands my sincerity in this. He takes note that my Jerusalem trip will be followed by a trip to Makkah and Medina.

Solemnly, Shalev apologises for delaying me and having to ask so many questions.

'I understand your need to ask questions. I hope you do your job well since I want to be safe in your country.'

'We are only concerned to ensure that we don't let people into the country who are going to work against it. You know there are still a lot of people in this world who don't like the idea of Jews having their own country.'

'Yes, I understand.'

'Thank you for being understanding.'

'I am used to this,' I sigh, estimating this to be about the twentieth border questioning I have experienced since 9/11.

I tell him about my American experiences, and others. I explain how the Americans appear generally more naïve in their questioning than the Israelis. Shalev follows this by suggesting that United States security officials are apparently quite nasty sometimes too.

'Not in my experience. They are never nasty to me, but they take a long time. Like you. You know Shalev, the questions don't need to be nasty. The uncertainty is enough to create an imbalance, a feeling of helplessness. If you turn me down right now, I will be very happy to go back to Jordan,' I sigh, throwing in some reverse psychology.

'No, no, Mohammad, you have come so far it would be a shame to have to go back. I am confident we can get you through successfully. Let us see.'

Now Shalev asks me about work, and goes into much detail. He takes the phone numbers of my superiors in New York, and others'. I decide to name two and call out the names one by one: Nausheen Narain and Joseph Eisenberg.

'It sounds like a Jewish name,' he says of Joe. 'What is his relationship to you?'

'Joe is my boss. He is a Jew. A very good, practising one. And a good man too.'

Shalev's eyes perk up. There is a new energy in him.

'Yes, in fact his children speak Hebrew, and he comes to Israel once or twice every year,' I add.

'How do you know all this?'

'I have been to his home in Connecticut. His family like me very much.'

My ploy to position Joe as my main boss works brilliantly. My credibility barometer shoots up a few notches and I begin to feel the situation is turning around. Evidently Shalev is quite touched that I work for a Jew, more than I would have expected from a calm and collected professional doing his job so dispassionately. I like Shalev for his professionalism, and for how he has played the game, and now I like him even more since he has shown a sense of fallibility, of emotion. He takes my business card and notes all of my personal email addresses, one by one. Everything goes into his database. He asks me if I have any questions at this point.

'Yes, I do. I have two.'

'Please, continue.'

'Firstly, if you grant me entry to Israel tonight, am I restricted simply to visiting Jerusalem, or may I go elsewhere? Ramallah, for example? To meet my teacher?'

Risky move, but I decide it is the time to press forward with this. I certainly don't want to be stopped later and questioned about my movements. I'd rather go back to Amman.

'Mohammad, Israel is a free and democratic country, and you are free to move about as you like once you are inside. We only recommend you don't associate yourself with people you don't know.'

It is the only time in hours with him that Shalev offers me an opinion.

16:50

I wait outside in the low-ceilinged corridor I was in before the search. Everybody has gone. Shalev and the others are inside and I sit alone staring at the security door lock to the cubicle with the curtains where I was questioned some three hours ago. The door handle has something written on it in Hebrew. I cannot make it out. Blinking with tiredness, I stop trying. I have no idea what will happen next. The keyhole is of a high technology. I noticed earlier before being searched that the lock itself had at least five levers on it, and it shut with a resounding metallic clunk.

17:35

I am woken by Ben. Shalev is right behind him. They usher me back inside. I follow Shalev back to his windowless office. His handset is off the hook, and the phone is set on loudspeaker.

'JOE? Are you there?' Shalev is speaking to Joe in the US.

I calculate it must be about ten o'clock Sunday morning there. He must be at home, a luxurious mansion in a leafy glade in Connecticut, about an hour north of New York City. Shalev ushers me to speak into the phone.

'Hi, Joe.'

'MOHAMMAD? Hey, Mohammad. Just wanted to hear your voice. Just wanted to make sure you're OK.' Joe's voice is shaking with concern.

Hearing Joe's panicked tones makes me feel for just a minute that I have gone through some sort of ordeal.

'I am fine, Joe,' I reply in a raised voice, my response as positive and upbeat as I can make it.

'Give me a call when you are done, Mohammad.'

'Will do, Joe. Thanks. See you in a few weeks.'

Another person dragged into this. More innocent names and numbers that will go into that database. Shalev switches back to the handset, says a few words of thanks to Joe and hangs up. Evidently they had spoken for a few minutes before I came in. Curiosity bites away at me but I decide not to ask what they had discussed.

'He is a nice man, this Joe,' Shalev observes. 'What was your second question, Mohammad?'

I am impressed.

'Oh, nothing. Nothing at all.'

18:05

I am released. The immigration hall is empty, bar two cleaning ladies wiping an already shiny floor with mops and yet another attractive Israeli woman in fatigues who for a final time looks over my passport. She is from the department that I still cannot identify. After a cursory shuffle through the rest of my papers, she stamps me in on a loose piece of paper as I have requested so that I can avoid having an Israeli stamp in my passport. Once done, I walk back into the baggage hall. Mine is the only bag left, sitting lonely on the shiny floor.

My eyes squint at the dull brightness of the late afternoon sunlight when I step outside, adjusted as they are to the softer lighting indoors. It is almost ten hours since I walked into the immigration hall off the bus from Amman this morning. The past few hours of interrogation have left me numbed and mentally exhausted. I hail the solitary, white Mercedes E240 taxi waiting at the cab rank outside, jump in and immediately ask the driver if I can use his phone to make a local call. Probably used to such requests, he quietly hands it over. As we drive off I am already speaking to my friend in Ramallah, broken down in stress by now, having not heard from me all day. Soon I will be at her house and enjoying some traditional Bedouin home-cooked maqloobah.* I nestle into the comfort of the taxi's firm leather seats, take a final look back at the immigration hall through the rear window. Ben never did get my picture, although his database now contained my name, address, phone numbers and knew that I was connected to monitored Syrian and Palestinian individuals.

---

* A traditional Bedouin dish enjoyed all over the Middle East. Maqloobah literally means 'upside down' as the dish is prepared in a large pot and then the pot is turned upside down to empty the dish onto a serving plate.

Four

Memories of Sylhet

'Tufael, you must redo that prayer. You read only two rakaat* instead of four.'

'Yes, but I read two rakaat because I am observing kasr† for travellers.'

I smile at the onset of this jovial debate, the endearing one that resurfaces each time I visit Sylhet. According to the traditions of the Prophet, prayer is to be shortened to ease the traveller's burden. Much guidance in Islam is based on practicalities, and there are specific guidelines offered as to when and when not to shorten one's prayer. The condition of kasr applies to one who travels over forty-eight miles from their permanent residence for a period of up to fifteen days. If a traveller stays in the same location for over 15 nights, they are no longer considered to be in a state of

---

* Rakah (plural *rakaat*) is a unit of prayer and every prayer consists of two, three or four rakaat.

† Kasr is Arabic for short, and refers here to the shortening of prayer as a dispensation to travellers.

travel. I travel to Sylhet for two or three days at a time, and it is around ten thousand kilometres' distance from my place of permanent residence in Melbourne. I offer shortened prayers whenever I go to Sylhet. However, the belief amongst certain family members is that since Sylhet is my ancestral root, it should never be treated as a place where one can be in a state of travel. To them Sylhet is home, my home as well as their home, and there is no kasr at home.

'Kasr? Sylhet is your home, Tufael. You cannot come here and observe kasr!'

'Chacha,* yours is an emotional definition of "home". Islam defines it practically, to lighten your burden when you travel. Sylhet is my family home, but practically speaking I am in a state of journey. I am away from my normal residence, which is Melbourne.'

Having spent most of my schoolboy life being treated as an outsider by the family, I found it ironic to be pulled up for shortening my prayer, as though the clan can dismiss me for being a foreigner yet expect me to behave as a local all at the same time.

'Tufael, you may on exception count London or Melbourne as your temporary home in this respect and also pray normally there . . .'

What I didn't appreciate was the emotional weight that issues such as kasr prayer carried with the murubbi. Sensible interpretation of the religion gave way to the feeling that Sylhet was the ultimate place of origin. But there was

---

* Paternal uncle; see also note to p. 157

great symbolism in coming to Sylhet, and not shortening one's prayers provided legitimacy to the concept of the mother soil, the base, the home.

Childhood trips to and from Sylhet were generously laced with such examinations as to how we, the ones born overseas, bridged our identities and origins. During my teenage years I dreaded as much as looked forward to our annual pilgrimage to this bustling town tucked away up in the hills. Surrounded by legendary slopes covered with lush vegetation, gas fields with flames flickering randomly out of the ground, beautiful people and miles of thick, mysterious jungle, the Sylhet division of Bangladesh (of which Sylhet town is the principal centre) offered much to discover. The main reason for our visits would be to spend time with Dadu, Abba's mother. We would also meet dozens of other relatives, dutifully doing the rounds of their homes during afternoon 'visiting hours'. Occasionally we would take excursions out of town too, to wander around a tea garden or drive up to the India–Bangladesh border posts of Tamabil and Jafflong, high up in the foothills of Assam.

Hazaripur is the labyrinthine locality where the Chowdhurys settled after leaving behind their spacious and landed existence in the village of Sonarpur some thirty kilometres away. By the early 1980s, Hazaripur was one of several areas clustered together to give the bazaars and alleyways of Sylhet the character of a squalid, overgrown town with an inanely located central jail right in the middle of it. A tightly knit community of half a dozen streets, Hazaripur had a smattering of shops each with its own pull-down corrugated tin shutters, and a mosque next door to the family home. Most people knew one another. Just about everyone knew Jamal Chacha, prominent civil contractor, local stalwart and manager of a hardware shop owned by my father, his eldest brother, in the thoroughfare of stores and ramshackle tea houses which lie along Hazaripur's dusty main street. This is the route which connects Sylhet to the suburb of Shipgonj, and the one we would take for our adventure trips to the lofty Indian border lands forty-five kilometres beyond.

In contrast to the freedom offered by rural Bangladesh or the anonymity of Dhaka, Sylhet town, with a small and congested centre of some 250,000 population, always felt claustrophobic, exacerbated by grimy smells and frustrating traffic on streets that were clogged like unhealthy arteries. Backstreets, barely wide enough for cars to pass and without footpaths, were flanked by the high whitewashed walls of well-to-do 'Londoni'* homes. As we walked past, I would stare at the Bengali-script graffiti or try to read the posters on the walls, mainly regarding elections and showing largely plump faces of corrupt, moustachioed local male politicians. The town was rife with slums and shanty areas strewn with crow-pecked mounds of uncollected garbage on street corners, and stinking open sewers by the roadside, regularly urinated in by passing men who would hitch up their lungis† for a moment and casually squat down, unbothered by anyone who might be looking.

---

* 'Londoni' was the Sylheti term used to refer to the many hundreds of emigrés to the UK. Sylhet accounts for well over two-thirds of all Bangladeshi emigrés to the UK.

† Ethnic Bengali clothing for men, resembling a sarong usually worn at home.

Sylhet has always tried to be different to the rest of Bangladesh in whatever way possible. Sylhetis pride themselves on their differences, centred on attitudes towards religion, their local vernacular, subtle variations in cuisine and stronger ones in social norms and codes of conduct. Whenever required, Sylhetis will proudly remind you that whilst British India was partitioned into India and Pakistan in August 1947, Sylhet only elected to join Pakistan in January 1948 following a public referendum. It isn't clear to me precisely how Sylhet governed itself between Partition in August 1947 and joining Pakistan in January 1948, or indeed how the plebiscite was administered, who voted, and who counted the votes. It is one of those dozens of colonial anomalies that I have discovered travelling through many developing countries. Until today, many Sylhetis base their business and social activities around proximity, be it by clan, class, family or ancestral village. When speaking with a fellow Sylheti, many will actively be gauging how authentically Sylheti the person they have just met happens to be, measured by how they speak and behave. Until recently even Sylhet's rickshaws used to have a distinctive design, in that the protective canopy for passengers came in the form of a square-shaped frame as opposed to the rounded arch prevalent across the rest of Bangladesh. If Sylhet had a state cricket team, it would have followed the old Yorkshire Country Cricket Club rule of only selecting players born within the state's boundaries.

Trips to Sylhet exacerbated the feelings of social exclusion I carried with me from Britain. As anxious to anchor my identity here as I was back in London, I practised Sylheti behaviours in a conscious effort to gain acceptance, so much so that today I am one of very few of the younger generation who wears the traditional lungi and one of the even fewer who can summon up traditional village vocabulary.

As much as I adopted the most visible symbols of belonging, I found conforming to stereotypical and closely defined group identities unnecessarily exclusive. Drinking beer to be accepted as English or supporting the England cricket team was as arbitrary a test of identity as was being able to speak Sylheti or wear a lungi without it falling down. Identity mattered to me since I had been travelling the world without finding mine, most of the time seeing people who had no question about theirs.

Each year the family clan, by now spread over several parts of town, would get to know of our arrival within a couple of days. We were one of the few British-based families who would visit Sylhet annually, and the regularity of our visits added to people's desire to see us. For our most senior relatives, protocol required calling on them immediately to let them know we had come and again before departing to beg their leave. From the moment of getting there, we would therefore be in a race against time to rush around to people's houses and greet them before they heard third- or fourth-hand that we had arrived.

'Yes, we heard yesterday afternoon that you had arrived,' would be the typical introduction to a ticking off. 'Khusru's wife told us you have come to Sylhet.'

Such rebukes would be delivered with a finesse only picked up by those conversant with the subtleties of Sylheti social one-upmanship.

'Yes, we visited Khusru yesterday,' Abba would smile as though oblivious to the obvious slight.

Centre stage for the family was Dadu's bedroom, the focal point of the Hazaripur household. Semi-rural in design, the house itself had black-painted cement floors chipped in many places and chalky, whitewashed walls, covered by a thatched roof inside and a tin one on top to keep out the elements. All the rooms were interconnected through a panoply of internal doors and windows, some of which opened out onto the interior courtyard, which was also the dining area. Paint-covered wiring ran along walls every-where, stapled to walls, connecting appliances through hazardous and dusty wooden switch boxes. The house had only the most basic utilities, with no running water, no air conditioning and frequent power cuts, day and night.

Dadu's room had large, barred windows on three sides, all of which would be left wide open throughout the day. Transformation from bedroom to living room was a rapid morning-time ritual. Mosquito nets would be folded away, window shutters reopened and bedlinen rearranged to leave an open quarter for daytime use. Both the flat beds would then be used as comfortable surfaces to sit, lounge or snooze upon. There were one or two other items of furni-ture plus, of course, Dadu's silver paan daan* and table.

---

* A silver box used for storing betel nut and its many accoutrements.

After the morning adjustments were done, by no later than eight o'clock, the daily procession of visitors would start to stream through. People would come and go all day, visiting Dadu to pay their respects because they had just come into town from Sonarpur, or dropping in because they had heard that relatives were recently arrived from London.

The bedroom was restricted to male outsiders from the immediate family, since Dadu was from the generation of women who observed strict 'purdah',* in her case by ensuring there were curtains drawn across her windows during the day so that she didn't need to wear her headscarf while at home. Contrary to modern day interpretations that privacy is oppressive to women, purdah wasn't seen by Dadu as a restrictive concept. Instead, in a world where women's needs for privacy were important and where outsiders could be unnecessarily intrusive, purdah offered Dadu the freedom to do as she pleased in her own home.

We would lounge in Dadu's room, chatting or watching her prepare betel nut plucked choosily from her paan daan. I would lie down and snooze, hoping that one of my aunties would start fanning me to provide relief from the sticky heat, or massage my head while I slept. Amidst everything else during this week of imprisonment, it was entertaining to sit at home and watch the rain, lying under the cool air of the fan and letting one's mind drift in and out of the living-room conversation. But at the same time, confinement to the house

---

* A level of privacy maintained by some women whereby they appear in person only in front of close relatives, and seldom in front of others. Literally 'purdah' means curtain in Bengali and a number of other languages.

during the rainy season provided constant reinforcement to the claustrophobia I associated with Sylhet. For hours on end I would lie and look out through the gaps between the window bars, whose dark colours contrasted sharply with the willowy vegetation swaying outside.

We would have to touch the feet of any relative older than us when we met them. Performing 'salaam'* was a customary tradition, as were many other habits which predated the arrival of Islam in Bengal a few hundred years ago. Touching the feet of an elder was so integral to showing respect that it became a proxy for respect itself, rather than a symbol for it. If you didn't touch someone's feet when you met them, you were disrespectful. Blending local customs of prestige, status and position with the Islamic greeting of peace, salaam had embedded itself deep into the ritual of Bengali Muslim tradition. Like many such habits, over generations salaam took on elements of subtlety, technique and variation. The most venerated relatives, such as Dadas, Dadus, Nanas and Nanis† would receive full salaam honours. This involved approaching the subject with eyes lowered to the floor, squatting briefly before them, placing one hand on their feet and using the other to salute each foot by touching it first and then touching one's forehead.

'No, no!! There is no need. No, no . . .'

There would often follow a feigned gesture of resistance from the elder, not intended to stop the action but to soften

---

* peace in Arabic

† paternal grandfather and grandmother, maternal grandfather and grandmother

the humiliation with a patronising pat on the head. A standard operation could take as long as four to five seconds per person, and covering several elders standing in line required a certain amount of flex in the knees and strength in the thighs to pull it off. As one would rise from the squatting position, typically the elder would play their part by helping you stand up and would say:

'Walekum as salaam.'*

The most arrogant would not assist you as you rose, nor would they reply to the gesture with the customary 'walekum as salaam'. These folks would simply stand awaiting homage, at times striding off before the exercise was even complete. Lesser variants, such as bending down from the waist and gesturing to someone's feet rather than going into a vertical squat, were acceptable for lesser murubbi, such as uncles and aunts, or those not too distant in age although performing the 'short-cut' method ran the risk of being pulled up and being asked to do it again.

Feudal, hierarchical and with a self-ordained sense of greater piety than other Bengalis, arrogance sat easily on the shoulders of many Sylhetis. We had numerous relatives who demonstrated a haughty side to their behaviour, anchored in their education, social or work status, hailing from a seemingly influential landowning family or from a respected village or family clan. Such relatives lacked an appreciation of what life might be like for us in Britain and how there were real challenges in integration and in balancing the contrasts

---

* And peace unto you.

of the different cultures in our lives. It didn't take long for them to judge us as being not well brought up, disrespectful or ignorant of Bengali cultural values.

I harboured doubts about salaam. As soon as I learned from Maulvi Sahib that in Islam any form of submission to another human being was forbidden, the only question that remained around rebellion was when, not if.

'Only Allah should be revered in such a way,' Maulvi Sahib would smile to us in the living room of our house in Grove Park Road. 'It is not right for us to lower our heads in front of anyone else.'

Maulvi Sahib was right, but I also understood that touching feet did not mean one was literally treating the other as a deity. Islam is so much about the intention and the principle, yet Muslim practise is so much about the practical and the literal. Finding compatibility between these two is an age-old test of life whether it be for kasr prayers, performing salaam or all sorts of other activities. There are many ways in which we 'lower our heads' to others in forms of deference not condoned by Islam. The main difficulty I had with salaam was the expectation that one had to do it, fuelled by symbolism which had gone too far. I disliked the hypocrisy of the action more than the action itself. For example, people from the higher classes would never salaam those from the lower classes, even when younger in age. Salaam had everything to do with status, and little to do with true love or respect. It had nothing at all to do with religion.

'Tufael, you must salaam anyone senior to you in age, even if by a single day.'

'So why don't we all touch Abdul Latif's feet then? He is older than everyone,' I would ask, referring to the bare-footed and elderly security guard at the house in Dhaka.

Neither Amma nor Abba paid attention to my dilemmas over salaam. In general, any inclination to probe into the logic of such actions caused irritation and was not appreciated. Amma was unwilling to entertain any discussion that performing salaam should be abandoned and dismissed my attitude towards salaam as the frustrations of an argumentative teenager. Some of my cousins had no objection to performing the ritual. To them, touching feet was an understood and acceptable way of showing respect. If the matter came up in conversation as we drove up to a relative's house, Amma would lead when we went inside to reinforce her point, offering full salaam honours wherever appropriate.

'See, Tufael. Look. This is how it is done,' she would smile. This posturing compounded a desire to hit back at the custom and fiercely reject it.

One evening in Sylhet, without much forethought or pre-determination, I cracked. It was a dinner party at the house of the eldest daughter of the Modhubazar branch of the family. A busy locality some three kilometres further into town than Hazaripur, Modhubazar was where Dadu's sister lived. Many prominent members of the family were present. On entry into the lobby, dripping with a few large raindrops caught from another monsoon downpour outside, I began by saying 'as salaam alaikum' to each relative. I went around to the murubbi one by one, offering my hand to each of the men. The moment was significant to all for being so visible and my abstinence from standard introductory custom was soon registered.

As I continued around more and more relatives, the fact that I was in mutiny became evident, and for Amma and Abba there approached the acute heat of imminent embarrassment. Whilst I had questioned salaam for a while, they had never expected that it would come to this. The first accusing glances were cast at my parents, not me, and without need for words the looks said:

'You two have failed to bring up your children properly in that heathen country where you have chosen to live, where young people do not understand how to respect their elders.'

The embarrassment for Amma and Abba was matched in similar measure by the people who didn't receive the customary feet-touching too; feeling that they had been singled out for a boycott which was unjustly meted out on them. I was never to perform salaam again, and over the next few months a number of my cousins followed suit. Their dastardly acts to reject salaam was partly blamed on me, and in turn my parents were fingered as responsible for their son's role in fuelling wider social disobedience in the clan. Amma was beside herself in shame that evening, and Abba carried his characteristic look of annoyance when he felt the wrong battle was being fought. Myself, I was merely disappointed that my parents meekly accepted blame and didn't try to help their relatives understand the context.

From then on, I would greet relatives by entering the room and saying out aloud 'salaam alaikum'. My words would purposely be clear and forthright, and I would be at pains to deliver them with a smile and a warm handshake wherever possible. My intent from the outset was to replace the fake salaam of old with a fresh and genuine energy of the future, something which elders accustomed to the reverence of old symbols could hold onto without impairing their sense of self-respect or stature. My respect for the murubbi was absolute, and my method had to offer something more genuine, less symbolic and more heartfelt. Today, touching feet is disapproved of by much of Sylheti society, eradicated by dozens of mutinies like mine. In some ways my revolt was another blow for the haughty landlords; not one that came from the hands of the village peasants but as a slap that came from one of their own bloodline.

The main reason I dreaded trips to Sylhet as a child was the physical discomfort of using smelly, squatting toilets. I simply could not bring myself to visit stinking, unhygienic and physically repulsive ceramic 'holes in the floor' without flush, which relied on the passage of fluids to wash away the solid, stinky deposits. The Hazaripur bathroom was actually quite spacious, with a smooth slate-coloured floor and latrine at one end, and a high washbasin at the other. But the floor was invariably wet, glistening and slippery, with no demarcation between the area for washing and that for toilet activities. With no running water, visitors would have to use a large pail of water in the corner, usually full and with a deformed plastic mug, or 'mog' in the vernacular, hanging over its edge, its chipped parts housing little speckles of grit.

Open commodes all over town stank of festering urine and faeces. Smells would flow both to and from the sewage line, and the intensity of odour depended on the physics of the prevailing air current, humidity and temperature. In the monsoon season, the smell would stick to one's face. I would sneak a bottle of bleach into the Hazaripur bathroom and pour copious, uneconomic quantities of it down the toilet to buy me a few minutes of smell suppression while I showered. I would spray my mother's eau de cologne ('odi-kolon') on my wrist before going, so that I could inhale its scent instead during longer toilet visits. Programmed from youth, I carry perfumed cream or ittar* in my pocket for protection to this day. Although the seven-foot-high bath-room walls afforded privacy from the sides, there was no bathroom ceiling and therefore the top of the cubicle was open. This limited sound insulation in the toilet meant that natural groans or other sanitary percussions had to be quelled, gulped down or let out with a slow, controlled release. Squat low on the commode, smelling awful smells, thighs aching, feet wet and with dodgy balance, it was dis-concerting needing to struggle with one's bowels whilst having full audio of the dining table conversation on the veranda outside. The thin wooden door to the bathroom was raised several inches above floor level and this meant that passers-by could spy whether someone was squatting on the lavatory, facing forwards or backwards by looking at their ankles. Half of the time I was in Sylhet I would have a

---

* Musk oil, usually perfumed with rose or other natural fragrances.

stomach complaint, and so the lack of toilet freedom exaggerated my sense of being trapped to the point where my bodily functions were closed up too. Each trip to Sylhet required a privately conceived plan of timing bathroom needs and restricting food intake. It didn't do my health a lot of good. My eating and drinking were distorted, and my bowel movements acutely suppressed whilst I juggled the logistics of how and when I might next make it to an English-style toilet with seat and flush.

The home of Modhubazar-er-Dadi,* Dadu's younger sister, and her husband, Modhubazar-er-Dada, was the only one we knew in all of Sylhet with running tap water and a flushing, upright commode. Modhubazar-er-Dada and Dadi had moved to Sylhet town from their village in the 1940s. Bestowed with the leftovers of the considerable wealth amassed by his landed father, Dada was one of the few Sylhetis to drive a car as early as the 1940s, an Austin Seven. Reflecting the experience and gravitas of his seventy-odd years, he cut an impressive figure. Fair-skinned and thick set with the family trademark broad nostrils, light brown eyes and sun spots and freckles on his upper arms and shoulders, he stood upright and spoke his mind with an authority and reverence that only some of the older generation possessed.

'No!! We will not accept that! This is our daughter you are talking about! There are plenty of accountants and doctors out there, and we are not desperate,' I remember

---

* literally the Grandmother from Modhubazar

him bellowing out once during negotiations to finalise the arrangement of a cousin sister's wedding.

Brando-esque in delivery, the edges of Dada's voice had been roughened through years of smoking a hookah* and cigarettes. Dada was one of the more educated people of the earlier generation in the family network. He had passed out of the Madan Mahan College of Sylhet with a Higher Secondary Certificate in the English medium class of 1926, unusual for a 'local' in a rural backwater to graduate alongside the children of his colonial masters. Dada spoke fine English and wrote erudite letters, although he had hardly lived outside Sylhet district in his life and never visited Britain until the 1980s. He was Chairman of his local village council, presiding over petty crime cases and other local judicial matters, and in his day had cut a dashing image with the ladies. His status was drawn from his father's landed title in their village, and from his elder brother's noted career as a civil engineer building bridges and pontoons for the British to help the colonial masters tame the angry tributaries of Bengal's colossal rivers. Dada and I would undertake meticulously planned hunting outings by boat every summer, plying many of the waters which he would tell me were once owned by his forefathers. Through the Combined Cadet Force† at St Dunstan's, I was a classified British Army first-class shot and understood the

---

* Bengali style of water pipe, similar to the one known as a nargileh or sheesha in the Middle East.

† The school CCF was a part-time activity where boys would receive basic military training in infantry manoeuvres, signals (radio) and engineering.

principles of how to handle his shotgun effectively. Too old to steady the weighty weapon in his own arms, Dada made me his proxy eyes, ears and trigger finger on those trips, relishing in watching me bring down a sitting duck at fifty metres. Judicious in my consumption of ammunition, I seldom fired more than ten times during a whole afternoon, and rarely missed. Years later, when confronted at John F. Kennedy Airport in New York by US immigration officials who asked whether I had 'received military training' before, I responded in the negative, thinking that if I explained about the CCF at school I would be hauled in for more questioning.

Frequent contact with grit was part of any Sylhet stay. Every morning, house staff would ensure that our beds had crisp, clean sheets, but with dust being blown around by the fans, and children running around day and night, climbing on and off beds and sofas, furniture would invariably be covered in little specks of grit and dirt. Paranoid about the appearance of more dirt, I would rub my palms on the sheets, feeling for the grit. Due to the unbearable levels of humidity, towels in Sylhet were damp and smelly. Rarely would I wipe my face and hands after washing them, preferring to flick the water off my cheeks and forehead and then fan my palms dry against the dank air. This would invariably leave me feeling even stickier, a modest price to pay for avoiding contact with the musty-smelling fabric. In her preparations for travel, Amma would pack us a set of fresh, scented towels before leaving Dhaka. The fragrance was usually of the naphthalene mothballs which she would buy at Boots Chemist in London and place generously around the cupboards we had in Sylhet House, our aptly named Dhaka home. I would guard my towel closely to ensure it didn't make it into general circulation.

Rather than engendering affinity and pride for my family origins, experiences in Sylhet would fuel a sense of wanting to be different. I loved most things about Dadu, Modhubazar-er-Dada and Dadi, but overall there was too much that I did not like. What disappointed me the most wasn't the lack of change or reform in Sylhet's ways, but the lack of attempt at reform by sons and daughters returning from places where they had learnt to live better.

But how to achieve change wasn't an issue for the majority of Sylhet's homeward bound diaspora. Reassuring the elders that after years abroad, they were still good Muslims and good Bengalis was of greater concern. Most would only return to Sylhet once every few years, and each trip would be a priceless opportunity to spend time with ageing parents and loved ones. Since nobody could predict when the next chance might be, sentiment would often draw returnees to treat every visit as the final one in which they would see their mothers and fathers alive. Treating the elders with tenderness and showing them that foreign climes hadn't changed them was more important than reform.

Both Amma and Abba understood my toilet-related reasons for going to Modhubazar. Abba probably hoped I wouldn't go, but he was a rational man who knew which arguments to pick with me and which ones to avoid. His greatest show of respect was to treat me as a sensible person who needed to be engaged through logical argument and reason. However, my moving to Modhubazar every few days affected the pride of Abba's brothers, who likely saw as an affront that one of their own should sleep in their aunt's house instead of their own mother's.

Since Sylhet town offered little prospect of escape, I relished trips to Tamabil and Jafflong, the twin border-crossing points to India along a picturesque three-hour-long outing from Sylhet town. The narrow, metalled road to the border twisted casually through an ascent into lush and romantic tea gardens. We would wind along the serpent-like route through the tea region, with seas of tea plants shaded under a canopy of dark foliage. Tea estates were a domain unto themselves, with a micro climate of heavy rainfall and social codes of conduct governed by an exploitative economic relationship between the all-powerful tea planters and the peasant underclass who for generations were fettered to the plantations. Tea pickers, dressed in cotton saris, would pluck silently at the bushes, oblivious to our stares as we drove by, their sun-darkened skin glistening under streaks of sunlight.

Staring at the Indian flag looking back at us from across the narrow strip of no-man's-land intrigued me. Border patrols lounged around, smoking and chatting with passers-by. The concept of a stand-off between opposing forces was irresistible, and I would search for clues as to how great was the enmity between the Bangladesh Rifles and their Indian counterpart, the BSF.[*] I especially resented British colonial history on border trips, since I could see how the divide

---

[*] Border Security Forces, the Indian border patrol

here ran exactly where the lower lands of what was then defined as East Pakistan met the lofty hills and mountains of India, drawn up no doubt in a meeting room in White-hall over a hundred years ago. From our inferior vantage point, we had to look upwards, and the elevated angle of vision from beneath irked me.

'Shillong* must be at least at one hundred metres higher in altitude than us,' I used to complain.

I longed to sneak across into India, to see how different the people could be by dint of the artificial partition of territories through imposed borders. I wanted to see whether they spoke Sylheti on the Indian side or something else.

Abba loved borders too. As on most matters, he adopted a positive perspective on our inferior position, explaining how we could collect the rocks that tumbled down from the Indian side into Bangladesh, which we could then use for essential building materials. Along with all its other resource shortages, Bangladesh is a country without stone – an asset that I never singled out as valuable until somebody told me the country doesn't have it. Abba invested in a trucking business which ferried stones from this very point into Sylhet town. The idea must have been conceived during one of these outings. We used Bedford trucks shipped from the same port in England from where we sent a Datsun Cherry once to Bangladesh all those years ago.

Years later, I was to fulfil my desire to cross the

---

* The principal Indian city in Assam close to the Sylhet border.

Bangladesh to India border on foot. On reaching a deserted border post at a jungle station near Khulna following a several hour bus journey south west from Dhaka, the Bangladesh Rifles wouldn't let us through.

'You gentlemen do not possess the correct visa for exit by road,' an irate border official announced to Andrew, Matthew and me as we stood incredulous before him, stating that we held valid Indian entry visas and should be allowed to pass.

'It is not matter of India visa. It is matter of incorrect Bangladesh visa. You entered Bangladesh by air, and according to your visa terms, you must therefore exit by air.'

Though it seemed odd to be refused to exit a country, technically we could see how he could be right, though I had never come across such a technicality before. After a few rounds of three nineteen-year-old students unsuccessfully negotiating with the official, the by now gruff man threw our passports onto his desk and stormed out of the room, leaving us sat there, wondering what we could do now. Return to Dhaka was out of the question, since it was almost dark and we were stuck at a dense and remote jungle outpost, miles from the nearest town. We were also barely fifty kilometres from Kolkata across the border, our target for the night. Accepting defeat now would deflate our enthusiasm as well as stymie our plans.

Hoping that he wouldn't return immediately, I leaned across his glass-topped desk and sneakily picked up the receiver of his desk phone. Carefully, using the rotary dialler from the opposite side of the table, I dialled our house number in Dhaka. By some fluke the line connected first time, and by another miracle Abba answered the call immediately.

'Abba. We are stuck at Benapole. Help. Can you call Uncle? Please. I have to hang up. Help.'

We sat and waited. Minutes later, the officer returned, presumably from a prayer or cigarette break, sat at his desk and continued with what seemed a mountain of paperwork for a post with such few travellers passing through it. Not knowing quite what to do, we continued to wait in the lame hope that as afternoon turned to dusk the officer might relent, take pity on these poor boys and let us pass. The office phone rang, and once he answered, he looked back at me, puzzled.

'It is for you.'

He handed me the handset, and as I leaned across and took it from him, now I too was puzzled.

It was the Duty Commanding Officer, Border Control HQ, Dhaka Cantonment. A kindly spoken man, he asked after my and my friends' welfare and then requested I hand the phone back to the officer-in-charge. What followed was an embarrassing and rather audible telephonic dressing-down of the poor man opposite us, who had only been doing his duty, by an HQ superior who had taken orders from his boss, the Director General, to get his poor little nephew out of a spot of bother on the border.

An hour and a sumptuous meal of curry and rice later, the Bangladesh border officials escorted us to the India side to a 3-gun military salute, after which we boarded a train third class which trundled us into the smoky metropolis of Kolkata. An embarrassing use of privilege to escape a sticky situation, this experience was to be my adult introduction to what was one day to become a life of nerve-racking border crossings, too often navigated by thinking on my feet to avert moments of risk and danger.

The tension caused by my bathroom-induced moves to Modhubazar became more visible with time. As it was never explicit that I was moving across town for sanitary reasons, as time went on I would resort to making empty excuses to go, and my behaviour would prompt questions and remarks that played on my differences. I had a nasty, fisty scrap with a distant uncle once, after an afternoon of being called 'Ingleesh' by him and another cousin and ridiculed for always having a bad stomach and constantly taking 'moshar oshod', or malaria tablets (the Bengali literally meaning mosquito medicine). Though both were a few years older than me, in a fit of anger I decided to have a crack back at them in a clumsy conflict where my uncle and I both inflicted a few blotchy blows on one another. It must have looked more like a frustrated amorous scramble than a real fight taking place on the front lawn of the Hazaripur house. Luckily none of the elders happened upon us and the contest was over within a few minutes. Neither called me Ingleesh again. Later we started secretly smoking together on the rooftop of Sylhet House, our home in Dhaka, playing carrom board into the early hours of the night and listening to Nazia Hassan* songs on the tape recorder. Years later the same uncle and I flew to London together after I had accompanied him to the British

---

* a popular Pakistani pop singer of the 1970s

High Commission in Dhaka for a visa interview. We sat in the plane and sobbed: he for leaving his beloved country for the first time and I to lament the end of another long, hot summer. Though I felt excluded in Sylhet, every year I dreaded the return to London too; to silence, bald trees and short evenings, and the impending resumption of exclusion experienced during school prayers.

Amma was often treated with disdain in Sylhet and differently to the other wives of Dadu's sons who were seen as 'pure' Sylheti women. I found this exclusion incomprehensible since Amma's mother was not only Sylheti but in fact Dadu's first cousin. In addition, Amma had grown up in Sylhet at the home of her uncle, General Osmani,* a family icon and national hero, the man who led Bangladesh's liberation forces in 1971 when the country won its independence from Pakistan. I couldn't see how anyone brought up in his household could be treated as foreign. But Amma's father was an Urdu-speaking West Bengali intellectual from Kolkata, and this was the reason why she was regarded as a foreigner by many Sylhetis. On more than one occasion someone or other pointed out to me Amma's cultural difference, referring obliquely to the fact that her late father was not Sylheti, making it clear that was a deficiency on his part.

'Your Nana was Urdu-speaking you know, he didn't speak Bengali much, let alone Sylheti. That is why your mother doesn't like it here, because she isn't one of us.'

---

* General M. A. G. Osmani, Leader of the Bangladesh Liberation forces in the 1971 civil war.

'Abba, why is Amma foreign? What is different about her?' I once asked my father. Abba did not answer, but nobody mentioned it again.

Matters weren't helped by the fact that until I was eighteen years old I didn't speak the Sylheti vernacular, only the 'shuddha'* Bengali of the educated classes from the capital. I was constantly reminded of my inability to speak Sylheti.

'Did you understand that, Tufael? Should we explain?' was the type of patronising commentary I had to put up with, as discriminatory as some of the racists I had to face up to in South East London.

Just as her room was the centre of gravity for the household, Dadu's silver paan daan was regarded as the focal point of her daily routine. I used to ask Dadu what was the difference between smoking and chewing mouthfuls of paan, tobacco and other narcotic ingredients throughout the day. She knew I was hinting at the hypocrisies of paan as being acceptable in society, whilst smoking cigarettes was not. Dadu was aware that most of her sons smoked but, observing an unwritten parent–child covenant that exists in many places, she turned a blind eye to certain of her children's bad habits. Abba was the only family member who smoked (his pipe) in front of Dadu and she told him regularly to give it up. Dadu liked my innocent style of asking off-limit questions. She didn't mind the salaam rebellion either, as she was one of the first to say, in front of all, that

---

* Shuddha literally means 'complete' and in this context is used to refer to classical Bengali as opposed to regional dialects of which there are many, and of which Sylheti is one of the most differentiated.

from that day on she certainly didn't expect me to salaam her again.

I admired Dadu for being one of the least formally educated in the Sylhet chapter of the family, and yet one of the most forward-thinking and independent. She was married in around 1925 at the age of eleven to my Dada, Mudassir Ali Chowdhury, a wealthy landlord and widower of around forty. Her one stepchild from Dada's first marriage was almost her age.

'Dadu, did you have sex as soon as you got married?' I asked her once, to the acute embarrassment of one of my aunts who being within earshot flashed me a look of instant disapproval.

'No, no, don't give Tufael the fish!' the same aunt would say. 'He will find it too difficult to sort out the bones, they are so fine here in Bangladesh. Not thick bones like English fish.'

'Leave him be and let him eat what he wants,' would be Dadu's statement, delivered without theatre or fuss.

'No. I was only a child. That didn't happen for many years. In those days we didn't think about sex as soon as we got married.'

As she chatted Dadu would often be peering into her paan daan, selecting the next betel nut to crack open with the special, plier-like nutcracker with which you could crunch open the hardest of nuts.

'Marriage was more like being handed over to someone to complete your process of growing up, the one that was started by your parents. Your Dada taught me a lot after we married. It was like having a new teacher and someone to look after me.'

'Yes, but when did you first have sex?'

'Much later. I cannot remember now, but your Fufu* was born about five years after my marriage, so it must have been around then. Then there was your father, then Mumtaz and Redwan, and then . . .'

Whenever we reached this chapter in her life, she would pause and look away, mouthing a quiet prayer from her lips for paradise to the two children she lost in between her sons Mamun and Jamal. Dadu's eyes were penetrating and wide open when she engaged in a story like this, and every now and then would give away a hint of her innermost feelings, usually kept private and remote. Although she was for years, the eldest and most senior of the family clan in Sylhet, oddly enough she was one of the most accessible. I didn't just admire Dadu for the simplicity with which she lived her everyday life, but I truly loved her. She, Modhuba-zar-er-Dadi and Dada all let me get close to them, and gave me faith that my attempts to close the biggest cultural gaps through closeness and sincerity would work.

On the surface Dadu was a stern woman, single-minded in her duty towards the projects and activities that most concerned her. Ibn Khaldun writes in *Al Muqaddimah*† about how the Bedouin are closer to being good due to

---

* paternal aunt

† *The Muqaddimah, An Introduction to History* was written by Ibn Khaldun around AD 1370. Chapter 2, Section 4 contains his theories about how the simplicity of the Bedouins' life keeps them closer to goodness.

the simplicity of their worldly interests and possessions. Similarly, Dadu was a person little concerned with the material wealth that a number of her offspring hungrily craved. Hers was an uncomplicated regime focused on the daily rituals of prayer, ablutions, receiving visitors and paan. Just as social activity in Hazaripur made Dadu's room its centre, so did she make prayer and remembrance hers. Whilst she remained in that room more or less the entire day, few realised that in essence her life was conducted through thoughts and visions located elsewhere.

'Your Nani' didn't go to school either, like me, but she was very well-read. She spoke Urdu and Bengali, and read Arabic with great fluency. I missed her so much when she moved away to Kolkata after her marriage.'

Dadu's eyes would be distant during these conversations, the limits of her physical confinement no barrier for an open mind. And so my richest source of enjoyment in Sylhet was to sit for hours with Dadu, drawing out from those betel-stained ruby lips more and more stories of my origins, every now and then catching the scent of her fragrant betel-soaked breath: her younger days, her early marriage, my father and his life in the village before the family was forced to abandon its lands and move into town.

---

* Amma's mother, my Nani, was Dadu's first cousin.

Five

City of Minarets

It is 2005 and a decade since my last visit to Istanbul. In the 90s, it was the tide of reform in the former-Soviet republics that swept me in and out of this city several times a year during those buccaneering days when Turkey seized its opportunity to revive the Central Asian republics, with Turkish Airlines extending from its Istanbul hub to recreate a late twentieth-century silk route into Baku, Tbilisi, Ashgabat, Yerevan, Almaty and Tashkent, fabled capitals of the Trans-Caucasus and further east. President Mikhail Gorbachev's final efforts to hold together the crumbling empire that was for seven decades the mighty USSR had finally heaved its way to a historic and monumental collapse. Over a dozen countries had been re-born as a commonwealth of independent states, and I had been part of the team deployed by the European Commission to guide these nations towards economic reform and modern-isation. Istanbul had become the gateway to the '-stans',* and

---

* Kazakhstan, Uzbekistan, Turkmenistan and Kyrgyzstan. Istanbul also served as a gateway to Azerbaijan and Armenia.

for me the favoured stopping point into and back out from lands of heady adventure, incalculable risk and inexpensive caviar.

History has moved on from that pivotal moment, and I too have come back now with different motives and seeking new adventures. This time, I am emerging from a few years of emotional turmoil during which I had decided to learn Arabic, wanting to complete the process I had started but abandoned when a graduate student at Cambridge many years ago. Having done some research, I enrolled for the Saturday morning class at the School of Oriental and African Studies (SOAS) in London's Russell Square. Taught initially by the disciplinarian Bilal, a sternly spoken Egyptian of over sixty who used to wear military-style shirts with epaulettes, I joined a class comprising a disparate bunch of students drawn from many backgrounds. We had an English archaeologist who had spent months on the trail of Agatha Christie through digs in the Syrian desert, a newly-wed Yemeni-British-Indian couple who were instantly intrigued by the unexpected colours of my pen ink (which would change by the week), an eccentric young Mauritian man who wore string vests in class on hot summer's days, a friendly American-expat lady working for a US multinational in Dubai, a straight-talking British-Pakistani computer engineer and myself. We mostly became close friends. For months and months, trundling through the basics of Arabic grammar and lettering, we moved each at his or her own pace but collectively pedestrian. With the aid of a special red-covered Arabic textbook, we studied Modern Standard Arabic, concentrating on 'fus-ha' or formal Arabic as written in books and newspapers. A year into the classes, I asked our teacher for advice on where I could go to develop my spoken Arabic skills by learning 'ammiah', that is conversational Arabic.

Unlike the other languages that I spoke, such as English or French, the spoken version of Arabic was quite different from the written version. Where in classical Arabic you might write 'Ana ooredoo shay' to mean 'I would like some tea', in Levant colloquial you would say 'bddi shay' to mean the same thing, or in Egyptian colloquial you would say 'a'iz shay'. If you were to walk into a sheesha bar in London's Edgware Road and say *ana ooredoo shay*, you would likely be met either with a cruel smirk or a sympathetic glance. As with any language, and I spoke a few, I desired to go deeper than transactional chit-chat. Not only is Arabic spoken differently, but almost every region across the Arab-speaking world has its distinct vocabulary, sentence forms and norms of pronunciation. Whilst fus-ha remains constant from Marrakesh to Baghdad, colloquial dialect in Iraq is largely incomprehensible to someone from the Maghreb.

'Go to Damascus and immerse yourself, ya Mohammad,' my teacher guided me, mopping her brow while inhaling desperately on a cigarette in the courtyard outside the SOAS buildings. 'Avoid going to where you revert to English on the street.'

English and Urdu-speaking Dubai just wouldn't work for me, and I wasn't a fan of the Cairene dialect. And so, I took the first of many journeys to Damascus in the summer of

2004. I returned many times, on the last occasion in 2010 with my family, barely a few months before the situation in Syria started to disintegrate into the sad shambles that it is reduced to today.

I was introduced to a lady in Damascus who was going to help me with conversational Arabic. But it turned out that Rita wasn't really a teacher at all. Rita Al Rahmani was one of Syria's most respected translators of Arabic into European languages and descended from a distinguished family. Rita meticulously created for me a customised curriculum of sight words and vocabulary, carefully converting what I had learned in the classroom in SOAS into street-friendly, conversational Arabic. The mornings would be spent at the Foreign Language Institute in the posh district of Abou Rummani, Rita's place of work, listening to the songs of Fairouz, the silky and unifying voice of Arab freedom, or reading newspaper articles and then discussing them. Day by day, I learned more about how to switch between formal Arabic and spoken dialect, and one by one we mastered basic topics of conversation such as nationalism, history, Britain, literature and economics. Speaking on chosen themes enabled me to develop a range of vocabulary as well as conversational confidence and depth. After the intensity of the morning immersion, afternoons would be spent walking around Damascus and chatting with all and sundry, encouraged by the invariably warm and curious reception accorded to me by most Damascene. After that first summer in Syria, returning to an autumnal London and a dreary SOAS classroom, my friends and teacher were startled by the sudden transformation of my Arabic skills. I briefly became a SOAS legend, a case study in how an absolute novice can master the language in quick time.

'Now I have given you the keys, ya Mohammad,' were Rita's prescient words when we completed that long summer of classes sitting in her atelier at the Institute.

On this occasion my journey through Turkey, Syria and Lebanon originates in Istanbul, where I am to attend the wedding of friends of mine. The rest of my itinerary is shaped around exploring how the Mediterranean wraps around so many interesting ports of call in the Middle East. I have planned to follow the coastline from Central Turkey east into Syria, where I can begin to practise my Arabic, onwards further into Lebanon all the way down to the border with Israel. Travelling for a few weeks with the sea at my side seems an enticing prospect and crossing plenty of national borders even more so. But as I am to realise, the borders I cross during these weeks are more than just jurisdictional ones. I can now view the region with the perspective of a Westerner, communicate in the inhabitants' native Arabic* and connect with them as a fellow Muslim.

While Istanbul clings onto the cliché of being the link between East and West, both sides of the equation have moved on. Tonight, the city's character brushes against me with an intimacy I have not experienced before. It is my first ever Bosphorus boat ride and I am impatient to see more.

'What do you think, Adam? It reminds me of looking at

---

* Arabic is spoken in the Hatay (Antakya) province of Turkey and throughout Syria and Lebanon. It is not spoken in other parts of Turkey where I begin my adventures.

Södermalm from the sound in Stockholm,' I say to one of the guests who has also just arrived from London, as we both look out across the waters to the mainland.

'Hey everybody, Mohammad thinks Istanbul looks like Stockholm!' In a prickly mood, I feel as though Adam is mocking me, and indeed his comment provokes a few chuckles from other guests.

Terracotta-coloured rooftops are the base from which Istanbul's visual highlights stand out. They provide a fitting foundation since these roofs give shelter to the ordinary folk on whose efforts the city's life is built. Low-rise and sitting on a series of undulating hills, the city appears like a freshly baked cake being held up to an admiring guest. In the dimming dusk light, the tops of the Istanbullu homes are too small to be singled out individually. Instead, I see countless rows and columns of buildings tracing jagged lines and oblique patterns. They are punctuated by the grand domes and pencil-sharp minarets of Istanbul's beautiful mosques.

With this perspective, the city beckons me to look deeper inside. The sensation is unlike that of New York City from the Hudson River, Abu Dhabi from the warm waters of the Arabian Gulf or Sydney from the Harbour. All those places present a vertical sheet of skyscrapers which relegate the waterborne observer to outsider status. It is the intimacy of Istanbul that takes me back to the riverside view of Stockholm.

The precise geometry of the domes and minarets echoes the fundamental link between Islam and the sciences, a relationship forged through the logic and reason upon which bygone centuries of Muslim glory were built, and in which the Ottomans played their own part. The mathematical symmetry of the domes shows a side modern Istanbul no longer possesses, a topic the Muslim world long ago surrendered leadership in. The sodium glow from the superbly lit domes emanates a feeling of warmth and safety, as though the mosques are watching over us. The sight of the mosques lifts me into a sense of emergence from a life which of late has lacked peace and spirituality.

Bobbing up and down on the Bosphorus, I salute Istanbul's magnificent minarets. They puncture the sky like slender pencils sharpened by the city's dwellers in an attempt to find a way into the heavens above. For the moment they offer me refuge from the wedding conversation. I think about the scrap of yellow-lined paper on which I scribbled a makeshift itinerary for my journey during the flight from Heathrow last night.

'Yes, yes. From London,' I reply, assuming the question is for me.

Much as I try, I am struggling to get into the party spirit.

'But can corporate strategy created by an external consultant really guide a large corporation? Do your strategic plans make any difference when you don't understand a company's inner workings?' the guest challenges me as I describe the nature of my work at the New York headquarters of my firm.

'Yes, interesting,' is all I can muster.

I am blending into Istanbul better than I did years ago but cannot escape investigation. The Istanbullus reject any notion that I am from England and the swift follow-up when I tell them I am British with 'where were you born?', or some such enquiry to seek out my true origins. Most crack open a toothy smile when I tell them that my origins are in Bangladesh, or that I am a Muslim, or that I am called Mohammad. Whichever of these, they sense a link and want to celebrate it. A link intangible and momentary, soon to be dissolved as I walk on to the next shop or turn the corner, and all the more heart-warming because of that.

Istanbul links me to the experience of those early work years in Kazakhstan, where driver Ahmet and I used to search endlessly for the warmth of shared identities. Like most Kazakhs I met in those days, Ahmet revelled in discovering that one of the Western consultants sent over to support the economic transition from Communism was a Muslim, just like himself. A proud man with a fierce and creased face and thick, spiky hair, Professor Ahmet Kadirbekov was the driver of our project car, as well as Chair of the Department of History at Almaty University.

Working in the 'stans' was a crazy and eye-opening, once-in-a-lifetime experience. These were the heady days of post-Soviet hyperinflation and plummeting living standards, and any opportunity to earn hard currency was not to be passed up. Funded by the EU and World Bank who were keen to showcase their support, I was part of a team appointed to advise the Kazakhstan Government on breaking up Communist-era monopolies, most of them strictly controlled by unions, cooperative, and the KGB. The former USSR intelligence agency was still a powerful force, even outside Russia and in the other former Soviet republics. In Azerbaijan they would confiscate my passport on arrival, only to return it two weeks later on the day of my departure.

Whilst we were careful not to provoke the KGB officers who tailed us around town, I once got myself well and truly on the wrong side of Kazakh border security. This was on the occasion that I stupidly entered the country using a Russian visa. I had been desperately exhausted coming off a snowbound Lufthansa flight from Frankfurt which had involved a fifteen-hour wait inside the aircraft in Uzbekistan when the plane's frozen wings could not be thawed out by Tashkent Airport's single, Soviet-era de-icing truck. Having landed at Tashkent for customary refuelling and offloading a few passengers, both our wings had iced up in the freezing winter cold. As the de-icing truck worked its wonders on one wing, the other froze up, and vice versa, until after a few futile rounds of failed de-icing, the frustrated ground crew gave up altogether. Not allowed to deplane, we sat in the aircraft, watched the slow drama unfold and made small talk with fellow passengers. In those days, almost everybody on such a flight had a story to tell, and the man sat next to me was an Uzbek-American Jewish tycoon from New York flying to Kazakhstan to invest in a new aluminium plant. He explained to me that my Russian visa, issued for a planned trip to Moscow which I was supposed to have taken that week to work on a project with a private TV station, would get me transit entry to Kazakhstan. When we finally landed at Almaty after almost thirty hours inside the same aircraft, I went ahead and used my

Russian visa to get in, head to my hotel, a hot shower and a plate of fresh, boiled vegetables. What I didn't appreciate was that the transit visa would expire after seven days.

On the day of departure, fifteen days later, the Kazakh passport official, sitting over me in his lofty cabin, refused to let me exit and board the once-weekly Lufthansa flight home.

'NIET! Do you not know that Kazakhstan is a sovereign country?'

I felt like a real idiot, as though I had insulted this nation through assuming a Russian visa would suffice for visiting there, as though I was oblivious of the fact that Kazakhstan was now an independent country.

'You cannot visit this nation and stay here under a Russian visa! Niet!'

I couldn't argue and deserved not to be let out, so to speak. But I also desperately wanted to leave. All that happened when I tried was that my passport, without the necessary exit stamp, was flung back in my face by an irate official who had better things to attend to than solve my problem. The Lufthansa ground staff only requested that my bags were off-loaded when I told them of my predicament.

This for me was a relatively early border-crossing quandary, but one that demanded quick thinking and provided training for the travails to come later on post 9/11. With barely an hour till my flight was due to depart, with my hard-earned business-class seat already given up and my bags taken off, I resolved that if I could rectify the root cause of my problem, I could still get out. Purposely oblivious to the fact that I was supposed to be waiting for my luggage which was about to be returned to me, and slinging the strap of my handbag across my chest, I jogged one kilometre in minus twenty Centigrade to the Arrivals terminal, miraculously worked my way 'back' to where incoming passengers come off the aircraft and bought myself a fresh, single entry Kazakh visa. The lonely entry officer must have been a bit puzzled when I placed my passport before him for a visa, seeing as he couldn't spot exactly where I had appeared from. I then ran back to Departures, presented my passport to the same and still irate official, who smirked with admiration and stamped me out.

Ahmet and my search for common cultural links focused on language. Our explorations would take place during the endless hours we spent stuck in traffic jams in downtown Almaty in Ahmet's Lada* Riva. Waiting for the roads to clear, in a game of language roulette we would each throw out words randomly to see if there was any hint of a match.

'Soap.' I would begin in English and Ahmet would nod, acknowledging the start of another etymological expedition.

'Saaban? Shabaan?' I would continue, speculatively providing the translation in Urdu and Bengali, the languages I could furrow most successfully for our purposes.

'Saaban? Saaban!! IT IS SAME! IT IS SAME!' Ahmet would yell out, leaning over the spindly steering wheel of his car in unbridled excitement.

The deep, cultural bond created through these journeys

---

* A Lada is a Russian car known for its boxy design and simple engineering and at this time was prevalent across the former USSR republics.

fortified us for many tests of character in those difficult and uncertain times following the spectacular collapse of the Soviet Union. To Ahmet and thousands of fellow Kazakhs emerging from behind the cloak of colonial communism which had shrouded their society for generations, the collapse of its planned systems and structures, whilst desired, had left them gasping for identity and context. For decades the Central Asian peoples had been subjected to a 'Great Game' between Britain, France and Russia, who had fought phoney wars over control of the region. By the early 1920s, a brutal Soviet regime run by Josef Stalin had mercilessly crushed Uzbek and Kazakh resistance, incorporating these 'stans' into the Soviet Union. Now, finally, they felt free and many were keen to establish and celebrate their links with other cultures and people.

To the ordinary people of Istanbul, the sense of a link with something 'eastern' in me furtively confirms that the debate over which way this city and country leans is far from over. With the world as it is today, the question of how 'east' Turkey is generally determined on a judgement of how Islamic it is deemed to be. And of course in Turkey's case, how 'west' it is, is critical to its ambitions of entering the European Union. The stakes are higher than when I was last here years ago. Back then when I used to visit the Blue Mosque to offer prayers, I would feel a weighty sadness over the fact that there were barely any fellow worshippers there. Once, homeward bound from another draining and wintry fortnight of World Bank-funded project work in post-Communist Azerbaijan, I snoozed in the mosque's vast praying chamber only to awaken and find it empty and desolate. To stand in one of Islam's monumental sites of worship and find worshippers out-numbered by tourists took the shine off this great spectacle. Marvel at the architecture I did, but I could only whisper to the souls of the long-departed Ottomans:

'For what purpose . . . ?'

This time I find rows of worshippers, men and women, during my midday visit, a manifold increase from my last visit. There can be little doubt that Istanbul has in this time uncovered itself to Islam. At the Topkapi Palace there is an imam dressed in velvet robes, fez and white turban, sitting rather pointlessly in the corner of one of the harem rooms, reading ayaats* from the Quran in an attempt to lend some spiritual ambience for tourists as they traipse about. Many more women have adopted the hijab, although it seems they are mainly from the working and peasant classes.

Within Istanbul the struggle between moving west and staying east roughly looks like a division between the well-to-do classes who are more Westernised and the working classes who are less so. Orhan Pamuk suggests in his Mem-ories of Istanbul† that this city has been divided thus for centuries. However, in Pamuk's perception both the elites and masses are united in their sense of 'hüzün', or sadness. This is emotionally portrayed by Pamuk as a nostalgic sad-ness which stems from the passing of Istanbul's glory, from being epicentre of its world into a present where the city is

---

* An 'ayah' (plural 'ayaat') is a verse from the Quran.

† *Istanbul: Memories and the City*, by Orhan Pamuk, Faber, 2005

hardly relevant. Removal of this hüzün must have been one of the motivations for Ataturk in the 1920s when he decided to inspire and uplift the people by replacing Ottoman with Turkey, empire with country, Constantinople with Istanbul, Arabic script with Roman letters, and removing the fez and hijab altogether. For the decades since Ataturk, Turkey has been on a mission of social and economic transformation to emerge from its staggering imperial demise into a positive, Western-oriented future. But the signals suggest that shifting westwards without the fundamentals of Turkey's national character properly in place risks becoming a stretch too far for much of the population. The struggles of the journey begun by Ataturk eighty years ago have resurfaced today as a choice between competing alternatives, more strongly than it has at any time in the intervening years. I wonder, if I am right, how the Istanbullus will deal with it.

Cubuklu 29 is perched on the edge of the Bosphorus. The wedding venue is a few steep steps up from the shoreline and dominated by a broad, open space adorned with an expansive marble courtyard. The sun sets soon after we arrive. I look around for signs of a place to offer Maghrib* prayers. Seasoned through years of practise of praying in unfamiliar locations, with a sweeping glance across the venue, I size up the possible options.

An expert at praying in parks, museums, offices and restaurants, despite being at a venue in a Muslim country, amazingly I am unable to find any such place. I approach

---

* sunset

one of the drinks waiters, dressed in a smart tuxedo and patrolling the poolside with a tray of champagne flutes balanced precariously on an outstretched arm. Upon understanding my enquiry, his face takes on a concerned frown.

'Come with me, please,' he beckons, breaking for a moment from his waiting duties.

He walks me to the drinks stand where he confers with the barman, who is busy mixing some fruity-looking cocktails. After some consideration, they decide that a storage room around the back and up the stairs will offer peace and quiet.

'I am sorry it is just a small . . .' The waiter's tone has changed from professional to personal and apologetic.

'No, no. Perfect. It will be fine. Thank you.' I am intrigued by the change in his manner.

The barman looks on. He too is now distracted from his mixing and shaking duties. Before we walk off he and the waiter discuss something and gesture towards a couple of the other waiters. Much to my amusement, they have quietly resolved that none of the team on duty this evening should approach me with alcohol. I am touched.

Entertained by the mini-theatre put on by Cubuklu's backstage players, I follow the waiter to the designated prayer spot around the back of the pool. As we walk over, I appreciate the finesse with which the pool and veranda have been laid out. Complete with hanging creepers and shapely vases, it resembles the Jannat al Arif (known in modern day Spanish as the 'Generalife') of the Alhambra in Granada. The would-be prayer room is being used for a baby's nappy changing by one of the wedding guests, and so I opt for a quiet corner downstairs. I place the jacket of my linen suit on the floor as a makeshift prayer mat and calculate the direction towards Makkah, the qiblah,* by the position of the sun over the horizon. I estimate that the sun is setting in the northwest segment of the sky, given that it is only a few weeks after mid-summer and that we are a considerable distance from the equator. I surmise that Makkah must be about one hundred and eighty degrees in the other direction.

'Must be about southeast from here,' I say to myself, trying to envision Istanbul's position on a map relative to Makkah's.

I stretch out one arm as though a compass and swivel it around turret-style in the appropriate direction. As I adjust my jacket and prepare to start the prayer, I am spotted by the bride and groom as they make their final preparations before coming and meeting the guests. Looking happy, she gives me a quiet smile as she puffs out the pleats of her dress with a final swish. She is gorgeous and radiant.

My enquiry about a place to pray seems to have reminded the staff of their Muslim identity. They channel their responsibility of care towards me through all the additional efforts they can muster, and in the event, their heightened solicitude means their attentions are sincere but at the same time a trifle overzealous.

Tonight's incidents rekindle my memories of Central Asia, a region so closely tied to my experience of Istanbul as

---

* Qiblah is Arabic for the direction towards Makkah, to which all Muslims point when they pray.

the gateway to those once mysterious lands. I remember Nur, head waiter of the signature Soviet-styled Hotel Azerbaijan's soulless restaurant in Baku. The Hotel Azerbaijan was the only half-decent place to stay in Baku at the time I visited, and the hotel lobby would feature oil barons, security police, arms dealers, foreign consultants, prostitutes and their pimps.

Nur was a simple and caring Azeri man of middle age with grey curly hair and a thin, bony neck which was too narrow for his ill-fitting shirt. He once insisted on feeding me a cooked meal in the middle of the night during a cold and desolate Ramadan* trip to this post-Soviet state in the throes of dealing with a collapsed economy, a complete lack of foreign currency to buy essentials and ravaged by a horrible war with Armenia which was to take one in five adult men's lives over the next few years.

'Ramadan. Ya ni znayu po-Russki.† Ra-ma-dan,' I had been trying to explain to him in fragments of Russian.

However it is pronounced, the word 'Ramadan' simply wasn't getting my meaning across to Nur in any form that he could relate to. So there I was all alone at my dinner table, wondering how on earth I could convey a clear reason to this waiter why I would like him to serve me one dinner now, and at the same time pack me another in the food container I had brought with me for this purpose from London. We spent moments scrabbling around in various

---

* Ramadan is one of the months of the Muslim calendar, during which all able-bodied Muslims are enjoined to fast each day between the hours of dawn and sunset.

† Poor Russian for 'I don't know what it is in Russian'.

tongues, mine restricted to languages which had no overlap with his strictly Azeri and Russian vocabulary.

'Raza? Arraza?' he tried.

'Da, da! Raza! Da!' I declared back to him, pouncing on his words.

I had no idea what 'raza' meant but instinctively I sensed a link with the Bangla word for fast which is 'roza'. Since some of Azerbaijan used to be part of Persia, I guessed 'raza' might be the word for fast in Farsi, and it was possible the Bangla was similarly derived since it was the Moghuls of Persia who brought the first wave of Islam to Bengal.* Rather like the Istanbul waiters tonight, Nur's way of observing the fast about which he knew so little was to help me undertake mine.

So it was, on a sub-freezing night in mid-January Baku with jagged icicles drooping menacingly from the edges of the Hotel Azerbaijan's rooftop and giggling Azeri prostitutes telephoning my room all through the night, Nur slept on the restaurant floor so that he could feed me a night-time meal ahead of my fast. It was 4:00 a.m. when I shuffled along the deserted sixteenth-floor corridor and knocked at the restaurant entrance. Seeing only darkness inside I wondered why I had been foolish enough to agree on this nocturnal meal deal, instead of insisting on a container full of dinner the previous evening. As I readied myself for the prospect of a day of fasting without nourishment and an afternoon of ministerial meetings feeling dizzy, a petrified-looking Nur

---

* There are many dozens of Islamic words in Bengali which come from Persian rather than Arabic, such as 'namaz' which means prayer.

sprang up from behind the bar, switched on the lights, beckoned me in and started frying an omelette. He was clothed in the same shirt and trousers he was to wear every day during my two-week stay. Bleary-eyed and dazed, Nur buttoned up his shirt front, cooked me egg and chips and poured me a glass of hot milk.

'Will you fast too?' I asked him in broken Russian as he spread the egg mixture around the base of the pan, watching over it as it started to sizzle.

'I'll give up the fags,' he chuckled confidently, pointing to a crumpled-looking pack of Marlboro Lights which I guess he must have received from one of the oil tycoons staying at the hotel.

Despite my efforts to observe the fast with as little drama as might be possible, my Azerbaijani Ramadan was soon to bring me within an inch of losing my life. The day after Nur was preparing my midnight snack, I had found myself at the Deputy Prime Minister's windswept hillside dacha,* invited to attend what appeared a Baku A-list barbeque party on a freezing cold afternoon. My team leader Bob, sick with influenza, sat in a corner wrapped in a dark blue blanket, shivering for most of the party. The Azerbaijanis, all men, were gregariously pumping themselves with vodka, cigarettes and kebabs. I quietly chatted with a couple of guests, observing the strictures of no food and no liquids in line with the principles of my fast. The Chief of Baku Police, a burly fellow with protruding stomach and bushy eye-

---

* cottage

brows, found my abstinence from intake not to his liking. He shot me a look of disapproval and then hastened to tell me to eat. After some discussion, when he realised that I could not consume anything till the darkness that comes with sundown, he switched off the light and shut the curtains. Laughter ensued all around. But then the Police Chief steadied himself, standing at my side, bumped me unceremoniously with his gut, unholstered his pistol and took it out.

'Eat! Now!'

Bewildered, I looked back at him, aware from my peripheral vision that the barrel of his revolver was not far from the side of my face. Rather than look hither and thither, I concentrated on maintaining eye contact with my adversary instead. And as I sat still, my life in his inebriated, podgy hands, all I could think of was why has this twenty-six-year-old London boy volunteered to live his life in an Eastern European freezer zone during Ramadan, instead of staying put at home like most of his friends and family to watch TV on a Sunday afternoon. As I was to learn from practise many times over during the next few years of my journey as a Western Muslim, staying on top of the moment of danger was most critical. As the moment captured everyone's attention, I remained composed and decided to sit still and wait.

Seconds passed, fifteen, perhaps twenty, until gradually the party bully cracked open a mischievous smile which then rapidly broadened out into a full-blown roaring laugh. A tad drunk, he had been testing me out, to see what I was made of. The ultimate test of the integrity of the faster, perhaps. As though the room itself had been holding its breath, there was an almighty sigh of relief all around, and the party moved on.

As the Istanbul evening wears on, the speeches give way to inebriated attempts at dancing and partying, a sight familiar to me from London on many a Friday night. I stare out across the beautiful Bosphorus, its ebony waters dicing the reflection of the moonlight which flickers on its surface. Free from the daily grind of being in London and feeling properly on holiday, I feel a sense of freedom and a readiness to find new reasons to be happy. This voyage across the Eastern Mediterranean lands will be a continuation of a journey across cultural borders that I have been on for a while now, one that originally took off for me when I went up to the dreaming spires of Oxford University.

Six

City of Dreaming Spires

By the time I went to Oxford in the autumn of 1986, I might have thought I had come a long way in integrating my Bengali, Muslim and British identities into some sort of coherent whole. But going away to university proved to be a big cultural wake-up call and made me progress a whole lot further in my journey of crossing borders. My university era didn't exactly start smoothly. When fellow schoolboys at St Dunstan's College were handpicked to sit for the prestigious 'Oxbridge' entrance exams, I was overlooked but secured places at Bristol and the London School of Economics (LSE).

My best friends Andrew and Matthew both got into Oxford as part of the selected cohort, to read History and Law respectively. I felt that I was no less a talent and was not prepared to have the school decide on my future on such an arbitrary basis, and so set about my own plans of gaining admission. Having secured sufficiently good grades in my A-levels, I applied through a 'seventh term'* entrance exam to Oxford without obtaining the school's consent, opting to take Philosophy, Politics and Economics (commonly known as PPE), with St Anne's College as my first choice. LSE and Bristol both agreed to defer my entry for a year, knowing I was appearing for the Oxford entrance exam. For some reason the Headmaster at St Dunstan's appeared not to be impressed. As soon as Michaelmas† Term commenced, he summoned me to return to school to meet him. Parading around in his study, he regaled me with a story of how he was selected for his Oxford college rugby team by drop-kicking a golf ball into a wastepaper basket during his entrance interview. When we finally moved on to discussing my future, he counselled me to drop the idea of Oxbridge altogether and consider my other options, suggesting these would be suitable and highly eminent institutions for further study. At the same time, he applauded my choice of picking arts and social sciences, saying that he never saw me as becoming a 'dirty handed engineer'.

I explained again that I had a yearning to study PPE, having discovered how versatile it was and how many great leaders had studied it before. Realising that I wasn't about to back down, he agreed to sign off my application with the official support of the school. There would be no further teaching however, so I was on my own. I prepared thoroughly, with some secret support from my economics

---

* A 'seventh term' entrance referred to students who would apply to either Oxford or Cambridge after completing their A-levels.

† autumn

teacher at St Dunstan's, did an impressive entrance interview and was accepted.

My parents took the phone call from St Anne's College to let us know. When I got home, we hugged and cried till tears were smudged across each other's faces. This was a monumental feat. In little over twenty-five years after coming to the UK with almost nothing other than the clothes on their backs, my parents had schooled one of the first British-born Bangladeshis to be admitted to what was one of the world's finest universities. It might have been my achievement, but more than this it was one of my parents' crowning moments of parenthood and a victory for the entire clan and community.

Grateful as I was to my parents, I couldn't wait to break out of the family environment and be free to do my own thing. With Abba away for prolonged periods during our teenage years, building a pioneering ready-made garments business in Bangladesh, Amma had been forced into taking a broader parenting role. Her well-intentioned approach had over the years become overbearing and protective. She would worry over the smallest of matters and rarely voiced the upside of any activity, trip or idea. Whilst I appreciated how much she did for us, I also buckled under Amma's risk-averse nature. The more she raised concerns about my leaving home, the more I became eager to strike out and find my own way. One evening soon after my Oxford entrance was confirmed, I stated an intention to move to Dhaka for the rest of the year and gain work experience in a private bank. Amma was against the idea, but Abba raised no objections, and I went off to Bangladesh for a last adventure before going to university. But when the time came to move out of the house in Grove Park, reality set in that I was leaving the Chowdhury nest and with it the safety zone provided by home and family for many years.

During my first term at Oxford, as the evenings were drawing in and turning colder and most Freshers* were busy partying and drinking, I endured a period of cultural and social isolation I had never experienced before. I had no desire to drink, party or find a girlfriend to sleep with, but just like any young person I wanted to be part of the fold. Never having been to a disco, bar or nightclub, I faced difficulty in knowing where I could make friends, since at Oxford these seemed the only places to do so. One night, visited by Andrew and his friends from Christ Church, we ventured down to the St Anne's Freshers' disco. I ordered orange juice and one of the others, about as socially handicapped as me, ordered milk. It turned out to be a quiet night, until when I decided to head back to my room and a sultry-looking Spanish student approached me as I made my way out of the make-do disco hall. She seemed friendly enough so I mentioned I was turning in and asked if she would like to join me for a coffee. Not realising that this was code for an offer of sex, I was gasping with shock when minutes later the young woman was climbing all over me in my tiny room as I was trying to sprinkle ground coffee into a filter cone. Almost giving in to the inevitability of losing

---

* First year students at Oxford are referred to as Freshers.

my virginity to this predatory woman, I was saved by a nocturnal knock at the door by a Russian undergraduate in my PPE class who had seen my light on. She left shortly after and never acknowledged me in town again.

My predicament was made worse by being allocated a room in a building where I was the only Fresher. My neighbours were either second-year students already set with their friends, or Finalists busy with preparing for their exams. But matters improved and I became good friends with Jamie and Meg, both senior students living in my building. First-class thinkers driven by curiosity and an interest in culture and identity, they took to challenging me like it was a new-found hobby. Influenced by their questions, I began to see from their perspective some of the illogicalities of my arguments to explain Muslim cultural practices and outlook. Even though I would be the one challenging the same points when in the home environment, I found myself defending such practices when speaking to my friends at university. In fact, Jamie would jokingly refer to me as a 'recruitment officer' whenever I spoke defensively about Islam. Whilst he never told me, I began to see that I was justifying my faith more often than just practising it. This was an important discovery. During these first few months at university, I entered a new phase in my journey, forced to accept that not everyone around me was going to agree with my beliefs. This new maturity was helping me come to terms with taboos, such as the sight of Muslims consuming alcohol, something that had always caused me deep anguish. I had always regarded alcohol consumption as forbidden to Muslims but now could see that if Muslims consumed it, they did so out of choice.

Studying PPE was like being a child in a toy shop. Whilst there were core subjects to study, we were given enormous leeway to pursue electives of our choice within the disciplines of politics, philosophy and economics. My philosophy tutors included Tony (now better known as A. C.) Grayling and Gabriele Taylor. For international relations I was taught by the late Professor John Vincent and paired up with a descendant of Georges Clemenceau, the French Prime Minister who signed the Treaty of Versailles in 1919. I was taught South Asia politics by Professor Gowher Rizvi, now foreign affairs adviser to the Bangladesh Prime Minister and attended lectures by Nobel prizewinners, such as economist Amartya Sen, in various subjects. But despite having great tutors, I couldn't master the art of writing a well-reasoned and structured essay until well into my second year. At school we hadn't been taught to break down and analyse topics and themes in the way that my tutors were expecting us to do now. I was unprepared for such assessment and in such a mess with writing that I had to retake philosophy Prelims.* After much hard work my articulacy improved and I did well in Finals but narrowly missed a First overall, one which I would never quite have deserved.

The awakening of my identity at Oxford beyond the context of the playgrounds of South London began with my induction into the Oxford Majlis, the South Asia society

---

* Prelims are the examinations taken at the end of the First Year.

founded by Indian students in 1905 as a body to canvas for British decolonisation and which continues to run today. Presidents of the Majlis had included Indira Gandhi, Prime Minister of India; Liaquat Ali Khan, the first Prime Minister of Pakistan; Kamal Hossain, the first Foreign Minister of Bangladesh; and Mrs Bandaranaike, the first woman to be elected Prime Minister of Sri Lanka. Amina, a Bangladeshi law student and now a prominent human rights lawyer, got me involved in the Majlis after meeting me at a Fresher's event. I admired Amina's sense of national identity and her zero tolerance of racism, sexism or colonialism. When the next round of Majlis committee elections came up, Amina encouraged me to stand even though I didn't think I was ready. I was elected as Treasurer. I quickly assessed that the society had a limited flow of funds and a dwindling paid-up member base and needed quick action to sustain an ambitious program. I got to work on a campaign to invigorate membership, pigeon-posting* people with Asian-looking names at the start and then becoming more sophisticated in targeting as time went on. I hit up local businesses to advertise in the Majlis' term card, exploiting my family-business training to convince a few Bangladeshi-run restaurants along the Cowley Road to sign up. As the funds grew, I started making trips down to London in suit and tie to seek more sponsorships. Being able to name drop Oxford and a few ex-Prime Ministers made the Majlis an easy sell, and I landed a memorable deal with Air India to give away a

---

* Pigeon-post was Oxford's archaic but amazing internal mail system whereby students sent each other paper messages for free, delivered the same day.

flight for two to Goa for winners of a raffle at our end-of-term dinner, a university highlight with sumptuous biryani, dal and kebab.

When I was elected President the following year on a joint ticket with a Pakistani undergraduate, the Majlis was running two events per week, had doubled the paid membership and commanded a small cash float in the bank. Second only to the famous Oxford Union in our ability to draw speakers and crowds, the Majlis was one of the most popular and active university political societies, with a list of speakers other student bodies were envious of. Leaning on our brand name, from the public phone at the corner of our staircase, I would boldly cold-call politicians, sports personalities and even Bollywood film stars to come and address us. Suffering from a new-found cockiness, I scratched out a hasty invitation letter to a respected author upon seeing his famous novel lying on a library table, only to be told by his publisher who replied that he had died several years earlier. I experienced my first taste of activism through the Majlis, getting involved in campaigns for the withdrawal of the USSR from Afghanistan, and the demands of Asians to be portrayed more fairly by the British media. The Majlis not only dodged bankruptcy but funded its way to a sustained period of stability and growth. My role in this did volumes for my self-regard as a South Asian, beginning to compensate for years of cultural exclusion I had felt with family in Sylhet. Majlis gave me a refreshed sense of identity. More than my relatives, I grew to appreciate the true reasons for the birth of Bangladesh and the partition of India in 1947, and eventually started to challenge my family on aspects of Bengali identity, history and culture. This didn't land well, as I was sometimes over-zealous in showing off my knowledge to a community that had treated me as an ignorant English foreigner for much of my childhood. Finally, my feelings of cultural inadequacy gave way to a new dynamic in my relationship with the clan. Left with no choice but to start letting me in, at last I started to earn their respect as well as their trust.

On the subject of Bangladesh's liberation, my interest was truly piqued. I read voraciously on why a country, founded in 1947 as a homeland for the Muslims of South Asia and modelled as a Westminster-style democracy, had to break up barely twenty-five years later, ravaged by years of human slaughter, famine and disease, until East Pakistan became Bangladesh. I learned about years of exploitation of East Pakistan's global jute exports to fund infrastructure development in the West wing two thousand kilometres away, and how Bengalis could not gain admission to the elite national Civil Service of Pakistan as it required passing an entrance exam in Urdu, a language that most Bengalis could not speak. The policy-clad racism of Pakistan was nothing short of the apartheid in South Africa, or other institutionalised variants. There was a lesson in basic politics here, which was that nations cannot be thought up as designs drawn up on pieces of paper and must be allowed to evolve.

On trips home to London, my ailing father, now suffering from heart disease, would tell me about how the Pakistan

Army had once gathered villagers, including some of his relatives from Sonarpur in a field and brush-fired them all dead in a matter of minutes. Men, women and children. The same was done in thousands of villages across the land, little different from the brutality of how Nazis murdered Jews in Europe, or how Pol Pot massacred Cambodians. Abba recalled tales of how General Osmani, my great uncle, had to flee into hiding, lest the Pakistan Army find and capture their prime target, and how the General and Jamal Chacha once spent a night bobbing up and down in a shallow lake to keep out of sight of passing soldiers. My Politics of South Asia tutor described to us how Bangladesh became independent, focusing on the roles played by the US, India and Russia and thereby giving the nine-month-long civil war a global context. He described the hand-to-hand combat and a mass genocide of civilian Bengalis by the Pakistani army which left hundreds of thousands dead, women raped, and children orphaned. These tutorials were the stuff of history, delivered by a passionate participant in the struggle for freedom who now lectured undergraduates and drove around Oxford in an orange Mercedes Benz with a chipped three-pointed star that looked like an Islamic crescent. Whilst he told us much, it was evident that to spare us the trauma of his own experiences he withheld even more.

In addition to gaining knowledge about my South Asian roots, I became more aware of intellectual and political interpretations of Islam while at Oxford, building on the basic grounding I had been given in religious belief and practise by my parents and Maulvi Sahib. Occasionally I attended meetings of the Oxford University Islamic Society, a superbly well-funded and run institution, but I was too caught up with the Majlis to put much time into intellectual pursuits to expand my perspectives on Islam. There was also the Middle Eastern Society, more political in nature and focused principally on regional issues in the Arab world, such as the struggle for Palestinian freedom, as well as throwing legendary and well-stocked parties brimming with copious supplies of hummus, wine and falafel. Their events were far more lavish than ours, funded by wealthy benefactors from Iraq and the Levant, but their core membership was as grounded and committed to political freedom as were members of the Majlis. I became more aware of the political challenges in the region, including the Lebanese civil war, Golan Heights occupation, Egyptian politics, and Israel and Palestine dynamics. Syria hardly came up and I wouldn't come to learn about it until I started travelling there for language practise many years later. Whilst we studied it, none of us had an idea of how significant Islamic Fundamentalism would become to world politics within a couple of decades. Studying the topic exposed me for the first time to thinking about Islam as a social and political force, and not just as a faith.

After my first year and the nervy retake of my Philosophy Prelims, I wandered somewhat randomly into enhancing my visible religious identity by keeping a beard. Initially the facial hair grew out of a laziness that kept me from shaving for a few weeks, but once the stubble had established itself into a fully thickened beard, I justified keeping it going for reasons of following 'sunnah'.* This was somewhat false on my part, since at this time in Oxford, my observance of religious rituals of praying five times per day had lapsed significantly for the first time since I had started praying regularly when I was fourteen. Nowadays I was praying only two to three times per day, and some days hardly at all. I continued to maintain other rituals and disciplines, such as fasting and eating halal meat, but the dereliction of prayer was perhaps the most important significant threat to observance of Islam I have ever experienced.

On my next trip back home, the beard caused an unnecessary amount of drama. Family members comprehensively chided me for keeping it, with my father and uncle saying it looked like I was becoming a radical, others telling me that it looked messy, and some saying that it would stop me from getting a job once I graduated. One relative even warned that the beard would expose me to racial discrimination and being stopped by the police. She was prescient, although it wasn't the beard that got me into trouble with the Thames Valley constabulary.

I encountered the police on Woodstock Road one evening when approaching my parked car opposite college. They were not happy with me having a sticker with Arabic writing on it on the dashboard, particularly since they had also found a suspicious-looking brown paper bag wedged against one of the front wheels. There was a police car and

---

* Habits and actions of the Prophet Mohammad

two officers standing by my Fiat Uno, one speaking into his shoulder-strapped walkie-talkie. I unlocked the car for them and surmised that the bag under my car was a Chinese takeaway left for me by a friend who hadn't been able to locate me in college. An odd place to leave a package, but I guessed (correctly) that this particular friend had decided to do just that. While they searched the glove compartment and gave the interior of my car a once-over, one of the officers reprimanded me for displaying Arabic writing on my dashboard. He said that it caused unnecessary suspicion and I was wasting police time. This was ironic, as the sticker depicted a prayer for safe travels. I argued that there was nothing wrong with what I had done and displaying suspicion towards Arabic writing was racist. The package under my car didn't exactly help, of course. Once they left, I sat in the car and ate my soggy dinner, and then I removed the sticker. I reasoned that God would protect me whether I had a sticker in my car or not, and that on the other hand, removing it might keep others' suspicion at bay given that we were (already) living in a world where the sight of Arabic writing in certain places raised concerns. This trade-off between expediency and maintaining religious principle proved to be an important lesson for the future.

Within ten years, the norm of being clean-shaven amongst Muslim men was replaced by a new normal of wearing a beard. By the mid-1990s, thousands had grown beards, and for the first time, a significant proportion of Muslim women had begun to cover their heads. The fashionable look of migrants in swanky, flared trousers and brogue shoes was replaced by men sporting straggly facial hair, wearing their trousers above their ankles and some even wearing Arab tunics for Friday prayers. Many women who had previously sported sleeveless blouses and figure-revealing sarees, were now donning a headscarf or a hijab, no longer applying nail polish and opting for long tunics or 'shalwar kameez'.* Some men kept a skull cap in their trouser pocket, plucking it out at prayer times. Long hair and trendy sideburns were out, shirt buttons were done up, and chains around the neck disappeared.

Up and down the land, Muslim homes started looking different too in a new-found tendency to highlight religious identity in the living room. Wood-mounted mementos of Dutch tulips or the Eiffel Tower came down, replaced by austere and neatly framed examples of Islamic calligraphy of stunning beauty, or woven hangings depicting the Kaaba in Makkah. Observing the strict Islamic tenet to not worship images or animate objects, many Muslims removed family pictures and portraits from display and packed them away into albums and drawers. In my view, hanging a picture of a loved one on the wall did not mean that they were being worshipped, but somehow the interpretation had come into people's thinking that photographs represented a form of salutation tantamount to worship. Some relatives discarded their cameras and stopped posing for family snaps, preferring to be left out. A few months following

---

* Traditional Pakistani dress which provides complete coverage of a woman's body, and reveals less of her figure than a traditional Bengali saree might do.

Abba's death, an uncle visiting our home got up off the sofa in our living room and carefully turned over a picture of my father so that it was face down on the sideboard where it rested. Abba's face could no longer be seen. Feeling hurt and seeing this as an act of interference in how we kept our house, I asked the uncle whether he would have done that in the presence of my father. He responded that he removed the image because he missed him so much, and not because it was a sin to show images. I apologised for questioning his motives. But I was confused and conflicted, overcome by all that was going on at this time and not quite sure what was motivating it. I wanted to fight this new orthodoxy just as I had with my salaam rebellion years earlier, another social ritual which I had found to be superficial.

I say superficial because people hadn't suddenly become more religious. On the contrary, people were as faithful or dishonest as they had always been. Those who observed Islamic rituals such as prayer and fasting regularly in the 1990s, had by and large been doing so in the 1970s and 1980s as well. And those Muslims who had been dishonestly claiming unemployment benefit while holding down a cash-paying job, continued to do so even after they grew a beard to exhibit their Muslim identity. People weren't becoming more Islamic; they were just wanting to show that they were Muslim. Some who kept a beard cited piety as the reason for growing it. I had a beard now too but I was clear that mine had not been kept for reasons of how religious I was. People started referring to others as a 'good person, he has a beard', something I found shallow and naïve. I could never accept someone as being a 'better' person just because they had facial hair. A sense of modesty might lead to someone keeping a beard, but it doesn't follow that keeping a beard results in someone becoming more modest. There was an alarming level of stupidity in such trends and judgements, although any mention of shallowness would be met with bristling self-justification and defensiveness. I saw these developments in the UK but the change applied to Muslims across the Western world.

The growing desire to show one's Muslim identity was also an important step in the integration of Muslims into the West, as it demonstrated that Muslims were becoming more confident of their stature and more willing to exhibit signs of their identity, something that their parents may have hesitated to do in an earlier era. The demonstration of identity needn't be considered as being necessarily problematic, because the fact that people are showing who they think they are also indicates a sense of being settled and comfortable. Beyond beards and hijabs, there are other examples of Muslims making themselves confidently more visible. Muslims' openness about celebrating and observing Ramadan provides an illustration. This is the month where Muslims strictly adhered to fasts, which in these years involves an almost nineteen-hour-long observance of fasting in countries such as the UK, mainland Europe and in the northern part of the US and in Canada. Almost every Western nation is nowadays fully aware of the onset of Ramadan, and people by and large are more and more aware of its spiritual significance, its hardships and the Eid celebration at the end of the month. I have had colleagues fast along with me for a day or two (usually it ends there) at times, and the month is usually accompanied by goodwill and moral support from those who are observing us as we fast.

Before gaining the confidence to become more visible, the first step taken by the earlier generation of immigrants was to basically assimilate into Western countries, something that largely took place in Britain in the 1950s, 60s and 70s. My parents' generation were assimilators, having come to the UK with a simple intention to make money and go home. Britain was a good place to do this since it was prosperous and booming as well as being the old colonial master where our people knew about its customs and laws. Few immigrants came with the intent to settle forever in this cold and foreign land with its short daylight hours, miserable weather, lack of spicy food and distance from siblings and parents. They certainly didn't come to the UK to talk about their identity, culture or religion either. In fact, immigrants were largely of different skin tone to the English and were often subject to racism and ridicule. My father once told me that in the late 1950s, a colleague at British Rail asked if he used to wear clothes in his homeland, or whether he learned to do that when he came to Britain. Abba humorously responded that he used to live in a tree house and wore a loin cloth. The immigrants knew that the more they fitted in, the better and higher paid would be their work. During the 1950s and 60s, immigrants worked in factories and services where they were hired and retained by indigenous white people, and they needed to convince them of their worthiness to be given a job. Assimilation was not a choice but a necessity.

This didn't mean that the immigrants discarded their way of life, not at all. They just enhanced it by learning as much English as possible, wearing English-style clothes and doing their best to learn about British humour, idioms and customs. Family pictures amply demonstrate the intent to assimilate, with my father and friends featuring in smart English suits and cloth caps, and the women in fashionable coats and shoes. Men combed Brylcreem into their hair and smoked Dunhill cigarettes, while some married English women and drank whisky and frequented clubs. When my father gave up cigarettes, he started smoking a pipe, and he converted his love of horses, from his days as a forester in the jungles of Bangladesh, into an annual homage to watch the Derby dressed in coat and tails and carrying German binoculars. Abba wore a Van Heusen shirt and tie every day, even when he was at home cooking.

As the immigrants settled and established themselves, the dynamics of assimilation evolved. For the elders, the fabled 'myth of return' set in. Financial conditions back home hadn't improved, and only a handful of immigrants had made enough money in the UK to retire. Most by now preferred the lives they had in Britain anyway, and could also see that their children saw the UK as home. Two of my wider family tried returning to Bangladesh, taking their teenage children with them. Both set up businesses and homes in the motherland but couldn't stick it out and reverted to more hybrid set-ups with one foot in each camp. In contrast, the second generation (that is, my generation) saw Britain as their natural abode. And whilst we experienced racism and exclusion, we were not prepared to accept it in the way our parents had. Instead, the second generation decided to assert its own, distinct, indigenous identity: British but not white English. Akin to Edward Said's observations in *Orientalism*, the diaspora now rejected the Western notion of immigrants in a stereotyped, oriental type* and established instead that being black and British was perfectly normal. Speaking at the Conservative Party Conference of 1985, a female nurse who was also a parliamentary candidate famously stated to a rapturous ovation, 'I am a Conservative, black and British and proud of all three.'† Whilst British Muslims experienced racism just as she had, religion gave them a distinct identity that they could positively express and shape their existence around. A Muslim identity gave people an opportunity to dress, live and behave in a way which would make them distinct. Muslims also had common needs, such as to find and establish places to worship, to secure a supply of halal meat and to make arrangements for religious tuition for their children.

As well as men growing beards and women adopting hijab, a visible minority of Muslims started to dress like Arabs. Of course, Islam was founded in Arabia, but it is not an Arab religion. The principles of Islam are universal, applicable in the context of any global culture. Wearing a

---

* *Orientalism* by Edward Said, Pantheon Books, 1978

† Ms Lurline Champagnie

two-piece Canali suit to a wedding in London in the late 1990s, I was asked by the host why I wasn't in 'Islamic dress' as had been stipulated on the wedding invitation. I responded that I was in Islamic dress, since the modest parts of my body were covered. He debated that Islamic dress included shalwar kameez, or an Arab tunic. My host was mixing up being Islamic, a concept underpinned by philosophical principles, with being Arab or Western, which are both examples of worldly, cultural identity. He was assuming that dressing as an Arab was necessary to being accepted as a proper Muslim. This was a rejection of the universality of Islam, a faith that doesn't impose boundaries of such a nature and one that has over centuries successfully assimilated itself into many different cultures across the Middle East, Africa, Europe and Asia. Many people at that time were re-envisioning Islam in a specific Arab cultural construct, discarding or demoting their own culture. This was not only inversely racist, but it wasn't even in line with the principles of the faith.

Dangerously, it was also something else. In my mind, the adoption of Arab culture by non-Arabs was raising a concern about radicalisation. There was a particular phenomenon fuelling the adoption of strictly defined codes of practise taken from Arabian religious traditions, and this was the propagation of such codes by scholars and preachers coming mainly from the Salafi, Wahhabi and Deobandi traditions of Arabia and India. During my childhood, Salafi or Wahhabi religious teachings were gaining more influence in mosques and via teachers all over the UK (and the world) prescribing a practise of Islam which followed schools of thought which had developed in Arabia* many centuries ago. The Salafi movement is an ultra-conservative school of thought which originated in the eighteenth century, to reform Islam by looking back at how the faith was practised and society was organised in the times of the Prophet. The term Wahhabi comes from the eighteenth-century Arabian scholar, Muhammad ibn Abd'al Wahhab, whose reformist teachings are closely in line with the Salafi school of thought. Wahhab came from the Najd region, deep in the interior of Saudi Arabia and the most religiously conservative place I have ever visited. From India, there was the Deobandi school of thought, taking its name from the town of Deoband in North-Central India (Uttar Pradesh), where the Darul Uloom of Deoband was established in the 1800s as a conservative school of thought which over time gained a significant following. The medium of propagation was the literature produced by scholars, but it really spread through the thousands of teachers who had been trained in the conservative ways and relayed this faithfully to their students. Some of the books we studied as children, such as Fazai'l e Amal or Bahishti Zewar, translated into English from the Arabic or Urdu originals, contained prescriptions that even at a young age I found questionable. For example, we had textbooks published in India that instructed us that the Shia were not proper Muslims and not to be trusted, that we should never befriend non-Muslims, that we should encourage small children to fast even if they cry for food, that

---

* Known as Saudi Arabia since 1932.

children who do not pray regularly from the age of ten should be beaten, and that we should never be the first to greet a non-Muslim but always wait to be greeted first. As a young man I was not aware of terminology such as Salafi or Wahhabi, or of the names of Deobandi scholars many of whose works we had studied as children. I simply had misgivings at the time of the danger of brainwashing through teachings which were prescriptive in nature and not reflective of the liberal spirit of Islam. It has to be said that the books we studied, on the whole featured helpful and well-thought-out fundamentals, and under Maulvi Sahib's tutelage, provided reasonable instruction. But there was an element of rigidly defined prescription in some of the guidance, and many of the arguments and justifications were not well researched or backed up by logic.

Our filtering mechanisms to work out what was acceptable and what wasn't came from my parents and Maulvi Sahib more than anything else. Since they were moderate and open-minded, I can count myself fortunate for having the ability to siphon out what was good. I didn't start praying regularly until I was fourteen or so, and whilst my parents encouraged me to observe my prayers five times a day, they certainly didn't beat me for not praying. In fact, they didn't beat me for any reason. But there would have been many children whose parents might have been less discriminating about how they were being taught or what they were taught, and who paid less attention to the orientation of the books they were learning from. With the lack of choice of Islamic reference materials especially in English, there was also a lack of alternative texts to learn from.

Many imams in Britain at the time had been taught in Islamic schools, known as madrassahs back in the subcontinent, which would have had a Deobandi influence in the curriculum and style of instruction. These imams subscribed to subcontinent-localised and rigidly applied interpretations which on examination would have had limited fitment to British life and culture. Such imams by and large were not well educated in other fields of learning, such as science, history or literature, beyond Islamic and Quranic studies, didn't speak good English, and only a few had a good understanding of what life was like in Britain. From many imams we saw giving sermons at Friday prayers, it was patently obvious that they didn't even like Britain, and regarded it as a forced sacrifice to live here (for economic reasons), and a place in which to live and get by somehow without giving in to local norms and cultures since these would compromise a purely Islamic way of life. Theirs was a life of resistance and attrition, whereas as British youngsters we loved the country and sought guidance on how to live happily as Muslims, not how to avoid enjoying and embracing the country for what it was. With Maulvi Sahib we were fortunate, but on the whole for young Muslims in Britain being taught by teachers with limited UK life-skills and a negative outlook on the host culture was deeply unsatisfactory. A fundamental tenet of practising Islam anywhere is to take Islamic principles from primary texts, such as the Quran, and then apply them in the context of culture, but this was not being done. Studying textbooks written in the context of other cultures had real limitations. To think that hundreds of thousands of British Muslim children like me were subjected to a similar experience in Britain in the 1970s and 80s is disturbing and goes some way to explaining why many have views which do not adjust easily to living in a secular society.

The adoption of Arab cultural influences started extending to other areas of life too. A prime example of confusion between what is Arab and what is Islamic arises in naming, since many Muslims regard 'Arabic' and 'Islamic' naming to be coterminous. In 2008, when we named our first son Ehsan, someone remarked that it was a good 'Muslim' name. I had to respond that it wasn't a Muslim name, but an Arabic name which means 'better' or, under some interpretation, 'spiritual', and that it is a name taken by Christians and Muslims alike. I continued that there are very few 'Muslim' names; in other words, a name whose specific meaning indicates that only Muslims are likely to choose it. Mohammad is one such example, since the name refers to the Muslim prophet. Jameel, Zaki or Haya,* common and beautiful names for Muslim children, are not 'Muslim' names since they do not have a distinctly Islamic nature to them. They are Arabic names with meanings that can be applied to people of any faith. What I also realised is that a good Muslim name needn't be Arabic either but can be taken from any language. I was to discover this in countries, such as Bangladesh, Kazakhstan and Indonesia, for example, where many Muslims have names with beautiful

---

* Jameel means handsome, Zaki means smart or intelligent and is the name of our second son, and Haya means life.

meaning taken from the local culture.

A number of other cultural modifications began to find their place in the Muslim community at around the same time. The first, and in my mind one of the most petty, was the replacement by Bengalis and Pakistanis of saying 'Khuda hafiz' with saying 'Allah hafiz' instead. Both terms mean exactly the same thing, which is 'May God keep you safe', and the farewell is traditionally used at the end of a gathering or phone call. 'Khuda' is Persian for God, and its use across the Indian subcontinent by Muslims reflects the introduction of Islam in the region by the Mughals who had migrated eastwards into India from Persia in the 1500s, bringing Islam with them. Many Persian words entered subcontinental languages (principally Bengali, Punjabi and Urdu) spoken by Muslim converts, including words such as 'namaz' which means prayer, and 'roza' which means fasting. On the face of it, substituting 'Allah' for 'Khuda' was a benign change, as the words mean the same. But I found the shift worrying as it reflected a new-found preference for the Arabic and it represented a broader shift in cultural attitudes towards looking and sounding Arabic. Almost half of Dhaka society says, Allah hafiz, nowadays and the other half 'Khuda hafiz'. Neither my father nor my mother ever adopted the term 'Allah hafiz'. This fascination with Arabic extended to other activities, such as the adoption of niqab by women which is an Arabian Gulf cultural dress, and my earlier reference to the wearing of the Arab tunic by men at social functions. This was worrying as it indicated a desire to be more Islamic *by looking more Arab*. As I had found during childhood, people in my community easily conflated being Muslim with being Arab. All of this has resulted in misunderstandings about how to practise Islam, and has rendered parts of the Muslim community impressionable to thinking that adopting Arab culture is the right thing to do.

People's desire to adopt a more Islamic way of life was exploited by businesses too. Some Muslims, like myself, desired to adopt a more Islamic method to finance our borrowing needs, such that we wouldn't have to pay interest on debt but would enter into risk-sharing arrangements with investors instead. This would be in line with the Islamic principle that capital-rich money lenders should not be able to exploit capital-poor borrowers. Planning to buy a house in 2000, I became one of the first British Muslims to negotiate Islamic financing for a new property purchase in London. For years I had been saving up to buy, not wishing to take an interest-bearing mortgage since by strict Islamic principles participating in any form of usury is not permitted. I was fighting a losing battle, since the rate at which I was able to save was outpaced by the rate at which house prices were escalating. So when a prominent Islamic bank in London launched a Shari'a-compliant* financing scheme, I jumped at it. Upon examination of the financing terms and conditions, I found that the arrangement calculated the 'leasing rate' for a property by taking the London markets interest rate and applying a mark-up. I had to provide the bank with a hefty deposit for the property, and the lease rate gave the bank a level of profitability

---

* Shari'a refers to Islamic law, and in this case compliance refers to instruments which avoid the use of usury, in other words charging interest for loans.

that any mortgage lender would have died for. Instead of helping Muslims buy a property by escaping market exploitation (the idea behind Islam's banning of usury), the instrument seemed to be exploiting Muslims even more than high-street banks did. It was almost as bad as buying a house on credit-card debt. I co-wrote an assessment of the instrument for the bank's Shari'a council, asserting that the bank had created a so-called Islamic financial product which might have looked Islamic in form but in substance was perhaps more exploitative than the alternative it was trying to improve on. The bank never sent a substantive response. Soon I exited the contract and went back to a high-street mortgage as I found it less exploitative and more transparent than the Islamic financing option on offer. But thousands of Muslims went ahead with such schemes in the belief that they were freeing themselves from usury, but in reality they were also taking on a much more substantial repayment burden and rewarding their lenders with a minimised risk profile.

It didn't stop there. A good proportion of Muslim men stopped wearing ties based on a view that the knot was a sign of the cross around one's neck. Whether true or not, the tie does not represent Christianity, just as an Arab tunic doesn't represent Islam, and a saree doesn't represent Hinduism. These items of clothing may associate their origins within a particular faith but they are not artefacts of faith. I have even met Muslims who stopped eating croissants on the understanding that the pastry's design depicts a Christian cross. I don't recall asking Abba but I am certain it would never have crossed his mind to stop wearing ties as he would not have associated such activities with an increased level of piety. He never desired to *show* religiosity. Amma was similar. She wore a headscarf and had been doing so at a time when few women in our family did.

Just before my university years, there had been a global political event that got us thinking about Islamic identity too, and this was the Iranian Revolution. The overthrow of the Shah of Iran in 1979 was a monumental political event, grabbing headlines all over the world with the romantic story of how a seventy-year-old exiled cleric stepped off an Air France jet from Paris to return to his homeland and depose the strongman who had thrown him out almost three decades earlier. The popular Western perception was that Mohammad Reza Shah Pahlavi, the Shah of Iran, was a noble king descended from a centuries-old bloodline, living in grand palaces built across the fabled civilisation of Persia, driving fancy sports cars and gracing the finest salons of Paris and London with his elegant wife. While partly true, this was a carefully constructed image which created a misinformed picture of the Shah in the West. It is well documented[*] that he was a brutal and at times evil dictator, a stooge of the Americans, the British and the French, who resurrected generous oil-supply deals with Iran at the expense of his own people and economy. The Shah was not royalty at all, but the son of a former army colonel who had

---

[*] Stephen Kinzer's *All the Shah's Men* provides a detailed account of this period in Iran's history.

led a coup in Iran in the early twentieth century, and who himself was a student in Paris when the British and Americans plucked him out and installed him as a king-like figure in Tehran in the early 1950s.

Like most people in the West at the time of the revolution, Muslims didn't know much about Iran under the Shah, and most Muslims were drawn in when he was overthrown. At first, many thought that a noble king had been overthrown by a fanatic religious leader. But over time some began to consider that the people of a large Muslim country had been set free from the rule of someone who had been both a tyrant and a Western puppet. Whichever way Western Muslims might have leaned, the Iranian Revolution brought many of us to a point of where we started to take much more notice of the Middle East. Most countries in the region, from Egypt to Syria to Iraq and Saudi Arabia, were still run by unelected autocrats known for their corruption, largesse and obedience to external powers. Seeing Iran get rid of the Shah began to look more and more to us like an event where the small man won against the brutal despot. My cousins and I started supporting the Iranian football team, since for the first time we had a Muslim country that was pushing its weight in a global sports competition. Watching the World Cup on TV, we had gotten tired of players from Christian countries drawing an imaginary crucifix across their chests after scoring a goal, and so whenever Iran scored, we shouted 'Allahu akbar'* and then

---

* 'God is great . . . God is great.'

fell about on the living-room floor in ironic squeals of laughter and celebration. But what would come next in Iran was decades of brutal rule by an Islamist leader who imposed a disciplinarian regime on the Iranian people and waged an angry war of words and deeds against the West. As the years passed by, many of us became disenchanted with how Iran turned out under the Ayatollahs, who merely replaced one repressive regime with another.

Instead of being forthright and adopting a new British Muslim identity, while at Oxford I was still in some confusion over religious identity and struggling to develop a deeper appreciation of my inner beliefs. Friendship and coexistence with thoughtful Muslims and non-Muslims was pushing me to define the boundaries of my beliefs more rigorously. But it took me a long time to work through my confusions over whether, when and how to practise and profile my faith in a secular society. This confusion resulted in behaviour on my part which I wouldn't repeat now that my sense of religious identity is more evolved and stable. After attending a book-signing ceremony by Salman Rushdie at Blackwell's bookstore on Broad Street, I confronted him for his insensitivity over treatment of the Prophet Mohammad in the *Satanic Verses* by writing him an open letter that was published by *The Times*. My letter requested moderation on affecting the sensibilities of religious groups in a multicultural Britain. In response I received numerous hateful (and some sympathetic) letters from readers, since *The Times* had unhelpfully published my college address. This included a robust response from a noted British intellectual also published in *The Times*. Having a St Anne's student named in a published response sparked excitement and debate across the college. One fellow student chided me from a second-floor window in college as being a 'mad Mullah', something which our Principal, an eminent constitutional and human rights lawyer, found unacceptable and had him apologise for. I am sure the beard and Arab tunic I had on that day played a role in provoking, though not justifying, the comment. Some years later I would no longer see a need to wear an Arab tunic, unless there was some specific reason to, such as that I was attending an Arab cultural event or desired the coolness of this comfortable style of dress in hot weather. My motivations in Oxford were different, though. My struggle with refining my understanding of my faith was pulling me in different directions – seeking truth while at the same time taking steps to overemphasise my identity. In that year, I wore a tunic at times, a Palestinian 'Yasser Arafat' style keffiyeh, and also let my beard become quite long and bushy.

I would not take the same stand against the *Satanic Verses* today, as I can now distinguish more clearly between the hurt of having my faith challenged or even insulted, and the rights of someone else to think, say or write such within accepted boundaries and protections which current laws generally provide in many jurisdictions. When a Danish journal published a cartoon mocking the Prophet Mohammad a few years ago, I was offended but found no need to react. I was on holiday in Damascus when the news came out and was sad to see that angry crowds had raided the

Danish Embassy in Abou Rummani, just near Rita's house, and set light to the building, also burning down the German Embassy which occupied an upper floor. If others are to criticise my faith, unless they are directly insulting or attacking specific individuals or using extremely inflammatory and hurtful language, I leave them alone. The Prophet taught us as much, saying once that if you find or see objectionable activity, use your judgement to determine whether you oppose it by actions, by words or, if the other options don't make sense, in thoughts. These people had used actions, where in this case I would argue that the judicious approach would have been to use thoughts or, at the most, words.

Despite reaching a few peaks in my academic endeavours at Oxford, I favoured days of activism at the Majlis and evenings of debate on social and political topics. When I did study, I tried to understand why some countries are poor and others rich, whether capitalism and socialism are really that different, and whether colonialism was such a uniformly bad thing and if not, then what good did it also do. I took interest in the works of John Rawls, Amartya Sen, Niccolò Machiavelli* and John Stuart Mill. During my Master's degree at Cambridge, I decided to focus more on my work than I had done at Oxford. While there, I developed a healthy scepticism for economic theories and ideas, aided by tutors who taught us how to no less than savage

---

* Niccolò Machiavelli was an Italian diplomat and political adviser and strategist during the Medici period in Florence, and one of the thinkers whose writing I refer back to regularly.

factual analysis by putting forward alternate facts that made another point. This forced us to always be ready to challenge the status quo. Whilst this helped me develop my strategic skills for economics and business, oddly this also contributed to my scrutiny of faith and culture.

I developed platforms for dissent against experiences from my childhood, questioning my parents and also my schools over how we had been provided with a skewed and historically revisionist view of topics such as the British Empire and the Crusades. We had been given a rosy picture of how Englishmen built roads and railways in Africa and India, but we weren't taught about how trade protection and tariff policy were used to undermine Indian exports of fabrics to let spinning mills in Manchester flourish, nor how the British used to slice off the fingertips of cotton spinners in Bengal so that they wouldn't be able to spin as expertly. By the time I left university I had started to develop my own voice, going beyond that of my family by reinterpreting my identity and recalibrating my understanding of history. I had become more conscious of having a dual identity as British and Bangladeshi, was more confident in my beliefs and conduct as a Muslim and had acquired the courage to challenge those who had rejected me as an outsider in the past.

Seven

Decline of the Dynasty

'Bloody fundamentalists,' I mutter under my breath. 'They give us all their big talk of Islamic morality and duties, with their long beards and hitched-up pyjamas, and then they cut soil away from underneath their neighbour's house.'

'The mosque extension is encroaching on our wall and the new foundations have damaged ours,' one of my cha-chas* says, as he sniffs the musty air of my late grand-mother's bedroom through his nostrils.

'And the hypocrites have the nerve to stand up to give the sermon on a Friday and talk about Jewish settlements undercutting the soil of our Palestinian brothers! Haraamza-dain!† Haraamzadain!' I add a couple more expletives, masking them only loosely under my breath.

'Did you speak to them, the bastards?' I blurt out in my

---

* Bengali for paternal uncle. In Bengali culture it is appropriate to greet elders by their relationship to you rather than only by name.

† 'Haraamzada' literally means 'son of the devil', but in cultural terms is on par in English to calling someone a 'bastard'.

roughest Sylheti vernacular, looking up at the green blades of the ceiling fan, out of commission for the winter and speckled with dust.

'Well, I said a few . . . No, not yet.'

The last time I visited Sylhet was to mourn Dadu's death after she had passed away in the family house in the locality of Hazaripur at the age of ninety-three, leaving behind five of her eight children and fifty-seven living grandchildren, great-grandchildren and great-great-grandchildren all over the world. My relationship with Dadu, innocent and loving in childhood, had deteriorated mysteriously following Abba's death. Once she had lost her favourite son, she was unable to set eyes upon me without missing him. From beloved grandson I became a symbol of my father's death. My presence before her became unbearable, and once again I came to dread visits to Sylhet, just as I used to when I was a child. Thankfully, in the past few years leading up to her death matters normalised and my final memories with her are pleasant ones.

Its rural expanses covered by a canopy of thick jungle, the heaviest of monsoon rainfalls and romantic tea plantations, Sylhet is home to some of the most scenic parts of Bangladesh. In Sylhet town, the region's modest capital, not much has changed. In the two years since Dadu's demise, the Hazaripur house has continued its long descent into disrepair. As I appreciate the mosque situation, my brow becomes furrowed, consumed by thoughts of strategies about how the problem might be handled. There are complications: the Hazaripur house's significance as a sentimental heirloom; the preference of some family members to fully redevelop the property; and the mosque next door which while building an extension has unwittingly caused irreparable damage to the foundations.

'The tiles are cracked on the ground floor, in one bedroom, on the staircase and upstairs,' my uncle continues. 'It's getting worse. They're already widening and when the rainy season comes . . .'

My uncle sounds down, staring at the knees of his khaki-coloured corduroy trousers, showing a glimpse of his bucked front teeth before my attention is diverted to the orange and white bristles of his henna-coated silvery beard. Although barely sixty, like many men in this community, he has aged quickly, graduating into the upper echelons of Sylhet's status-obsessed religious murubbi. All of his life he has spent in the shadows, shepherding his siblings' property interests and nurturing the Chowdhury base whilst others ventured overseas to seek their fortune. Loyal to the end, he has lived a life paying insufficient attention to his own needs, visions and capacities.

Dadu's once legendary room is feebly lit by a pair of naked forty-watt bulbs whose illumination is not strong enough to reach the nooks and crannies. Pools of darkness spread from the corners, rather like the anger that now seeps from my heart through my brittle, jet-lagged body. In the rafters up above us an intricate cobweb glistens, one end of it dangling from the thatched ceiling and waving gently with the air current that flows through the vents in each wall. Gone is the era of jollity and business when Dadu held court here.

This trip to Sylhet has ambushed my plans to spend time relaxing in Bangladesh. It was barely two days ago, in the office in London that I had been finishing off my final conference call for the year before heading to Heathrow for the thirteen-hour flight to Dhaka.

'Forty-four,' I compute and say back to myself, as usual obsessed with statistical analysis of every passing detail. 'Forty-four hours and . . . twenty minutes since I left the office.'

It has been a good year for me, seeing through my side of the billion-dollar acquisition of a software company, the one we were discussing on that final conference call. Tonight, the same call bridge that I used then will connect the global Chowdhury clan together for the first time into a single phone conversation. I look at my watch. It is 6:28. Despite blowing one hundred thousand of my hard-earned British Airways air miles to fly out in the comfort of business class, a faint feeling of tiredness still lingers inside my head. I am giddy and in need of some air.

The Chowdhurys set up home in Hazaripur in 1960, following a tumultuous final decade of decline in the family's all-powerful history. Sylhet had a predominantly rural and agrarian society ruled by a few hundred mighty jamidars,* including the Chowdhury clan who exerted influence over many villages with their thousands of inhabitants. The

---

* Bengali for landlord or landowner

jamidars' methods are not remembered fondly, built as they were around perpetuating almost two centuries of class division and a carefully administered system of local peasant taxation. My grandfather's ancestors came from Pahargonj, about ten kilometres from Sonarpur, the seat of the Chowdhurys' feudal power since the 1800s. The Koronshi clan, as they were known before the Chowdhury title was bestowed on them by the British, traced their origins in Sylhet to the time of Hazrat Shahjalal, a Mughal envoy and religious saint who came to Bengal in the 1600s. It was Hazrat Shahjalal's influence that spread Islam in east Bengal and neighbouring Burma.

Dada moved to Sonarpur on his second marriage, to my Dadu, around 1925, but Pahargonj remained the Chowdhury epicentre. My father and his living siblings were descended from Dadu, with one elderly uncle from Dada's first marriage who resided in Chittagong and was just about the same age as his stepmother. In both villages, peasants who would walk past the Chowdhury house would have to present gifts, close their umbrellas and remove their shoes as they passed by the boundary wall. Those who defied such humiliating customs would be castigated and punished. Based on the revenues from their land income, the Chowdhurys lived for decades like local kings, wanting for nothing and rarely doing an honest day's work. Resented by most and pitied by none, the Chowdhurys' life of privilege charted a rapid demise after 1947 when the British partitioned, decolonised and departed India, their Jewel in the Crown. After Partition the Pakistan Government displaced the role of the jamidar in Bengal by implementing locally administered taxation measures with collection by a District Commissioner. By the mid-1950s, time had run out for the landlords who, without taxation revenue and too idle to work in the fields, were scarcely able to sustain their once lavish lifestyle. Increasingly out of favour with the villagers and with no education to speak of in the family, Dada resorted to selling off the family land to his subjects in the village and at rock-bottom prices. Years later, relations and friendships were resumed with the villagers on a more even keel and ultimately with a good rapport, but with the backdrop of a history which was seldom recounted in proper detail.

It was my father as the eldest son of eight siblings who decided in 1957, in his early twenties, to migrate to Britain, having left high school in 1954 to take up a job in the Pakistan Forestry Department. In London, he would spend the next decade doing three jobs and sending most of his wages back home to support the roost. After marrying in 1964, both my mother and father would toil away in the Curry Queen, his Indian restaurant on the Lee High Road in Lewisham, carving out a meagre living for themselves from the leftovers of their earnings. Meanwhile back home, my grandfather was left with little option but to sell the substantial Sonarpur family home and accompanying final few acres of land and move to the then fledgling town of Sylhet. Following the shame of their rushed departure, the Chowdhurys were never to return. The family laid its roots in the comparatively modest suburb of Hazaripur. Constructed as a makeshift dwelling on a plot of barely 500 square metres, the Hazaripur house was built with limited funds and mixed feelings about how long the Chowdhurys would live there. Forty years on, the temporary base remains, and the house looks dishevelled with its cheap-looking windows and doors, rudimentary plumbing and corrugated tin roof.

'You are on the Mosque Committee, aren't you, Uncle?'

'Yes, I am.'

I look at the hairy backs of my uncle's dark hands. He wears no jewellery and a make-do, chunky watch. As I wander in and out of my thoughts, I stare at its analogue dial. 6:40.

'Years ago, when the peasants used to walk past our home in Sonarpur, they would have to hold their footwear above their heads as they went past,' murmurs Jamal, relating once again the familiar story of the obligatory show of respect incumbent upon villagers whenever they would pass the jamidar's house.

'And then there are the days of your General Nana; in those days too we were respected.'

General Nana, or General Osmani as he was known in public, treated me with great affection as a child. Later on, staying at our house whilst undergoing medical treatment at St Bartholomew's Hospital in London, he inspired me to try for Oxford, telling me about how one of his father Khan Bahadur Mofizur Rahman's elders had read Law at Pembroke College in the 1890s. General Nana was commissioned in the British Indian Army in 1942 and became the youngest Major to serve in the British Army in India. Later on, during World

War II he was captured by the Japanese in the jungles of Burma, and later still went on to become the most senior Bengali in the Pakistan Army. After leading the liberation forces to Bangladeshi independence in 1971, Prime Minister Sheikh Mujibur Rahman appointed Nana to his first cabinet as Civil Aviation Minister, and then to Defence Minister. As children we used to visit him in his official ministerial house, and in turn he would oversee the construction of Sylhet House, our new family home in Dhaka.

Sylhet House was the first residence to be built in the nation's capital by a member of the Chowdhury clan. Completed in 1974 and funded principally by profits from the Curry Queen back in South London, this was a grand, two-storeyed villa, with large bedrooms, a clutch of verandas and a garden with enough space for a badminton court and plenty of coconut trees. Over the next four decades, Sylhet House played a critical convening role for our family network, analogous to that of the Curry Queen in London; it served as a guest house, office, meeting point, social centre, wedding hall and occasional car park for dozens of our relatives. Whenever we visited during holidays, the house would be invariably packed with daytime guests as well as a few staying over with us too. Of all my traumas of visiting Sylhet as a child, a compensating factor was the fun and freedom we enjoyed as children in Sylhet House. I even learnt to drive on Sylhet House's driveway, aged thirteen, during a school holiday.

Fearless, bloody-minded and eccentric to the core, more Englishman by behaviour than Bengali, but with the beating heart of a Bengal Tiger, Nana remains an inspiration to the clan and to the nation. He tried to instil some of his courage in me, calling me 'Mr Taffy' in his posh English accent and pushing me to strive harder. Nana was dead by the time I got into Oxford, having passed away in London in 1982 after a few hard months of treatment.

'And now, in this city, we are nobodies. No respect, no voice, nothing,' Jamal continues, his tone not haughty as it used to be when he retold this story dozens of times before, but lost and defeated.

I look back at my uncle and realise why I am feeling angry. I have returned to a place associated with the roots of some of my deepest frustrations, and the resurfacing of stories about the background of the Chowdhury clan is something I do not relish. Like many others, it is a topic in which I share little of the elders' pride and less of their rose-tinted nostalgia. Over the years, I have attracted the displeasure of many of the murubbi due to my resistance to embracing the glorification of the village days.

For a moment my ire is eclipsed by my affection for this simple man and his current predicaments. His loyalty to the family cause is astonishing. Truly has he served his kith and kin, most of all his mother whom he tirelessly looked after for many years. But as we continue to talk, my mind wanders back into its archives, conjuring up distant memories. Since my youth I have experienced many Bengali behaviours and practices that irritated and disappointed me, and these trips to Sylhet regularly serve to rekindle some of those memories.

'Please don't talk about Sonarpur, Uncle,' I implore, lamenting how the old blood still thinks in the traditional ways of the feudal master. I drift into a recollection of some of my frustrations, focusing on the notions of hierarchy which I dislike the most.

Phrases such as 'Tar jat bala na' epitomise this frustration. Meaning 'His breeding is not good', this would be a typical response to a marriage proposal from a seemingly unworthy candidate. Although Muslims in India, Pakistan and Bangladesh pride themselves on not being divided along caste lines as Hindus are, in reality the concept of jat approximates to such divisions very closely since they distinguish people by education and landownership. With traditional Bengali society having limited mobility between classes until more recent advances in economic opportunity, such jat patterns were often perpetuated across several generations and applied to Muslims as much as Hindus.

'Tar baf dada hokkolti maimol-or-jat', meaning 'His father and grandfather are all fishermen stock', would be typical of the khati* Sylheti commentary that can accompany conversations concerning marriage, or business or any matter which might involve the prospect of social interaction. Such unashamed attitudes of high-handedness have always stood out as distasteful behaviours to me. Such positions have been entrenched in the clans for generations, from the land owning stalwarts on my father's side to the technocrats and educated types on my mother's. In fact,

---

* Literally means genuine or true, and when referred to with the vernacular means the language which is from the village, that is, the 'true' language as spoken at its roots.

haughty arrogance is a game that everybody can play in Bangladesh, so stratified is the society, so divided on class and caste lines. As a good friend once remarked to me, in Bangladesh everybody from the Prime Minister to the lowliest street cleaner has somebody that they can look down on.

During childhood visits to Bangladesh, I would see that many relatives would not eat the same food as their servants nor ever sit at the same table; dark-skinned people would be referred to as being 'moila', which in Bengali means dirty, and fairer-skinned as 'porishkar' meaning clean. Elders and higher-class people would always refer to others with the 'tumi' or 'tui', familiar version of 'you' rather than the 'apne', more respectful variant.*

There was also the belief amongst Bengali adults that children understood little, but had much to gain by listening to the murubbi and following obediently. In the living rooms of Bengali homes in London, children would be expected to sit to the sides and never to cross their legs or point their feet in front of an elder. Talking back to a murubbi would be castigated as 'beaddobi.'† In mosques run by Pakistanis or Bengalis, kids would be banished to the back at prayer time and parents who wanted to pray next to their children had to retreat with them.

---

* Bengali has a second-person-singular personal pronoun that is differentiated in a way similar to 'tu' and 'vous' in French; only that in Bengali there are three variants, 'apne', 'tumi' and 'tui'. 'Tui' is reserved for use with minor children, servants and people undertaking menial jobs and is sometimes used in anger.

† behaviour which demonstrates no respect

The stratification of Bengali society was not restricted to home turf. When I grew up in Britain in the 70s and 80s, racism extended well beyond white people. There was a lot of it amongst the Bengalis and other Asians we knew, and in many ways more venomous and practised than the more occasional racism that I saw from English people. Most of my relatives discouraged their children from having English friends. The 'Ingleesh' label was used conveniently and disparagingly to refer to all white people, as well as to all non-Muslims. Distinctions between such groups were deemed unnecessary, since most fell into the 'we don't want to mix with them' category. As a result, any anomalies, such as white converts to Islam, or Bosnian (i.e. white) Muslims for example, would be subjected to strange looks in mosques from many Asians who would pray in the same places. Whilst I was uncomfortable with the lazy logic of such categorisations, I was more irritated by the refusal of my murubbi to address or even discuss it, especially given the Islamic principles we had been taught of equality between all humans as creations of God. Again, I saw simultaneously the faults of both sides: how the English categorised brown people as somehow less civilised and cultured, and how Muslims regarded white people as unbelievers (referred to often as 'kaafirs', literally the Arabic word for non-believer).

I would rankle at the two-facedness of those who earned their living off people they referred to disparagingly as kaafir, but to whom they behaved so obsequiously in person. To me this was hypocrisy, since we had been taught that God is the only judge of mankind, and that it was not our role to judge who is and is not a true believer. This racist attitude was illustrated most strongly in our restaurant, the Curry Queen. Staff would occasionally refer to West Indian customers as 'kala bhai'* while smiling at them as they came in. Most would despise the 'kaafir' action of drinking alcohol, but then a number would actively encourage greater consumption of it enabling them to take home even more profit from their business.

'Arokhta moot dhalo!'† the head waiter would shout to me from in front of the bar on a busy Friday night. He would be asking me to pour another pint of lager, only using 'moot' to refer to it, meaning urine or effectively piss in the coarsest Sylheti slang.‡

The Curry Queen was a Chowdhury family institution and the landing pad for many a Bangladeshi immigrant to the UK. Few of our relatives in Sylhet had ever seen it, but they all knew the Curry Queen by name. In the days of my childhood, the consumption of alcohol was generally abhorred by Muslims in the UK. There are many more heinous Islamic transgressions than drinking, but since it has a high visibility, it came with a heavy social taboo too. I saw gross inconsistency amongst some Muslims, who despised drinking yet engaged in all sorts of other misdemeanours, such as double-claiming social security whilst

---

* Sylheti slang for black brother.

† Literally meaning 'Pour me another glass of piss!'

‡ 'Peshap' is the general word in Sylheti (and Bengali) for urine. 'Moot' is used more coarsely, and its closest English equivalent would be 'piss'.

earning a decent living, dodging tax by under-reporting income or overcharging invoicing costs, cheating business partners or relatives, or taking a second wife back home in the village. Such hypocrisies, with the backdrop of the lecturing we received on religion, led me to regret how wide the chasm was between Islamic principle and Muslim practice.

People of other faiths would be looked down on by Muslims, who, so we were taught, were the only people destined for paradise. Christians and Jews, or 'Yehudi', were seen as 'people of the book' and accorded more respect than Hindus, who it appeared to me were despised more than any other faith due to their worship of many deities. Jews were disliked more than Christians due to the lazy association many Muslims made (and still do) between people of Jewish faith and supporters of the statehood of Israel.

To me, we all believed in God and the Prophet Mohammad being his final messenger. Regarding religious differences, there were many statements bandied about which were plain and baseless brain-washing, such as that Shia commit adultery, that Jews are never to be trusted, that Coke contains drips of alcohol in a disguised attempt by Christians to inebriate Muslims, and that Christians made up that man has flown to the moon. These statements underlined the gulf between many Muslims and non-Muslims in the West.

Every now and then, these beliefs would result in actions of social and cultural defiance, too. In the early 2000s, a new and sugary-tasting cola drink by the name of Mecca

Cola was launched to great fanfare in France, the UK and a number of other countries. For a short while, Muslim families who bought into the Coca-Cola-being-spiked-with-drips-of-alcohol theory purchased the new drink in copious quantities, consuming it by the crate load with the satisfaction that they were defying a global conspiracy to confine Muslims to the hellfire for a lifetime of drinking alcohol. Other variants came up too, including Qibla Cola and Zamzam Cola, all with messages on the bottle to show Muslim unity, and support of Palestinians, by consuming this drink. Devoid of taste, these drinks suffered a quick demise.

The subject of alcohol created its own world of Islamic guilt-induced distortions to deal with. One evening, before opening time at the Curry Queen, one of the waiters instructed me on how to wash beer glasses whilst making minimum contact with the forbidden alcoholic contents. Carefully he dipped a glass in and out of a basin full of hot soapy water and then expertly dried it immediately afterwards, starting from the inside, with a dry cloth. He fished the glass out of the water with a flourish which belied his pride in a perfected, non-alcoholic-contact technique for washing beer glasses.

'Tufael, you know that any part of your body that comes into contact with alcohol will not enter paradise, until it has been purified in hellfire.'

Heavy stuff, but the first thought that came to my mind was the absurd one of a body going to heaven minus two hands and forearms, which went to hell to burn for a few hundred years instead.

'What if the alcohol was touched with no intention of drinking it, but to do a job such as this one for my managers who have decided to sell liquor?' I asked.

This question would hurt, and normally be followed by a glance away from the elder it was directed to.

'If you touch it by mistake, you will be forgiven. But you cannot be forgiven for this. This you are doing wilfully and knowingly.'

Selling to others something which is strictly forbidden to Muslims on the grounds of good health didn't make any sense to me. I couldn't see how glass-rinsing techniques could in such a context be the most relevant issue. Whilst the washing methods seemed logical, in the grand scheme of things, the techniques seemed a guilty distraction. I didn't follow the advice for long, preferring to give priority to washing glasses properly, since I felt that our ethical responsibility to ensure customers ate and drank from clean utensils should take priority over keeping my hands free of diluted dregs of alcohol which I had no intention of consuming. When reminded of my delinquencies in the cleaning department, in other words that I was washing more thoroughly than I needed to, I replied that as a juvenile I bore no responsibility for touching the alcohol and that the account for this had to rest between my employers and the Almighty.

Not drinking alcohol was one of the clear-cut compliance issues that could be easily categorised into lists of Muslim 'dos' and 'don'ts'. But what I found difficult was how to deal with behaviour and attitudes where the dividing lines were harder to define, and judgement was needed to decide how to act. The more I thought about it, the more I found issues touched this more controversial category. As time passed and my life became more integrated into British culture, the lists of 'dos' and 'don'ts' that my parents and religious teachers had painstakingly rehearsed for me appeared increasingly exclusive. Throwaway comments by relatives regularly criticising Christians, Hindus and Jews did not help. Most of my friends then, as today, were not Muslim and yet had impeccable moral and ethical behaviour. I found such discrimination against non-Muslims to be distasteful and mean-spirited.

Admittedly, the dilemmas over profiting from the sale of alcohol caused grief to many of my relatives, originally driven to such measures by a need to find ways of making a better living. When my father opened the Curry Queen, he had worked for years in lowly paid jobs which afforded him nothing more than a meagre lifestyle. His ambition went way beyond that, as did his capacities, but he lacked the professional training and polish to be given a well-paid job. Business was the only way to go and restaurants were becoming a proven formula. Bitten by guilt, one by one most of the family withdrew from the licensed elements of the catering business, though not until some had made a neat profit by holding onto their businesses until the 1990s UK property boom had peaked.

For many, attitudes against the English went beyond differences in religion and drinking alcohol, and revealed at times a deep-seated, predetermined grievance against a people who they saw as somehow responsible for the predecessors who had ruled over their forefathers for many decades.

'Ingleesh don't look after their elders when they get old,' a relative once sneered when we discussed how sad it was that our next-door neighbour, Uncle Bob, was putting Aunty into a nursing home. 'They let their mothers and fathers die in old people's homes. Shame on them.'

Uncle Bob moved his ninety-three year old wife to Morden College nursing home in Blackheath when she became so frail that he, himself in his upper eighties, was too weak to attend to her. It wasn't because he didn't care. He did, and this was evidenced by how the decision took its toll on him. Logic drove his actions, not sentiment or a 'what will other people think?' attitude. Ironically, it was Uncle Bob who behaved truer to Islamic tenets of balanced decision-making than the more emotional Bengali ways would have resulted in. In short, many of the attitudes of British-based Bengalis towards white people might just be referred to as plain racist.

But there were aspects of British culture that didn't work for me. There were the obvious areas which were out of bounds for an observant Muslim, such as drinking, girlfriends and partying, all of which clearly went against Islamic codes of conduct, but there were less obvious and more subtle issues which were more challenging to come to terms with, and more fundamental in fuelling my sense of exclusion. British society seemed to me one in which people were much less involved in each other's lives compared to what I had been brought up to believe was right. The English appeared less communal and more detached. Most of the English children I knew were less influenced by the wisdom of elders than I had been brought up to expect, and I saw them having less respect for the older generation. For example, I didn't understand how some of my friends could address their parents on a first name basis, or how a number could even swear about them behind their backs.

The majority of English people I knew were ambivalent about the colonial injustices that still afflicted the existence of millions around the world. This was principally out of ignorance, though there was still a healthy dose of colonial nostalgia in Britain in the 1980s which bordered on eulogising and celebrating Britain's great recent history. Mainly because they had not been exposed to it, English people did not understand as well as us – with all our experience from annual trips to Bangladesh – what real poverty was. Many of my English friends and teachers didn't have a clue about how imperial Britannia had exploited the lives of the colonised, and some took a patronising, pitying stance towards me, as though having been born brown-skinned was somehow unfortunate. Regarding itself as a fair and great nation, there was duplicity in Britain's glorification of her often shameful past. This bothered me, since many of my own family had been affected by colonialism's consequences. Later I appreciated that the Chowdhury jamidars were actually beneficiaries of colonialism, since the British presence in India safeguarded their life of feudal mastery all the way up until midway through the twentieth century.

The relative lack of emphasis on sanitary privacy and cleanliness in British culture meant that visiting bathrooms, like communal changing, could be an awkward experience. Physical cleanliness is seen as a path to spiritual cleanliness in Islam, and toilet hygiene is one of the most important aspects of maintaining cleanliness throughout the day. Growing up in Britain, stand-up urinals which spray back speckles of urine onto one's trousers and toilet cubicles without wash-basins were all sources of daily anxiety. Bathroom challenges of course weren't restricted to my experience in Britain, as challenges extended to trips to Sylhet as well as countless incidents in other places. When I grew up in London, no bathroom offered facilities for rinsing one's genitals properly after a visit to the lavatory, and many users would leave the bathroom without even washing their hands. To avoid contact with urine-smeared bathroom appliances, I developed techniques for not coming into contact with door handles, locks, flushes, toilet seats or anything else. The methods used are so honed that now my senses are keenly attuned to dealing with almost any sanitary layout or arrangement.

Fellow students at Oxford University would snigger when they'd see me going to the bathroom with a 'bodna'* in my hands; as fellow holidaymakers did once when one of my cousins and I did the same on the Isle of Wight. What possessed us to spend half-term in a holiday camp near Cowes with hundreds of half-drunken teenagers, I don't quite remember. In those years we were less confident of

---

* Bengali for a plastic water jug with a spout designed specifically for use in bathrooms.

our cultural differences in regard to bathroom behaviour, and so we would hide the necessary water vessel in a Marks & Spencer polythene bag. Cultural differences concerning attitudes to hygiene fed a strong feeling of exclusion from British society, and the ridicule attracted from being different in such personal matters was acute. The resultant pressure to conform was strong, since the cost of not doing so was to be made to feel even more foreign, inferior and uncivilised. Being occasionally referred to as a 'dirty Paki' added a laughable yet unfunny irony to the situation. The same cousin who visited the Isle of Wight together with me was spat on once by teenage girls on the number 141 bus coming home from Catford. As they giggled off to their seat at the back, my cousin and I were too shocked to react, and too gentlemanly to do so with girls, concentrating instead on wiping embarrassing bubbles of spit from our faces before others would notice and ridicule us further.

In the grand scheme of life, bathroom behaviour may seem a trivial matter, but in Britain (for different reasons to bathroom challenges in Sylhet!) it was an element of the daily challenge. Going to the toilet, eating, praying five times a day, all meant that being foreign wasn't an occasional challenge; no, we were foreign all day long. Successfully visiting a 'hole in the floor' toilet at Karachi Airport some years ago, this time dressed in a hand-cut Cerruti suit from Bond Street which emerged spotless and neatly creased from the experience, is one of thousands of more recent successfully executed bathroom operations over the years. Once upon a time a fearful ethnic minority secretly performing acts of toilet hygiene, today we are easy-going masters of sanitary cleanliness. As time has gone on, our toilet traumas have been transformed into technical execution challenges, negotiated using a carefully constructed compendium of tools and techniques to suit almost every circumstance. Buying water bottles from a street vendor before going to the toilet, keeping perfumed ittar and loose tissues in the pocket, and being able to hook open a toilet door with one's shoe being just a few. No contact is the objective and failure may result in a swift trip home, a shower and a change of clothing.

Being made to feel foreign extended to other fields too. When Pakistan beat England in a cricket match at Lord's in 1990 and their opening batsman Mohsin Khan scored a magnificent double century, my encouraging cheers to applaud their victory were met with stony stares of silence by the English fans sitting around me in the stands. I was supporting England as usual, but felt happy to see the underdogs win a contest that levelled matters between the two teams; all summer Pakistan had been subjected most uncharitably to accusations of cheating by sections of the tabloid English press. As I trudged back to the Baker Street tube that night, I felt bitter about backing an England team whose fellow supporters didn't even trust me.

'If it had been a white man applauding Pakistan in the stands this afternoon,' I thought as the escalator steadily descended down into the depths of London's underground, 'it would have been regarded as hearty sporting behaviour.'

Back in 1990, I was years ahead of my time in the way that I was already comfortable with a multiplicity to my identity. I was happy to be British, and to support and encourage the success of Pakistan and saw no truck in this combination. Whilst this caused no issue to me, because of my skin tone it created a negative reaction from white English people around me who judged my responses as somehow ungrateful or foreign. It wasn't me who failed the famous Norman Tebbit 'cricket test' that day, but the Englishmen sitting around me.

Using cleansed fingers to break, sort and eat food was another case in point. In Bengali culture using hands for eating is quite commonplace, and is somewhat more practical than using cutlery when it comes to negotiating fiddly elements of food such as fish with a large number of fine bones that could easily be choked on. In the context of a culture of cleanliness, eating with fingers was of course as hygienic as using cutlery, only more practical. But some of my English friends and colleagues at work regarded it as either dirty, or uncivilised. Once I met two professionals from the British Council in Dhaka who explained to me the purpose of their cultural project in Bangladesh was to 'to teach the locals how to be civilised and use knives and forks to eat with'. Similar to our humiliation over toilet activities, eating with hands was too often also seen as a way of being somehow different, foreign and inferior.

Whilst each had drawbacks, these seemingly opposed ways of life offered fundamental attractions. The English culture offered the qualities of logic in thought, fair play in attitude, equality in opportunity, respect towards children, as well as acceptance of change and openness in behaviour. The

Bengali one offered the values of broad familial affection, deep social respect, valuing elders and personal cleanliness. I felt a pride in and affinity for each and, before I got the hang of playing the bicultural card, I often found myself stuck in the middle stubbornly defending one flank from an attack by someone from the other.

I did not wish to choose between these worlds but wanted to retain both as my own. I wanted everything integrated, interchangeable at will and personalised. So the challenge wasn't the difficult one of compromising around the middle ground, but the harder one of actively bridging the space between all the aspects of my confused, kaleidoscopic world. I needed a foundation that glued together all the compatible elements and left out all the ones incompatible with my core values. For this reason, the countless instances of cultural accommodation illustrated by other Muslim kids worked for me as little as the touch-free glass-washing techniques of Muslims serving alcohol.

One evening during a CCF summer camp, the boys in our dormitory ganged up on a South-Asian-looking boy from another school, caging him between a pair of radiator grilles which they cleverly padlocked together once they had forced him inside. They slid him on his backside around the shiny floor, pushing and shoving him about as though an ice hockey goalie stuck inside a 360-degree net. They chided him, letting their spittle drool from their lips onto his entrapped head. Shamefully, I didn't have the guts to confront a roomful of boys behaving in unison in this way. The poor kid's reaction to this humiliation was to head down to the local off-licence and return with a dozen cans of beer, handing them out to all and sundry, and downing one himself. It looked like it was the first time he had drunk alcohol, and it made him the dorm mate of choice for the evening. But it seemed to me that they broke him that night, forcing him to cross a cultural divide and opt for belonging to one side.

I remember the drive months later to a cricket match in the team bus, and some of the boys who had been at the camp chanting Paki songs to pass the time. One other Asian boy and myself were the targets, I guess 'Brown Girl in the Ring' made another appearance too that day. Maybe the boys just thought it might result in them being offered more free beer. One thing was clear to me: no amount of beer would ever buy you the right to be left alone for being an outsider and might never buy you rights to being an insider either.

I spotted Ali, a Pakistani boy from my school, at Catford Mosque some weeks later, praying with his ailing father. I despaired because he was another one who wasn't taking the easy option of shifting across to the 'Western flank', so to speak, but instead was trying to carve out a way of life in between a traditional English and a traditional Pakistani and Muslim one. Like me, Ali too looked like he was entering that lonely zone on the social hinterland, living a life of two incompatible halves, a culturally undefined and socially ambiguous something that I saw as a path to unhappiness. At times Ali seemed to look down on me too; I imagined that in his eyes I was a Bengali from inferior and less literate stock to the fairer, taller and more educated West Pakistani stereotype.

I breathe a deep sigh, emptying my lungs as I look around Dadu's room. I had tuned out into a world of day-dreams as my uncle continued to mumble on about the cracks in the house. I recalibrate to the conversation and my surroundings, still angry and now also disturbed from the dredging up of memories that this trip has triggered.

'There are a couple of shontrashis* in the area and we cannot oppose them,' he continues, as I realise he has moved onto a new topic. 'They are too strong. Last year one of the gangs set light to the Hindus' house opposite after attacks on Muslims in India after the London bombs.'

Bicycles and rickshaws shuffle past the black front gates of our modest Hazaripur home. The evening traffic is heavy as people rush to get home or finish errands before the early shutdown that contrasts this conservative, home-bound city from the night-owl culture of the nation's capital.

'Driver!' I spot an empty rickshaw.

The rickshaw wallah† slows to an easy halt a few metres past me and a subtle nod of his head towards the empty seat behind him indicates that he's available. Not bothering to fix the fare, I jump on.

'Amborkhana. Dhire shuste jawka,' I suggest we go nice and easy. 7.39. There is time.

The back of the driver's turbaned head bobs up and down

---

* 'Shontrashi' is Bengali for a local troublemaker or mobster.

† driver

as we wind through the localities which make up Sylhet's haphazard city centre. A lazy evening mist is settling, hinting at how it will shroud us in a cosy fog by the early hours. As we traverse busy intersections, I reacquaint myself with the familiar small-town sounds of Bangladesh. The chatter on street corners, the banging of steel on steel from the workshops and garages that line the roadsides, and the sawing from furniture shops in between. Men stand around in small clumps watching passers-by, breathing out cold mist in most cases mixed with lungfuls of cigarette smoke. Some have mufflers rather oddly wrapped around their heads.

There is hardly any part of the city which is not overcrowded nowadays. The sprawling hutment has grown more congested and with it more squalid; its narrow and winding thoroughfares bursting at the seams with rickshaws and carts, its open drains more smelly by the year, and the overhead views strangled by a criss-cross of power cables and knotted phone lines connecting shanty buildings with dusty junction boxes.

'Our average speed must be about twenty kilometres per hour,' I compute, with a series of mental calculations that momentarily distract me.

Assuming a ten-hour shift and fifty per cent chargeable utilisation, I work out that the average rickshaw puller must be covering a good hundred kilometres a day. As we progress, I calculate the average fare per ride and the average daily income. An LED clock above a shop's signboard beams out. The red numerals radiate through the light mist. 7:57.

I crook my neck around as we pass by to see if the read-out will also display the temperature. It doesn't, but I guess it must have dropped to about eight degrees above zero by now. I notice that the time reads the same backwards, too. Forty-six Fahrenheit, I compute, continuing to play mathematical acrobatics in my head, as we soldier on through the crowded evening streets. I wonder what mood the clan will be in tonight.

A couple of kids jump about in the water in Dufardigirpar, slapping their hands on each other's backs. 'Dufar digi' means 'cleaners' pond' and the 'par' denotes that this is the area right next to, literally on the banks of, the pond used by the laundry people. They have left it late to be having an evening dip. Like most shared facilities in this overcrowded country, the laundry lake is another scarce resource that is destined for multi-purpose, round-the-clock use. The air smells cleaner and purer than in polluted Dhaka, and I enjoy the breeze brushing against my face as we hit some open road and gather pace. I sit back in an effort to relax my tired thighs and knee joints.

'Egaro gonta aiz,' the rickshaw puller tells me that he has been on duty for eleven hours.

I revise the arithmetic around how much he will make today, deducting vehicle rental and police bribes from his daily trip fees, and leaving him with a take-home pay of around five US dollars.

'Dekhoin!! Look out!!' Another rickshaw pulls out right in front of us, jolting me out of my reveries and bringing me right back to the crowded street scene in front of us.

Alert, my driver has it under control, skilfully leaning over to alter our centre of gravity by just enough to avoid a collision. It is standard riding practise and the moment passes without incident. One of our back wheels drops into a pothole due to our need to manoeuvre off course. When I wince at the shudder in my hip joint from the impact, I notice my mobile is ringing.

'Yes, this is Mohammad.'

It is the New York office. I wonder what they want now, two days before Christmas. It must be 9 a.m. there.

'No, I can't help since I am on leave till . . . . . . yes . . . no, in the new . . . Yes, OK. And the same to you. Bye-bye.'

It's the major deal we have been working on. I consider the acquisition critical to my company's telecoms industry offering, filling a gap with which we would otherwise have lost out on important opportunities.

'Ji, ekh-sho-fonro.' I say to the driver that the number of flights I have taken so far this year is one hundred and fifteen. We speak about life in London.

'Computer bechte parben?' I joke with him about whether he could sell computers when he asks me if there are any opportunities for migration to Britain.

Digressions continue to flow through my mind, mainly involving numbers and formulae, as we undulate through the shallow dips and inclines of this hilly part of town. At 8:10 the rickshaw pulls into the Amborkhana alley where my cousin Mosaddeq lives with his wife and children. Lush green moss coats the walls of the narrow lane which leads into the property. The rickshaw wallah looks wide-eyed at the handsome tip which I hope will persuade him to buy some extra food for his family, clock off and have an early night.

'We are holding ourselves back,' Mosaddeq regrets. 'This mentality of rejecting modernisation, technology and science is halting our progress. The mullahs don't want to have TV or computers in the schools, saying that it will introduce Western influences.'

We are chatting about how his life has changed since retirement, about his eldest daughter in New York and about his welfare projects.

'That's absurd. It's the same in some of the madrassahs* in Britain,' I lament, thinking briefly of my experiences in London, working with a Muslim school.

'We need to reconsider the logic on that one again,' I add. 'The mullahs are intelligent and like all of us they need to come to conclusions themselves, rather than have answers forced upon them.'

'The timing of Eid came up again this year and as usual the mullahs were not interested in using a telescope to look for the moon, arguing it is sunnah† to spot it with the naked eye.' My cousin looks goggle-eyed and kind through his bifocal lenses.

'It's the same in England. Some people refer to Meteorological Office timings to determine if the new moon is

---

* Literally the Arabic for school, but in the context here meaning Muslim school.

† Actions which are known to have been practised by the Prophet.

visible after sunset, while others follow pronouncements from Saudi Arabia.'

My voice is rising again. Presenting at Cabinet meetings and answering to border security officials waving Kalashnikovs doesn't unsettle me, but domestic complications are a different matter, and I have never easily dealt with hypocrisy from the local mosque. I take a deep breath. My chest aches and I poke my ribcage with the tips of my fingers to check if the pain is really there. I notice the light green fridge standing in the corner of Mosaddeq's living area. Commonplace to the Bangladeshi living room, the appliance squats on a block of wood designed to give it enough ground clearance to remain well ventilated.

'The mullahs in Sylhet are confused about all this. But it's not their fault. They are just like goats following a shepherd, only there isn't one. We have no leadership, no guidance.'

'We've been lost since the fall of Cordoba, and that was five hundred years ago.'

'Six, since the real decline began,' he corrects me. '1492 was just the bitter end.' Mosaddeq Bhai looks crestfallen, as though ready to give up. 'Saladin gave us leadership too, from Damascus against the Crusaders, but that was even longer ago.'

Mosaddeq Bhai is referring to how the Muslim civilisation in Southern Spain, or Al-Andalus as it was named, declined and was finally obliterated in 1492 as a result of the reconquest of Spain by Isabel and Ferdinand.

'Brother, I have to tell you about the most interesting

conversation I had during a recent trip to Beirut, with a shoe shiner on the street.'

'Oh, really? Shoe shiners and barbers are generally full of wise observations. What happened?'

'Well, the most interesting thing is that this shoe shiner, who happened to be a Muslim, had a copy of the Quran in his shirt pocket, and as we talked he would every now and then pluck it out and . . .'

Just as we start discussing what I had learned from this shoe shiner, another uncle walks into the room, having heard of my arrival. His entry interrupts our flow of conversation and within minutes we are discussing the pros and cons of watching television, from a religious perspective. It transpires he has discouraged the use of TV in his own household. Some traditional, backward-looking Muslims believe that looking at any image or likeness of a human is tantamount to creating an idol of it, and therefore unacceptable from an Islamic perspective. These Muslims tend to ban TV watching altogether in their homes. Others do not approve of some of the violent or adult content, and discourage watching anything with such material. We look at the uncle, expecting him to throw more light on his experience and to help us understand which camp he is in.

'I didn't ban it. But I have suggested to everyone that it's not a good idea. And I've stopped going to my daughter Farah's for dinner if she has the TV on while we eat,' he explains, with a hint of smugness on his face. 'After all, capturing and displaying any image is tantamount to idolatry.'

'There is so much rubbish on air these days.' I decide to curry favour while preparing the ground to challenge him.

Much as I would like to stay for the debate, I see that it is 9:06, and I need to head back just as the conversation is unfolding. I look over to my cousin, hoping that he will pick up my thread from here. But he doesn't catch my glance, our connection not as instinctive as the ones I enjoy with some of my closest friends and cousins. I notice the camera phone balanced on my uncle's knee and smile to myself at the irony.

The driver on the way back is quiet and I engage him less than I did the chap on the way over. There are fewer people out on the streets now. Shopkeepers are busy closing up, replacing the earlier evening sounds of industry with the shrill, violent bursts of steel shutters as they come crashing down before being locked up. I wonder if the house phone has a speaker button.

'Ekhtuk joldi khorouka bhai,' I urge the driver to speed up. But the acceleration demands energy levels from his bony body that will exhaust him for the following few hours, so I ask him to slow down again.

We connect at the first attempt, the international line working without a hitch and taking us straight onto the conference bridge. Relatives look on bewildered at the array of numbers being dialled into the keypad to activate the call and set it up. The speaker functions fine and the cord is long enough for us to place the phone on Dadu's paan table.

'Welcome to AT&T conferencing.' The woman's recorded voice has a booming, upbeat tone that I am familiar with from countless work teleconference meetings.

'Please enter your pass code, followed by the pound or hash key.' She sounds like she is speaking down to us from a considerable height, as though a schoolmistress standing on a stage.

A young cousin sister brings out paan and tea for everybody and quickly disappears.

'She will be doing the same soon, when the suitors arrive,' I think to myself.

I change hurriedly into a lungi* and T-shirt and, as we wait for the participants to log in, I seat myself cross-legged next to another uncle on one of the beds.

There is a series of beeps on the line, and through the speaker we can hear that somebody has joined. Hoorah!

'Khe khoira? Who is speaking?' I ask, speaking loudly right into the microphone.

'Ami Julie.' It's Julie, my aunt from Manchester. 'Salaam alaikum.'

'Alaikum as salaam,' we all chant back.

Right on the hour, one of the elders recites prayers to conclude our call. Returning to the atmosphere of frivolity with which we opened, everybody wants to know how I will spend the rest of my time in Bangladesh. I explain that I have finally decided to seek out my family origins and visit

---

* A traditional Bengali man's garment worn across the country and seen in other parts of South East Asia. It is a simple piece of stitched cloth, often with a chequered pattern, tied around the waist and hangs down like a skirt.

Sonarpur next week, the countryside seat from which the Chowdhurys were uprooted half a century ago and where hardly a soul from the family has spent a night since.

'Now that he's gone, this family will slowly fall into disunity.'

As I enjoy the family banter on our call, I think about Dadu's words a few weeks after my father's death fifteen years ago. I am confident that she will not be proved right.

Eight

Welcome to the No-Fly List

I feel rudderless as we pass through Iskenderun and approach the historic city of Antakya, better known outside Turkey by its Biblical name Antioch, the last Turkish settlement before we cross into Syria. I stumble off the coach at the otogar* after the overnight journey, rubbing my eyes as I hear taxi drivers shouting in Arabic. Still half asleep, my first thought is that I've arrived in Syria already. I have read already about Antakya's transfer from Greater Syria to Turkey in 1939 but did not appreciate that Arabic is still the dominant local tongue here. The transfer of this region was part of a pre-World War II deal struck between France's General Gouraud and the Turks in return for which they were to support France in the war. In the end the Turks didn't support France and sided with the Germans instead, kept Antakya anyway and renamed the province Hatay. Whilst this hastily hatched territorial division proved to be

---

* coach station

a bad deal for the French, they were able to walk away from it. But the transfer of this land to Turkey was a loss for the Syrians that they have had to live with ever since. Damascus does not recognise Antakya as a possession of Turkey, and Syrian tourist board maps denote the border with Turkey as 'temporary', with the 'international' one including Antakya and Iskenderun within Syrian jurisdiction.

I hadn't expected that much Arab culture would survive here into the 21st century, but it has and with no shortage of pride either. Most people speak Arabic, including the younger folk who are second- if not third-generation Hatayans. In the little square outside my bijou hotel, old men are gathered around a table, silently duelling over backgammon, muttering every now and then to praise a tactical move. I photograph them discreetly, though there seems to be nothing I can do from my balcony which is not detected by the locals sat at their stools watching people go by. Founded as Antioch in the 4th century BC by one of Alexander the Great's generals, at its peak this settlement rivalled Alexandria as the chief city of the nearer East and was to become the cradle of Gentile Christianity. A city with a grand history but when I visited it, the place had an intimate, small-town feel and was nothing like the overrun holding post for thousands of refugees that it has become today.

At the Ulu Camii at sundown prayers, I receive a tongue-lashing from a fellow behind me once I have completed the obligatory prayer behind the imam. An elderly gent with unkempt, blackened toenails, he prods me from behind and gives me an unsolicited briefing on the correct method for standing in line for prayer, animatedly pointing out that I have been standing too far forward. Like the Hazaripur Mosque in Sylhet, the Ulu sports a front line of old-timers, as though next on the subs' bench to the skies. The old fellow's comments mirror similar conversations I have had in Sylhet and in various mosques around London. I study my stance and realise that he is right, but I wonder why it is that he is angry with me, rather than sympathetic or helpful in how he offers advice. I guess like Bilal and so many others, this is another seemingly frustrated old man seeking to make a point about something.

Bilal seemed to me to have issues of his own. A proud and highly educated Egyptian intellectual from an established Cairene family, at times he looked like he was carrying a personal frustration over the ignorance of students about the literary greatness of Arabic language. This bred what seemed like a haughty animosity towards those who didn't appreciate it. Bilal would at times castigate us for our shortcomings in reading or writing, even though we were all beginners. He would mercilessly expose an individual's failings to the group and drive us through a strict regime which occasionally involved sitting in lessons for over three hours without even a single break. Since the toilet was two corridors' walk away from our classroom, most of us would hold out till the end and then rush off to the facilities as soon as class ended. In what I imagined was perhaps a personal revenge mission against US hegemony in the Middle East, he sometimes seemed to pick on an ever-so-positive American lady in our class. This enthusiastic student was making a committed effort to learn Arabic, a tongue completely foreign to her. I felt ashamed of our teacher's behaviour, falling into the trap of assuming responsibility for another Muslim's behaviour given that I too am a Muslim. Outside class, Bilal was a different man. Whenever I would bump into him in SOAS' prayer room by the library on the lower ground level, he was the picture of sweetness; a mildly mannered and kind-hearted man who would always insist the other should lead the prayer.

Earlier, in the ablution area at the Ulu, I watch the young man in front of me vigorously brush his gums with a stick of miswak.* Evidently, he chewed on it earlier to soften its edges since the bristles now appeared as flexible as those of an extra-firm toothbrush. He is following the practise of cleaning his gums regularly throughout the day, just as the Prophet Mohammad did himself. I remember trying this once during a period of zealous effort to adopt Sunnah† into my life. I was fourteen and it was during a weekend trip up to Dewsbury in Yorkshire to attend a young Muslims' ijtema‡ at the vast Jamia Masjid there. Maulvi Sahib used to encourage me to accompany him to ijtemas up and down the country, so that I could learn about the practise of Islam and how to live in the ways and habits of the Prophet. Maulvi Sahib was active in the work of dawah§ through the

---

* A twig of soft wood which was used like a toothbrush by the Prophet and his followers to keep the gums clean and firm.

† Actions which are encouraged from examples of the personal practise of the Prophet.

‡ Arabic for gathering and in this context refers to a religious meeting or congregation.

§ Arabic word which literally means 'invitation' and refers to evangelical activities to invite people to take more interest in Islam.

Tabligh-i-Jamaat* (TIJ), and would often head off in his Hillman Avenger to far-flung parts of the UK, to attend a gathering or join a group which had gone out to spread the message of Islam. Whilst I liked the idea of learning more about Islam, I was nowhere near committed enough to get involved and would usually have a ready excuse up my sleeve. Every now and then, after I'd said no too many times, I would give in to guilt and go. In those days, the Dewsbury Mosque was one of the largest in the UK and a stone's throw from Bradford, the Yorkshire town that went on to become one of Islam's heartlands in Britain and a centre for the Tabligh-i-Jamaat effort, as well as one of the best places outside Pakistan to enjoy delicious Pakistani food. Down at the Markaz Mosque in Whitechapel's Christian Street in East London, I would sometimes accompany Maulvi Sahib to the TIJ's thick-carpeted private offices upstairs which served as a nerve centre for the global dawah movement. Away from the hustle and bustle of the main prayer area below, there was a peaceful hush in the TIJ office. Here, long-bearded TIJ stalwarts would sit and discuss their plans, some lying down on the carpet and stretching out after a long day of prayer, debating over where to deploy the next dawah team. Some would huddle around large trays of ghee-laden pilao and korma. A large political world map was pinned to the wall, with green marker pins showing where current teams were visiting.

---

* A movement founded in the 1920s in India focused towards bringing spiritual awakening and practise amongst Muslims, strictly non-political and not an officially recognised group or association.

Johannesburg, Amman, Madrid, Milan, Glasgow to name but a few; the breadth of coverage was mind-boggling, the organisation precise and clinical. Not only is this mosque located on 'Christian' Street, but to add further irony the building used to be a synagogue and was purchased from the Jewish community when their needs for a prayer place in this part of London had diminished. By the 1970s, most of East London's Jews had moved out of this impoverished area and settled into more affluent parts of North London, such as St John's Wood, Muswell Hill and Hampstead. Meanwhile, the Muslims, especially Bangladeshis, were just moving into localities such as Whitechapel, Poplar and Mile End.

My gums ached that day in Dewsbury, lacerated by the sharp bristles of miswak that I had tried to softened through chewing, and I spat blood during ablutions. Some of the older guys did better since they were miswak experts, a few with smooth beards since they had never shaved and one or two with piercing, confident and amazingly peaceful eyes. A number had developed a nonchalant, hands-free miswak action, skilfully rolling the branch around from one side of the mouth to the other without even dribbling on their shirts. They looked cool, chewing and occasionally spitting as they chatted. These boys were in their element in the mosque in Dewsbury. Unlike at school or on the streets, where they faced racism and exclusion, here they enjoyed recognition, respect and camaraderie. The rigours of early morning miswak may have been tough on me, but to these young men the rituals developed a much-needed sense belonging. Haughtily flashing their white teeth as they gnawed away, they would remind me of Clint Eastwood chewing on a fat cheroot in a spaghetti Western more than of any doctrinally inspirational character. These dudes lived for these weekends away at the mosque. They didn't just make religion magnetic, they made it feel sexy.

There was something isolating about hardcore dawah devotees, about how they viewed their involvement in the life of missionary effort. Many who spent time in dawah were troubled characters, misfits in society and rejected by their family. Contrary to the standard socio-economic analysis of who are the radicalised Muslims, these boys weren't necessarily less educated or unemployed; some were university graduates and had good jobs. But I suppose they were generally young people who were looking for a place to belong and feel valued. It was well known that some Bengali and Pakistani families would send 'troublemaker' children, the ones they couldn't control or discipline at home, to Islamic boarding schools. This made no sense, since a lot of these boys were marginalised due to experiences of racism and bullying, and needed more, not less, parental guidance and care. Sending them to boarding school was more a cop-out from a parenting responsibility than a sincere act of encouraging children to learn more about Islam.

My cousins and I attended ijtemas without any such burden of isolation or bullying carried over from home or school. We were relatively adjusted kids, balancing the tensions in our lives and learning what we could about the faith. We were able to both participate in and observe the proceedings at arm's length; we had the judgement to take what was useful from the gatherings whilst resisting getting too drawn in. But around us there was a blind, almost frightening faith in dawah, where young men in need of finding and expressing their identity were highly receptive to the call of religion, and the unity and sense of purpose religious activity offered.

This zeal was best illustrated during 'recruitment' sessions for brothers to go on missionary activity, the visiting groups despatched to towns and cities in Britain and around the world to spread the word of Islam. Such missions were intended to be peaceful and harmonious, and often involved groups undertaking huge personal sacrifices of sleep and home comforts to endure a few days' of being on the road to visit a few towns. While doing my Master's at Cambridge, I joined a group staying one night in a local church nearby, where the group leader spent much of the evening in discussion with the local priest who was their host. But as always, I remained a transient visitor to such groups. At the end of a typical ijtema lecture, the session leader would stand and open up the dreaded recruitment logbook. Every ijtema gathering had a book to record the names of brothers and sisters who were willing to devote more time to the path of dawah. I feared these sessions, since I had no interest in committing anything more than the odd weekend, and that too was only fuelled by a feeling of obligation.

'Now then, brothers, who would like to step forward and give time in the path of Allah?' was the standard opening question.

With appealing arguments expertly articulated by persuasive orators, the exhortations were irresistible, the logic difficult to overturn, and the guilt it provoked strong enough to quash any normal desire to resist the invitation. I avoided having my name put down mainly through staring at my ankles and knees throughout the sessions, ensuring I did not make eye contact at the critical moment. Of those that stepped up, some reluctantly at first, many were then inculcated into the doctrine of dawah, a life on the road inviting others to the faith. In the hall of Dewsbury Mosque, going into prostration with my face close to floor level, it seemed as though the recurring patterns on the carpet stretched out for miles in every direction, their symmetry mesmerising.

Still standing in line at the Ulu washroom, I realise that this man has already taken up several precious minutes and even more valuable litres of the water that flows copiously from the tap he is crouched in front of. Like the Dewsbury boys, he too looks cool. Single-minded in his intent to perform a pious ablution, he is blind to my need to wash and careless of how much water he is wasting. I have but a day left before leaving Turkey and crossing into Syria, and my time here is now coming to a close. My irritation at the man's selfishness with time and space shows that I too remain merely a traveller on the windy path to wisdom, a man whose real destinations remain distant and as yet unseen.

Before the outbreak of today's bloody and heart-wrenching civil war, few places on earth could have been as idiosyncratically endearing as Syria. Memories of my first overland border crossing into Syria from Turkey are restored to sharp focus today when I see footage of the latest carnage happening around the northern city of Aleppo and the small towns and settlements around it. Call it Yayladagi or call it Kessab, depending on your direction of approach, this is a border crossing on the road less travelled, perched as it is on a mountainous outpost some fifty kilometres south of Antakya and around the same distance due west of Aleppo. Steeped in rich history, the crossing separates varied peoples with a shared past: Orthodox Christians and Catholics, Sunni Muslims and Alawites, Armenians, Turks and Arabs. The picturesque checkpoint is served by broken roads not immediately connecting anywhere significant on either side. Kessab consists of a small but strategic town that sits in the expansive shadow of the regal Mount Aqra, a beauty spot in a staggering landscape which would, in any normal era, merit a visit just for its own sake. Being an important border post, Kessab became a sensitive target during the Syrian conflict and a prized control point for both Al-Qaeda and Syrian government forces. After being taken over and occupied by Al-Qaeda and Islamic State forces in 2014, Kessab was retaken by Syrian government forces some months later.

Sheltered from travellers of varied nationalities, the smartly clad Syrian immigration officer has his work cut out with my passport as he struggles to decipher my true identity. When ten minutes have passed and he is still asking me questions about my parents, I begin to wonder whether this diversion off the beaten track is going to become a point of departure from my mission to discover the Turkish and Syrian coastline of the Mediterranean Sea. He is a mild-mannered man with clear blue eyes and a dense crop of fuzzy, grey-black hair. I feel like reaching across the counter and patting the officer's head to see how bouncy it must be. Oblivious to my musings, he continues to assess my documents with keen interest.

'The man must be more accustomed to reading Arabic,' I think, as I notice his eyes scanning from right to left.

As he finds out that I am not only British, but have Bangladeshi family connections too, matters become a little trickier. In keeping with Syrian custom, his manner is friendly and courteous, more like that of an Istanbullu shopkeeper than a border official. He concludes that he needs to satisfy himself of my Bangladeshi credentials before he, or I for that matter, can proceed. This poses a problem, since I am not carrying any Bangladeshi documentation with me. Not accustomed to reading English, when he reads a 'No visa required for Bangladesh' seal in my passport and assumes it means 'Not allowed to enter Bangladesh', matters go downhill. His English isn't up to it and I don't want to explain in Arabic, lest he starts wondering why I speak that too.

'I was born in Britain and have lived there all my life,' I explain. 'My parents moved to England from Bangladesh around fifty years ago.'

Satisfied, as well as intrigued and entertained, this dutiful guardian of Syrian territory proceeds to further tapping on his keyboard. By the time we finish, he knows the birthplaces of both my mother and father, their birth dates and when each moved to the UK. The questions are no longer procedural, more an inquisitive chat to engage and wile away some minutes of what I guess is an otherwise event-free afternoon.

'What is your profession?' he asks.

'Eee . . . ec . . . economist.'

'Economist . . . hmm.' Picking up on my hesitation, he seems unconvinced.

'What sort of company do you work for?'

'Sharika teknolojia,'* I respond, watching him scan his finger down a list of professional categories on some sort of form in front of him.

'Hmm . . .' He pauses, eyeballing the options.

'Ah! Computer salesman,' he announces and, not giving me an opportunity to debate, types it straight into his database.

Land of process, due process and connections. For me only the first two apply, but for the gentleman who waltzes into Kessab's sleepy immigration office, slaps the officer on the back with a crisp ten dollar bill and marches out all stamped and ready to go, connections are the only way to travel. The satellite navigation system in his BMW will ensure he will be smoking a cigar in distant Damascus long before I crawl into nearby Latakia and negotiate the next two nights' hotel deal. The Syrian experience is coming back to me loud and clear. The penchant for showing

---

* Arabic for 'technology company'

incredible amounts of kindness; a habit for doing things calmly with a pedantic insistence on following due process; a heavy reliance on information, bureaucracy and control; and a quiet sophistication and sincerity in the turns of phrase used in everyday conversation. Only this country effortlessly combines all of these facets into one frustrating and endearing mix.

The melange is unique partly because the Syrian Arab Republic has always been run in a pretty uncommon way. An errant outlier in this 21st-century world of real or would-be democracies, the autocrats who have shaped Syria for the past few decades claimed credit for some fine nation-building in a region where most states are riven by underlying conflict and strife. But it is Orhan Pamuk's theme of the Ottoman hüzün which hangs over Istanbul that I would like to borrow as my sentiment for this country. Unlike Istanbul though, my sadness here is not drawn from a sense of lost history, but from the spectre of a lost future.

Whilst in some ways Syria appears a civilisation carefully preserved, in others it seems pent up, like a locked-up teenager, bristling with energy but with nowhere to let it out. This is exactly how it feels in Latakia, a place which seems artificially restrained, subdued from the productive vigour that its young and talented people should be exerting themselves to. The city feels robbed of the purpose of the neighbouring towns and ports in Lebanon or Turkey, because Syria's economy is so much more sheltered. Latakia was, prior to imperial France's ill-planned break up of Greater Syria, larger than the Mediterranean ports of Tripoli or

Beirut (both now in Lebanon), Tel Aviv or Haifa (both now in Israel). Latakia's decline parallels the fate of other once great maritime cities which have now been eclipsed by the incessant march of history. I think of Liverpool or Lisbon, colonial trading centres in their past but now relatively minor cities on a global scale, as other examples.

Despite its limitations Latakia is an open, friendly and festive place. In a crowded downtown café on a Friday night, dating couples sit cheek by jowl with mums in hijab and dads who have brought the kids out for an ice cream. The openness of Latakia is endearing, as it illustrates the simple niceties of how Muslim families can go out and enjoy themselves without inhibition whilst maintaining Islamic social values.

This balance is something I grow to love about the Levant, a trait that contrasts with other places in the Middle East where people's freedom is stifled in the name of protecting the same Islamic values. Unaizah is a small town nestled in the arid and orthodox Wahhabi region of central Saudi Arabia. I visited my cousin Tina and her family there once whilst advising the Saudi Government, just a month after the 9/11 attacks in the US.

'Let's go for dinner!' I exclaimed on turning up unannounced at their apartment, following an exhausting three-hour evening dash across the desert in a taxi from Riyadh.

'Dinner? Here?' my cousin replied, rather bewildered.

Once Tina and her mother, Khala,* had gotten dressed in

---

* Bengali for mother's sister

the black niqab dress which shrouded them from head to toe and rendered them completely unrecognisable even to me, we headed for Unaizah's foremost restaurant. The arrangements were the local standard for ensuring families would eat in complete privacy: a windowless cabin in which we sat all alone; a buzzer in case we needed to order anything; and a serving hatch for passing dishes in and out. Whilst travelling to and from the venue, in evening temperatures of 45 C, the women had to remain fully covered with not a square millimetre of skin showing; only in the secluded cabin of the restaurant were they permitted to remove their head scarves. Incredulously, on return to my cousin's apartment, there was a knock at the door from the local religious police to ensure we were not going to miss our evening prayers. Not having expected them to be so inconvenienced through a restaurant outing, I apologised, having understood why they had suggested we just eat at home.

As I walk about Latakia remembering Unaizah, my thoughts turn in more general terms to extreme Muslim practices which paint such a restrictive picture of my faith. I recall the words understood to have been said by Cat Stevens, a famous convert to Islam:

'I am glad I found the religion of Islam before I discovered the practise of Muslims . . .'*

Many of the specific ways in which Islam is practised in the interior provinces of Saudi Arabia reflect local cultural traditions. In my mind, there is no particular reason why

---

* Yusuf Islam, formerly Cat Stevens

such a lifestyle should be imposed upon Muslims in other parts of the world as a precondition for practising Islam correctly.

But what's interesting about my remembering Saudi Arabia whilst walking around Latakia is the similarity, on a separate level, between the two places. This is because like Syria, Unaizah too seemed a place where the people are not being permitted, let alone encouraged, to fulfil themselves. Many Saudi townships are inhabited by communities who are underemployed, in an economy that is oil-rich and poor in the wider diversification of activity, surviving on a mix of low-paying professions or business topped up by generous handouts from the state.

Smoking on a nargileh,* I feel light-headed from the rush of apple-flavoured tobacco in my nervous system, my hookah tonight seeming endless. I ask the coal man how is it that sometimes the pipe smokes for hours and other times it runs out within minutes. Holding up his hand, he twists his wrist back and forth as though coaching me on a slow bowling technique, winks and, leaving me none the wiser, walks off.

My driver for the next day as I explore the now war-stricken Aleppo and its surroundings by car, is a man of bulky proportions and few words. A pleasant companion, Aus dwarfs the pint-sized Daewoo car he drives. He speaks a vernacular which is easy to understand. We approach Qala'a Salah ad-Din, the great warrior and leader Saladin's

---

* Arabic water pipe, otherwise known as a shisha

Castle, an immense 11th-century crusader-built fortress squat on top of a rocky ridge surrounded by wooded valleys. Ten centuries ago, thousands of tonnes of solid stone were hacked away to give the fortress sheer, smooth walls thirty metres high. One of the original Crusader builders was Robert of Saône and the site used to be known simply as 'sayhun', which is how Lawrence of Arabia refers to it in his memoirs.* Aus' face cracks open into a cheeky, vengeful grin as he explains how Saladin took Saône from the Crusader armies in 1188. I reconsider what little I know about the heinous and brutal activities of the Crusaders. This was the most significant example in recorded history of a mass, religion-inspired, extremist political movement that caused untold death and destruction to thousands of people across many countries. Hundreds of years before the rise of Islamism, it was England and France that gave the world a century of state-sponsored terrorism carried out in the name of religion, Christianity in this case. Yet in our English school curriculum, we were instructed that the Crusades were a 'civilising' action of Western Europeans in the Near East. Even the Christian community service club at St Dunstan's College bore the name 'Crusaders' with a noble-looking knight-on-white-horse symbol that went with it.

Setting aside the bleakness of the Crusaders' past, significantly to this day Saladin remains one of the few figures in post Prophet Mohammad Islamic history who commanded

---

* *The Seven Pillars of Wisdom*, by T. E. Lawrence, 1926

the respect of Shia and Sunni Muslims, and even Christian Arabs. Indeed, Saladin's unifying position of leadership amongst Arabs regardless of faction is something that no other leader in this region has managed to achieve in the 800 years since his death. This vacuum of inspiring leadership is one of the many reasons why politics in the Arab world remains so dysfunctional. I asked a Christian in Damascus why they supported Saladin, and the response was that they preferred to be ruled by an Arab of their kind rather than brutal Europeans who happened to share their faith but savaged their women and usurped their lands and artefacts.

Earlier in the day, I receive a talking to of a more serious nature than my burly taxi driver's lectures on Syrian unity. Wandering around a fish market near Latakia's port area, I take a snap of a sale negotiated through some truly outstanding haggling. On the click of my shutter, two of the customers morph into suspecting onlookers watching my every move. Sensing trouble I move on, feigning aloofness and wandering towards some vegetable stalls. One of the two men approaches me from behind and taps quietly on my shoulder. Middle-aged and ordinary-looking, he stands close, leans into my face and hisses:

'Inta sahafi?'*

The 's' sizzles on his tongue like a rasher of bacon on a hot frying pan. It reminds me of how taxi drivers in Ghana used to call out to gain attention. The first time I walked out

---

* 'Are you a journalist?'

of Accra's Kotoka International Airport, I was met by a sea of hisses which made me feel distinctly uncomfortable, unaware that this is simply a way of getting someone's attention. I half-expect this plain-clothed man to produce a Secret Police identity card, hold it in front of his nose and roll his eyes from side to side.

'No, no,' I reply, purposely in a voice slightly louder than his.

'Where are you from?'

'From Britain,' I smile, walking slowly, thinking that stopping to talk would prolong the conversation, and walking too fast might imply panic.

The smaller the town, the more amateur the mukhabaraat.* I recall flying into Dallas, Texas in 2005 and experiencing something similar to the small-town ambition of the Latakian intelligence officer. Most of that Sunday afternoon at Dallas/Fort Worth Airport was spent in a futile interrogation by a pair of clueless US Immigration and Naturalization Service officers, who appeared to have little idea as to where their quizzing was leading them.

'And what exactly is this, Sir?' was the accusing question when one of the officers discovered my Modern Standard Arabic textbook from SOAS, and a diary including an entry from a visit to a mosque in Beirut.

The burly American was a tall, bald man and like his younger, hirsute colleague, he was dressed in the official dark blue shirt and trousers of the US immigration authorities.

---

* intelligence services

After I had deplaned off the flight from London Heathrow, the authorities had 'randomly' asked me to step aside for a routine round of extra questioning. How their eyes lit up when they opened the textbook to see pages of Arabic script, their gazes to each other telegraphing their thoughts:

'Look! We've got one of 'em right here!'

A half hour later, as the interrogation continued, I feared the afternoon I had planned to spend with my cousin's brother and his two little kids was being frittered away. Knowing my leverage was limited, I cooperated fully and decided to ride out the minutes in the hope that I would be free soon.

'That's a temple, Sir? Is that right? A temple for Muss-lims?' The officer was kind-hearted and genuinely curious, but clearly he had no idea what a mosque was and this was worrying.

Whilst touched by his humane attitude, I was alarmed by his amateurism. His approach to nation-defending could not be in greater contrast to the cunning games played by his Israeli counterparts, carefully trained to figure out how to effectively protect their borders.

'Yes, that's right. Muslims pray at mosques,' I responded. 'Rather like the way Christians go to church. We call them mosques, rather than temples, though.'

As the official and his largely silent colleague continued to leaf through my papers and ask more questions, they carefully unpacked the rest of my luggage and laid out the contents on the aluminium-topped table between us. Wearing the customary white nylon gloves, they handled each item carefully and methodically, even the most innocent-looking articles of clothing, as if each piece of underwear could explode at any moment.

'And why did you visit that mosque, Sir? What was your business there?' The question was generated from a casual flick through the manuscript for this book, commenting on a particular mosque visit in Beirut.

'I went to pray there and to meet the priest, who I know from earlier trips.'

'So, Mohammad, can we ask you a question?'

'Sure, be my guest.'

'Are you a Muss-lim, Sir?' His hesitation in how to pronounce the word made it hang in the air between us.

'Is that correct? Is that why you go to the mosque? Because you are a Muss-lim?' he continues.

'Yes, I am a Muslim.' I sigh quietly, lamenting that after an hour or more, these two have managed to work out that the man named Mohammad standing opposite them is a Muslim.

For defenders of US borders at a major international airport in the wake of the 9/11 attacks on the nation, this degree of ignorance was alarming.

'And what was your business in Lebanon, Sir? And in Syria?'

'They are lovely, friendly countries, full of history and interesting places. I go there for tourism. I am learning Arabic and they are great places to go and practise the language. Do you know that in Syria . . . ?'

'Yes, Sir. But do you really believe it is a good time to be visiting these countries?'

As on so many occasions during border interrogations, I feel now that I am being offered advice on a topic beyond the officer's grasp and remit.

'Erm, is there any reason why you believe I should not be going to these places right now?'

'Well, Sir, with all the events and difficulties we currently have, perhaps there are more sensible places to visit in the world than Syria.'

'What exactly is not sensible about going to Syria? Is there something specific you would like to tell me about? It would be very helpful if you would tell me, if there is.'

'No, Sir. There is nothing specific to mention, Sir. It is absolutely your choice where you visit, Sir.'

'You have told us you have a meeting in Atlanta, Georgia tomorrow. So why have you flown into Fort Worth today, Sir?

'To visit my cousin and his family. They live in Dallas. I am catching a connecting flight to Atlanta at nine o'clock tomorrow morning.'

'And how exactly is he your cousin, Sir? Isn't it tiring for you to take another flight tomorrow morning, again? Would it not be easier to have gone there directly?'

'My cousin's mother is the eldest daughter of my late father's second-oldest maternal aunt. So he is my cousin a couple of times removed. He is four years older than me, and when I was a teenager, he was a hero to me. He taught me all the capital cities of the world when I was eleven. I haven't seen him in years.'

Their questioning had lost direction by now and the

search had yielded nothing more than a few notes about a mosque in Beirut and some handwriting in Arabic.

'Do you have proof he is your cousin, Sir?'

'Proof? I don't carry around documented proof of who my relatives are, I am afraid.'

Layer upon layer of memories of incidents concerning Arabic light up in the corners of my mind as we continue, from Brussels Airport where I was told the variety of foreign-looking stamps in my passport would be used as a 'case study' for future officer training courses; Woodstock Road in Oxford where the policeman advised me not to display an Arabic sticker on my dashboard; to the mezquita in Cordoba, Spain where local police all but arrested me for praying in Arabic in a church.

'I haven't got my cousin's address since he is collecting me from the airport,' I explained. 'He is probably waiting outside for me right now, with his wife and two boys.'

I looked at the clock on the wall facing me, the one the officers had their backs to. It was 3:40 p.m. now and I finally remarked to the officers how my plan to spend a precious afternoon with my cousin had all but slipped away. I notice next to the clock the INS charter to release all visitors within the shortest possible period of time.

'And you haven't seen him for ten years, Sir? So why do you want to see him now? Isn't Dallas a long way to come to see a cousin twice-removed?'

'It's pretty standard for my family and rather expected in my culture.' I sighed and wondered whether he might make another statement that goes outside his remit, implying that

I shouldn't have relations with people so distant from me. 'He was one of my role models when I was a child, as I said. I couldn't possibly visit Texas and not see him.'

'How old is he precisely, Sir? And what does he do for a living? May we have his cell phone number, please?'

I explain that he works for a bank as a senior IT specialist. Almost two hours and a few phone calls later, I was released. Malik and his wife Jennifer were concerned for my welfare, and as soon as I emerged from Customs they were relieved to see that I was all right. As we climbed into his family people carrier, Malik confirmed that he received a call a little while ago. As I was to discover the next day when checking in for my Atlanta flight, the Dallas episode led to my name being entered onto the US Department of Homeland Security register commonly known as the 'No-Fly List' and maintained by the Terrorist Screening Center. As a result, and until today, I am routinely questioned when I check in for a flight within the United States. Despite writing letters to the US Government and US Ambassador in the UK, neither my American employers at the time nor my local MP in London have managed to get my name removed. I was offered an option to apply for a US visa to be stamped into my passport, and a special reference for travel, meaning that I would not need to be questioned on entry. However, I felt that to accept such a 'special' visa would be a retrograde step on my part. After all, I am a UK citizen and entitled to travel to the US at any time, courtesy of the visa waiver scheme that exists between both countries. So I didn't see why I should obtain a special visa, which might allow the Americans to monitor me in some other way. As far as I know, my name is still on the list now and mostly I get questioned when I travel to the US. President Trump already had me in the database of Muslims he called for after being elected. But the list was created many years before he took office. With my name still apparently on the list, logic suggests I continue to be relevant to the US Government as a potential terrorist.

'Sorry? Er, yes. Yes.' I tune into my Latakian fish-market questioner again, 'This is my own camera.'

The intelligence official takes a long look at my camera and for no evident reason, turns it upside down, as if to check what type of tripod fitting it has. After a few more seconds, realising that he is fishing in the wrong pond, he lets me go.

Back at the Meridien Hotel, bobbing up and down on the warm waters of Latakia's Shatt al Azraq, I feel hungry, hungry to push south to the furthest reaches of my journey. I want to move away from the watchful eye of Mount Aqra and touch with my fingertips the limits of my possibilities, as though this voyage is going to answer all of my questions and set my concerns right. I peer along Syria's short Mediterranean coastline, less than three hundred kilometres long, struggling to keep my head above water. I look north to the serene mountains and then rotate to face south towards Latakia's port, squinting into the distance to eke out every last kilometre of visibility. I wonder whether from the top of Mount Aqra one can see as far as Lebanon. I want to move away from the Latakia mukhabaraat. The incident at the fish market has rattled me, and shown again how thin the veil is between normality and suspicion here in Syria, as indeed it has become so across much of the world.

Nine

Dangerous Doodles

After flying into Cairo for a short holiday in spring 2005, I walk out of the hotel into the hazy morning sunshine to explore the local vicinity. Leaving the leafy enclosure of the Nile Hilton Hotel and entering the Midan* Tahrir, I am stopped by a police officer dressed in a starched white uniform and sporting a dark blue beret. He is stationed at a barricade placed across a street running between the hotel and the Egyptian Museum, right next to the midan. Brazen, camera-laden Western tourists traipse about, headed in all directions. Tahrir Square, as it is better known around the world today, is unforgettably etched in our memories since we associate it with the Arab Spring uprising that led to the overthrow of Egyptian President Hosni Mubarak in 2010. But this is a few years before that. A trail of tourists wanders through the wrought-iron gates of the museum, shepherded in by eager tour guides. A shiny new coach unloads a troupe

---

* an open area within a city

of European travellers just a few metres behind where the police officer stands.

'Min feyn?'* he asks in a friendly way, in Arabic.

'Min britani.'

'Tatakallam arabi?'† he seems happy. 'Min feyn?'

'Min britani. B-skon bi London, wa b-dros al lughat al arabi bi kulliya hunik.'‡ I smile back confidently, justifying the Upper Intermediate Arabic status accorded to me by SOAS in London.

'Feyn jawazak?'§

'Ma ma'i jawaz. Bi ghurfati.'¶ I point to the concrete bulk of the hotel looming large behind me, the once fashionable rendezvous of 1960s Cairo and the scene of countless Arab movie scenes.

The officer asks what I am doing in Cairo and, bizarrely, enquires whether I am Palestinian. I say I have just arrived and want to go for a walk around the area. Continuing in Arabic, he explains that I am not allowed to proceed past the barricade. Even though streams of people are walking past freely, tourists and locals, and none are being stopped by the police. Puzzled, I look at the officer. The coachload of what now appears to be Scandinavian tourists are on the other side of the barricade too; some walking our way, some the other.

---

* 'Where are you from?'

† 'Do you speak Arabic?'

‡ 'I am from Britain. I live in London and study Arabic at a college there.'

§ 'Where is your passport?'

¶ 'I don't have my passport with me. It is in my room.'

'Su mushkila?'* I ask finally, a touch exasperated at the differentiation in treatment.

The white-uniformed officer smiles and says there is nothing wrong, but that going in this direction is prohibited. He recommends I go in another direction. I survey the options. To my left, the museum gates. To my right, back to the hotel. Behind me, a quiet street running down the side of the hotel towards the banks of the Nile. I decide against a visit to the museum itself, but see people sitting out in the grounds. Compared to the deserted street this looks the more inviting option, since all I want to do is relax awhile. I thank the friendly officer and head towards the gates.

As soon as I walk through, I am approached by a throng of would-be museum guides, four or five in all, shouting across each other in a bid to gain my attention. Another barricade and another guard, this one standing by an X-ray security machine, separate me from the hungry hoard. The guides proffer a volley of meaningless offers, including ticket and photo deals, history lessons and guidebooks, baying to get at me as soon as they can once I cross security. The museum security officer waits for me to pass through, but as the touts continue their barrage of offers, I decide that the quiet street down the side of the hotel is more appealing after all. Still jet-lagged off the New York to London flight from the day before travelling on to Cairo, I am in no mood to be hassled by tour guides. Within seconds I am stopped by two policemen.

---

* 'What is the problem?'

'Where are you going?' they shout in Arabic, more assertively than the smart officer a couple of minutes ago.

'I don't want to go to the museum,' I explain, preparing to walk off.

'Why have you changed your mind?' It is the white-uniformed officer again, more official in his tone now.

'I didn't change my mind,' I explain. 'I said I just want to go for a walk.'

The three officers all gather around me, asking questions all at once, which instantly becomes more difficult to understand. Before I know it, there are four or five men encircling me, most in blue and one in white. The scene rapidly takes on the air of a brewing incident. An intelligence officer appears, tall and dressed in a smart brown suit, dark shirt and tie. Mirrored shades hide his eyes from me. He looms over me, sun glinting in the backdrop, feet close together, leaning in like a lamp post which has been hit by a lorry. He grins and then shoots a couple of questions at me, first in Arabic and then in English.

'Why are you running away?' is the opening question after he switches to English.

I tell him I am British, on holiday with my mother and staying at the Nile Hilton. I explain that I arrived last night and want to go for a walk. He asks me where I work and I tell him I work for an IT company.

'Why are you running away?'

'I'm not running away.'

'You are running away. Why don't you want to go to the museum?'

I repeat that I just want to go for a walk, that I don't wish to visit the museum, and that I only went in that direction because there was no better alternative.

'I don't believe your story. Where is your ID?'

I explain I don't have it, take out my wallet and show him my Hilton Honors card as the best proof of ID I can find on my person. I indicate my name on the card and then somewhat unconvincingly point my finger towards the top of the hotel, saying there's my room, right up there.

'You are not British,' he announces.

'What type of name is "shoodoori"? Whatever it is, it is not British.'

I respond I was born in Britain, but that my family is originally from Bangladesh. He doesn't seem to know where Bangladesh is and is irked by this. At this point he notices the black Moleskine notebook in the left leg pocket of my cargo pants.

'What's this?' he asks, motioning with his finger for me to hand it to him.

'It's my diary,' I explain as I hand it over.

Ignoring me, he undoes the elastic band that keeps it shut, flips it open and starts flicking through pages of my scrawled handwriting. He hands it to one of his assistants to inspect it in detail. I don't know what it is, but I sense something is about to go wrong.

'Why do you speak in Arabic?' The intelligence officer questions me further, irritated now.

I answer while I am watching my journal being examined. I am relieved that the officials aren't stopping to read through all my personal thoughts, since these are mostly neurotic commentaries on the state of my mood.

As they leaf through the diary, working their way towards my more recent entries, I recall my trip to New York City earlier this week. And now I realise why something feels wrong, and my heart begins to pound faster.

It was on Wednesday morning in the Big Apple that I had scribbled a sketch of the Manhattan skyscrapers while having breakfast on the twenty-first floor of the Times Square Hilton Hotel.

'Where did you learn?'

As I picture my hand-drawn sketch of New York's recently violated skyline, I feel an air of inevitability about how my scrawl is going to be seen.

Choking in anticipation, I descend into a parched stammer as I continue to answer questions, more of the contents of my diary being revealed, page by painful page. The sun beats down on my forehead.

'Where did I learn what?' I squint, distracted and wondering how on earth I will handle the situation which is about to descend upon me imminently.

'Arabic. Arabic! Where did you learn it?'

'Oh, fuck,' I think to myself as I keep picturing that latest entry, mumbling my responses now and feeling a trickle of sweat collecting on my forehead. 'Well, I have been taking lessons at . . .'

'WHAT IS THIS?' The officer doesn't bother to look at me, gaping at the drawing he sees in the open book before us.

The blue-shirted officer has reached the last entry in my diary, a purple-ink doodle of a line of Manhattan skyscrapers. In my own seemingly criminal handwriting, the sketch is titled 'New York City, April 3rd 2005', rather like the guilty signature of a villain whose blueprint for murder has finally been revealed. Like magnets drawn to the direction of the North Pole, the officers lean in simultaneously, pushing against each other to get a better view; their sharp shadows fighting it out on the blanched page open before us.

'Oh. Shit.' I think of what might happen now, and also of how farcical is the situation that is developing.

My usual countdown begins – the countdown to resolve a security situation before it descends into an unaccountable disaster. Israel, London, Almaty ... I have seen it before, and each time I have had to think two steps ahead of security to come out unscathed.

'What's this?' One of the officers stoops forward to get a better look before gazing back up at me, his white gloves a familiar sight for me now on my travels.

The gloves add a hint of ceremony to the tension of the moment, and remind me of the similarly attired officer at Logan International Airport in Boston, who had once taken a keen, post 9/11 interest in my travel adapter. I had just spent a week at Harvard Business School and was on my way to Montreal to visit an aunt before returning to London. Bristly haired and with a serious face, the officer scrutinised the converter plug inside and out, frowning and feeling along its edges as if he was about to discover something that could be detonated. I stood before him feeling somewhat humiliated – the only Muslim-looking person at the gate for the flight – shoes removed, trouser belt loosened and pants sagging below my waist. That particular search ended when, after a minute's poking around, the officer looked up at me. His gaze gradually worked its way up to my chest, then my throat and finally rested upon my face. I stood waiting for our eyes to meet, conscious that my trousers were now uncomfortably drooped around my hips. When our eyes met we held our respective stares for a brief moment, each of us wondering what the other was thinking. I couldn't hold back any more, breaking out into a tentative smile. To my surprise the young officer started to grin and, as soon as I could confirm that he was, so did I. We started laughing, harmonious and spontaneous, following which with a heaving effort to regain his composure, he put the adapter back together again and wished me a good flight.

But I have little reason to smirk now. The facing page in my diary is ominously blank, bar a small title-heading at the top which says 'Cairo'. We must all be wondering what the entry there is intended to say. Accusation hangs in the air. We all stare down at the open book glistening under the sun. The New York skyline drawing looks suspicious, even to me. Like the policemen, my eyes search the page for a doodle of an aeroplane about to fly into the buildings, as if my notes provide the blueprint for another terrorist attack and I am its grim author. The purple ink, a gimmicky colour theme of mine which is ridiculed by friends and colleagues, adds a layer of mystery.

'You can search me if you want.' I'm not sure why I make this self-implicating offer.

'Yes. We will.' They immediately agree to take up my suggestion.

Too often at times like this I am left to rely on chance to deliver me into the hands of a calm and reasoned questioner, rather than an impulsive or nervy one. I look at the intelligence officer's face, wondering what will be his next move. I cannot see his eyes, only a distorted reflection of my panicked face in the mirror of his shades.

They begin the search there and then. I am about to suggest they at least accord me the dignity of a private cubicle, but thankfully stop myself from making such an inane suggestion, realising it is of course better to be out in the open. Tourists sidle past, either oblivious or purposely steering clear. The white-uniformed officer who had first greeted me at the barricade looks on, his rank now eclipsed. His shoulders have stiffened and his smile is now steely. The body search reveals nothing but a Waterman fountain pen clasped into the leg pocket of my cargo pants. They don't like the look of it. I feel like James Bond being found out for carrying one of the gadgets that Q has given him before his latest mission. Always time for fantasy, even in moments of adversity.

The intelligence officer looks increasingly bothered, as though losing a chess game which he has become too committed to winning. His puzzlement is rapidly turning to further irritation, and this in turn fuels an increasingly confrontational line of questioning.

'I don't believe you,' he repeats, still managing to smile down at me through his mirrored shades.

'I don't believe your story.' Story. The word hangs in the air. I invite him to come with me to the hotel. I point to the building behind us, the hotel, as if trying to touch and feel the distant haven that it has suddenly become.

'You are lying, and I don't believe you. And yes, I will come.'

In my travels I now regularly face situations which turn from normality to a heightened state of tension in a moment.

'No. I will send my assistant with you.' A reversal of strategy. His chess game is going a bit wrong, and this worries me. The last thing I want is for him to feel that he losing control.

'Why doesn't he come with me himself if he thinks he's caught a terrorist?' I wonder.

Perhaps he doesn't want to risk looking stupid, greeting my mum after a knock on the door. What if she invited him in for tea and biscuits or something? Maybe he is too senior to traipse into the hotel with a suspect. He'd rather have a lackey do it, someone whose reputation is dispensable. Someone in a white uniform perhaps.

'Well, if you are not lying, then why are you looking so nervous?' he challenges me.

'Because I have just arrived in Cairo and now I am surrounded by eight police officers asking me lots of questions,' I smile back at him, letting out a nervous laugh.

A few beads of sweat have developed on my crown as the

sun beats down. The officer insists that something is wrong and that's the reason why I am nervous. Getting his permission and moving slowly, I pull out my driving licence from my wallet, having spotted its pink edge as I was replacing my Hilton room card a few minutes ago. He looks at it, surveying the EU flag on it and comparing the photograph to my likeness.

'Why didn't you show us this before when we asked for your ID?' he quizzes. His suspicions, like his brow, are on the rise again. Knight to Q4 and check. Game on.

'I just noticed that I had my driving licence with me,' I explain, speaking in English now. He asks me again why I speak Arabic, and why I am learning it. He asks me why I do not speak in Arabic now.

'You can go,' he declares, but somehow I cannot believe it is over.

'Which way?' I ask. 'Everything seems to be blocked.'

I explain that I have no option left but to go back to my hotel. He says I can go any way except past the barricade, the same one that dozens of people are still walking past every minute.

'How about that way?' I say, pointing down the quiet street.

'Yes, that's fine.'

The quiet street really is quiet. Cairene men sit along the pavement, chatting and smoking. There are no tourists here. The men watch me as I walk past. I feel that it is not just they who are watching me, but I don't look back. As I reach the end of the street and turn the corner onto the bustling

Corniche-el-Nil, I begin to feel that the ordeal might finally be over. Traffic bustles past, taxis darting in and out of lanes in an endless quest for the quickest way through. The Nile flows past, its colossal history leaving me feeling insignificant in its presence. The air feels fresher here than it did back near the Egyptian Museum. It must be the river effect. I take in a deep breath and ease up to a slow amble. But the situation doesn't feel right.

'Hey! You!' A voice of authority shouts out in Arabic from somewhere behind me.

I look back. It is another officer in blue, motioning to me, a walkie-talkie gripped tightly in his palm. He has been following me, probably for the couple of hundred metres from where I left my questioners. I wait for him to catch up. As he approaches, he starts asking me the same basic questions again, all in Arabic. I can see he speaks no English at all. I explain. He asks for my passport. I say I don't have it and tell him it is in my room in the hotel, the Nile Hilton. He speaks into his walkie-talkie.

'I have the British guy who speaks Arabic. What should I do with him?'

He asks me to accompany him.

'Su mushkila?' I ask again, repeating the question I had asked the first officer I bumped into a few minutes ago in Tahrir Square. He says nothing, grabs my upper right arm and motions me to walk with him back towards the barricaded area.

I remove my shades and look at him, waiting until his eyes rise up to meet mine. Our gazes lock, and when he has held my stare for a second or two, I glance down slowly until my look is resting on his hand gripping my arm. He lets go. I smile, slip my shades back over my eyes and set off by his side. We walk back down the quiet street, back past the smokers and chatterers. As we approach the barricade, my accompanying officer grabs my arm again, needing to show he has his ward under control. I don't resist this time and instead from behind the privacy of my shades, I turn my attention to scanning the scene for the sharp-suited intelligence officer. He is nowhere to be seen. I recognise only the white-uniformed officer amidst a clutch of blue shirts. As we reach them, my escorting policeman dissolves into the background, and I am now preoccupied with sizing up a new intelligence officer.

This man is dressed in a crisp blue-striped shirt and he too wears dark, expensive sunglasses. As he rattles off the same questions, and I the same answers, I can see that he is more polished and experienced than the previous apparatchik. Clearly the replacement has been briefed, since his questions flow naturally as though he knows what he is looking for.

'Why are you running away from us?' The 'from us' is a neat and threatening touch, one which I realise holds an important clue.

I think about situation resolution, before this gets out of hand. I examine the questioning process in an attempt to understand the strategy behind it. The first issue I have to grapple with is what their cause for initial enquiry was. As I continue to answer questions, my mind races, computing their tactics.

'It had to have been the X-ray machine at the museum gates,' I suggest to myself, recalling that they first took real interest in me when I turned back from the museum gates.

Now I slow down and decide to illustrate my thinking to my questioners in much more detail, to articulate what my options looked like at each step of my walk.

'Could we start again, please? From the beginning?' They agree.

I go into detail to show them that I was avoiding the onslaught of tour guides, and that I wasn't running away from the security procedure or the X-ray machine. The officer's shoulders relax as he realises that I haven't been running away from them after all. He speaks good English. I cannot see into his eyes, but instinct assures me he is more reasonable than the previous one. Par for his rank, he has his own assistant, another man in a blue shirt, carrying the trademark notebook and pen. I don't notice his face, just his shirt and his organised note-taking style. I help him by answering his questions in Arabic. Meanwhile, the intelligence officer leafs through my notebook. A loose note flies out from the book and he catches it expertly before it blows away. It is a note I'd written to myself to record a bad dream I awoke from a few days ago. He gives it a cursory glance, puts it back, shuts the book and clasps the black elastic back around the covers.

'Where did you come from?' his assistant asks.

'London.'

'Did you come from Palestine?'

'No.'

'Are you going to Palestine?'

'No.'

The intelligence officer asks me about my Arabic, and so I explain I am learning in a college in London. He warms to me. Meanwhile, the assistant notes down all my answers in his notepad. He examines my driver's licence, and I hear them calculating my age as 'tissa wa talatin'. Thirty-nine. Overestimated by a whole year, for once on the increasingly touchy subject of age, I decide not to argue. Room 1117: they note that too. It is my mistake not to have my passport with me, but by now I feel relieved to be without it since it contains numerous stamps that would have raised even more suspicions. The assistant has a loyal, kind-hearted face and writes with a diligent hand. He reads out my first name, Mohammad, and asks if I am a Muslim.

'Na'am,' I confirm. He breaks into a simple smile.

'Salaam alaikum,' he grins and I respond in kind.

'Welcome to Egypt,' says the intelligence officer, changing tack upon concluding that more pressing matters of state need attending to than questioning me.

'There's no need to fear,' he reassures me, when I tell him I am finding my stay rather frightening.

He applauds me for learning the language of his country and our religion. I ask him if he will accompany me on my walks around Cairo's historic streets, to make sure that I am really safe.

'Sure,' he says, as we shake hands again.

Ten

9/11 and Other Shocks

In 1991, within a year of completing my Master's and just when I was starting to flourish as a young man, Abba was dead. As he was breathing his last at Guy's Hospital in London, I was desperately begging my way onto a Pakistan International Airlines flight from Islamabad to Heathrow without even holding the right ticket, barely three weeks married, my last gasp effort to somehow see my father as he approached death. Miraculously the PIA crew let me board a flight to Copenhagen, and after I came stumbling into the intensive care ward at Guy's Hospital in London many hours later, Abba's pulse dropped until the cathode ray oscilloscope showed the lethal straight line on its screen. The doctors said he hung on just for me, as everybody else who mattered to him was around his bed already. I chose to believe them. In that moment, my father was gone from my life, taken from us in his mid-fifties and before I had turned twenty-five, and years before I was to realise how much of a pillar he was in my life and a shining beacon for my journey. I was left in shock for months, staring out of the windows at work and feeling a constant, wretched hollowness in the pit of my stomach. I remember him all the time, not out of ritual but from memories triggered as I scratch my way through every day. My younger son Zaki, who calls me Abba, asked me recently who *my Abba* was, and I responded unhelpfully by falling apart in tears. Thousands came to Abba's funeral service in London. Already decorated by the Bangladesh Government for his services to the liberation, for the local community and for our global family network, his departure left a huge void; a godfather-like figure who served many through deeds the breadth of whose impact remained unknown till after his departure. For he was one of the few men who said little yet committed the boldest of actions to achieve untold amounts of good for people around him. After his death, a friend of his came to me to repay a loan my father had given him, which none of us were even aware of. My mother was completely devastated, for she lost the only person who truly understood and stood by her. I don't think she ever recovered from losing her life partner until she died in 2013.

Finishing off my Master's at Cambridge, I joined as a Research Associate in the Policy and Economics practise of a global consulting firm in their London offices located by the Old Bailey courthouse. It was a dream job. The firm was one of the few employers that emphasised the global nature of its projects and activities and counted agencies such as the World Bank amongst its clients. My first boss, herself a PPE graduate from St Anne's College two generations before me, instilled in us an irritable intolerance of mediocrity and a scepticism of the obvious.

'I knew we had someone joining us from St Anne's, but I didn't expect a fella!' was her first comment to me upon joining, referring to how St Anne's had only recently become a mixed-intake Oxford college.

From forecasting the impact of a new terminal at a major UK Airport,* to figuring out how Dubai might become a global hub when its oil ran out, to how to privatise Pakistan's energy sector, I was exposed to strategic topics that required analysis as well as an ability to envision different outcomes across varied cultures. As a young graduate, the permission to even think about these kinds of subjects felt like a privilege. Whilst we were a talented group of professionals, I saw myself as different and having something unique to offer. Most of my colleagues were from privileged, white backgrounds and had seldom experienced social exclusion, whereas I constantly had to deal with cross-cultural, racial and religious obstacles to get ahead in life. I was also familiar with my father's garments business, which by now employed four hundred people and had export deals to America and the EU and a supply chain in India and Korea; as well as with the Curry Queen and our other restaurants, where I had hired and fired staff, redesigned menus and run local marketing campaigns.

Within a couple of years of starting work, I was advising a number of Central Asian and Trans-Caucasus

---

* I worked on the economic case for Terminal 5 in 1992 and it took almost 20 more years before the terminal was built and operational.

republics on opening up centrally controlled former USSR economies into bustling capitalist ones. In Almaty, the then capital of Kazakhstan,* we realised that our particular project wasn't going to be as 'easy' as providing economic advice, since the officially defunct but still ever-present KGB were monitoring our every activity. As the populist President Nursultan Nazarbayev attempted to tighten his slippery grip on power, the threat of a counter coup and a KGB-driven return to Communism hung over us, even as we worked through our project to advise on economic reforms. Security operatives would trail us around the city in their rectangular Ladas, following us into meetings and watching intently as we puffed on cigarettes in a desperate bid to transfer a bit of warmth into our fingers and freezing lips. To placate them, Mike, an inspiring partner in the firm who fearlessly led our forays into the East, and I would pay respect to the achievements of socialist economics by deriving from its tenets the fundamentals of supply and demand in a capitalist system. Ironically, our meetings were held at the Marxist-Leninist Institute, the only building with half decent heating and a conference room with flipcharts and a board. Adam Smith might never have imagined he'd be discussed so keenly in a centre with such a name. At these tense times in the region, our work to coach senior officials on the mechanics of how to embrace capitalism played no small role in stemming the temptation to return to the old ways of the Communist Party, the servitude to the Politburo

---

* Kazakhstan's capital is now Astana.

and the draconian controls of the KGB. Life across the dark waters of the Caspian Sea in Baku was no easier, since the Azeri KGB tracked us daily. On one occasion our team had almost been blown up when a bomb went off in the Baku metro several minutes after we exited. This wasn't Islamic terrorism, but the result of an internecine feud between neighbours Azerbaijan and Armenia over a disputed piece of land known as Nagorno-Karabakh, a stand-off between these nations which re-emerged during 2020. We learned that a significant percentage of Azerbaijani men aged under twenty-five died in the ensuing war. When it came to our request that we pause our project until the war was over, our clients at the European Commission instructed us to bear with it, keep calm and carry on.

The Central Asia and Caucasus work was not just a cultural challenge but a uniquely demanding analytical one too, where our ability to explain mathematical proofs of economic theories became currency for cultural acceptance. I spoke a little Russian, having done a year of it at St Dunstan's. Fragments of language and the intrigue of my Muslim identity both helped us win acceptance. Every evening in Almaty, over cheese and biscuits at the picturesque Communist Party sanatorium where we stayed, built for President Leonid Brezhnev's summer holidays, we would plan out the next day's workshop. Frozen by day, by night the stern Scottish Presbyterian professor who was an expert on our team would urge us to walk in minus twenty degrees Centigrade 'for some honest fresh air', trudging our way to Russian ballet concerts, gaining admission for a few roubles or a dollar or two.

In the former USSR, mostly my Azerbaijani and Kazakh clients took interest in my Muslim identity, something which they themselves aspired to reclaim. One evening in the remote city of Chymkent in Western Kazakhstan, almost the most remote place I have ever visited, the local city mayor wept as I read to her in Arabic from a copy of the Quran she had kept hidden in her home for years, as it had been ruthlessly banned in Soviet times. Her forefathers had endured much suffering, including the mass and largely unrecorded slaughter of Muslims in cities such as Tashkent in the 1920s, when Stalin made efforts to quash Muslim opposition to Communist hegemony in the 'stans'. This dignified lady had never heard the language of Quran before, as this was the first time anyone had ever read it to her. I used to find the Central Asians' Russified Arab names, such as Kadirbekov, Aliyev and Mohammedov, fascinating to interpret.

In early 1990s, corporate London, bonus-rich bankers and consultants often frequented wine bars after work. Practising Muslims like myself who didn't drink or party didn't have much choice but to assimilate, or be left out. Champagne Charlie's, inconspicuously nestled under the arches at Charing Cross Station, was a favoured firm hang-out. Sipping on orange juice, I would spend time in casual discussion with colleagues who were fascinated by my background, quizzing me as to why Muslims fasted from dawn to dusk and prayed five times a day, and whether Muslim men were really allowed to keep four wives. Having had a few years at university where I was praying only two or three times daily out of the stipulated five, I was now back to being regular with prayers, so at least I could speak of my own practise when I engaged on the subject of prayers and fasting. More innocently put than the same questions I was to field post 9/11, I saw these conversations as opportunities to break down barriers, but also important for building trusted relationships with seniors upon whom I had to depend for a diet of quality projects. I needed my colleagues to appreciate that I was no different from them, despite having different cultural and religious roots. This was an easy task as my colleagues were open-minded, informed and a pleasure to work with. Most grew to not only accept but also respect me for maintaining my differences.

Whilst many Muslims complained of being cultural victims in pursuing careers in the West, my exploitation of identity was emerging as an asset. When he first met me, the Chief Executive of our client in Dubai couldn't see past the Bangladeshis who cleaned his office bathrooms, but eventually grew to trust me so much that he would drive me around the tiny Gulf state in his Range Rover and treat me to high tea at Claridge's Hotel when he visited London. Late for a meeting once with the emirate's Chief Economist, he recklessly raced his car down some stairs to cut through a traffic jam. These were heady days of high-level meetings and unexpected situations, and too often I felt like I was living my fantasy of playing James Bond. Years later in Saudi Arabia, a senior official requested that the Englishman managing our project be replaced since they seemed to feel there wasn't sufficient understanding of their particular concerns being shown. With no better alternative, the team requested me to take over the project. Over time I had earned the Minister's trust, accompanying him to the palace of the Crown Prince for briefings. On occasion, the Minister even requested me to lead prayers at the ministerial offices, a spectacle which my British teammates found most entertaining. Once, at a meeting in the United Arab Emirates, a Dutch colleague sat aghast as he watched me remove my shoes and socks in the office of the finance director. What he didn't appreciate was that the client had requested me, in Urdu, to perform ablution with him before standing together in afternoon prayer. Clients' trust didn't just result in cultural connection but extended to the business of winning more work, since we were showing them that we understood them and their markets better. Conditioned by years of adjusting to challenges and turning many to my advantage, I encouraged Muslims who complained of being discriminated against in the Western workplace to do what they could to turn their differences into advantages. I also understood that my situation was different, since working in a global capacity gave me more opportunity to differentiate myself compared to a Muslim who might be in a role which is based in the same office or work location on a day to day basis.

As my post-Soviet projects completed a natural cycle, I was sent to manage the firm's World Bank unit in Washington DC. Life in the nation's capital was a fresh and empowering adventure. I joined the Bangladesh association at the Bank and became like a secretary to senior Bangladeshi World

Bankers and IMF staff who would order me about to run errands and organise meetings. Through this apprenticeship I gained their enduring trust, and even today I am occasionally called upon by the Bangladesh Prime Minister's Office to provide advice on digital and technology policies. While Washington was engulfed in gossip around President Clinton's alleged dalliance with Monica Lewinsky, my own cultural and intellectual horizons continued to expand. I had joined a World Bank team that advised the Vice President of Ghana on the approach to privatising the economy and, spending time in Accra, learned about Kwame Nkrumah, the country's iconic founder who had created the Non-Aligned Movement of nations that helped countries such as India and Indonesia stand up to their former colonial masters. I worked with an IMF team on structural reforms in Nigeria and gradually became accustomed to presenting details directly to Cabinet Ministers myself. Often performing without visuals and slides, I was forced to learn how to convey complex issues with conversational ease by internalising data and key facts, an asset which years later would help establish me as an analyst for news channels such as the BBC.

After three years in Washington, including turning down a mysteriously unsolicited job offer from the Bank to work on projects to influence transition in emerging markets, I made a teary-eyed and ultimately bittersweet return to Britain. Along with the by-now significant struggles I was facing in my marriage, I was also conflicted between pursuing a future in America and the Bank and a dutiful return to London to be reunited with the rest of my family and be more present to look after my mother. I don't think there was a pressing need for me to return, and neither my mother nor sister suggested it, but I just couldn't deal with the guilt from the comments of many elders.

'Tufael, when are you coming back to London, son? Are you going to just leave your mother here and not do your duty properly?'

The guilt pangs would be worse some times, depending on what people said and what frame of mind I was in to receive their comments.

'You know it is your duty in Islam to look after your mother, now that your father is dead.'

I told myself that I preferred to be back home as the work was technically more rigorous in Britain. This was a self-defeating lie. In truth, I had returned out of a feeling of guilt and now that I was back, I felt trapped. But it was too late. Consumed with bitterness, I didn't even provide the emotional support Amma needed and constantly fought with her and other relatives instead.

Ironically, some of those who used to criticise me for abandoning my mother and living the high life in Washington, would now ask why I left the great United States and returned to sorry Britain, where the prospects didn't seem as good. Whilst work was mercifully exciting and more stimulating than I might have expected, I was close to depression and started to break down in tears at unexpected moments, struggling to reconcile the gaps between my worldview and that of my community. Driven by artificial tokens of what seemed like I was doing my duty,

I realised that I had taken on too much, was overstretched on too many fronts and trying to force-fit myself to live up to others' expectations, rather than define my own life priorities. Things were beginning to crack.

The more I worked internationally, the more I got involved in projects which had a nation-building focus and this motivated me to do more. Compelled by the power of digital technology to empower societies and promote greater inclusion, I signed up for my firm's telecommunications practice. They asked me to focus on designing industry reforms and liberalisation around the world. Over the ensuing years, my work was to contribute to the mobile and technology revolutions happening in Africa, Asia, Europe and the Middle East, whereby hundreds of millions of people who had never dreamt of having a communications service, started getting affordable access to mobiles, and through that all manner of life-changing services. On a month to month basis, I would land in a new and often relatively little-known country. In Ljubljana, Slovenia I attended Cabinet meetings as a project adviser, whilst using haircuts and taxi rides in the city to banter and learn. In Addis Ababa, Ethiopia I briefed the Deputy Prime Minister over tea without the comfort of any slides tucked under my arm, and did similar in many other countries, as diverse as Poland, Zimbabwe, Oman and Slovakia. I am applying some of the thinking from this experience to solving similar problems today in Australia, where I live now.

One evening in Muscat, Oman's sleepy capital on the coasts of the Straits of Hormuz which separate the Arabian Gulf states from the almost visible Islamic Republic of Iran, my colleague James and I were convinced we saw Osama bin Laden, seated and holding a stick, in a private room at the back of a traditional Omani restaurant where we had wandered in uninvited. Shocked and independently coming to the same conclusions, hastily did we both back out and do a rapid about turn, comparing notes on our nervy experience once at a safe distance from the venue. It might or might not have been the man himself, I still cannot be sure. But it was perhaps the second time I would be close to one of his hideouts, as I once visited the Pakistan Military Academy in Abbottabad, Pakistan, the town where bin Laden was to be killed by an American drone attack a few years later.

Occasionally, work could still conjure up unsavoury experiences which took me back to my playground nightmares at school. At my induction training upon joining the firm, I was informed that a beard didn't look professional.

'Please could you shave it off, and don't wear a brown suit.'

This was my first week at work, and whilst I hated these strictures and was angered at how they had been conveyed, I ignored the advice and suffered no consequences. Having resisted 'joining one camp or another' through childhood and university, I wasn't about to give in now. In Washington I had been asked by a senior British colleague visiting from London to play, in his own words, the 'little Indian' in a meeting while he would be 'white man who will tell them how it needs to be done'. I was incredulous. It is difficult to imagine that these were actually his words. A traditional Englishman, I don't think he intended to be racist but unconsciously he was being just that. He blushed profusely when I repeated back to him what he had just said, and he changed tack for the meeting itself, giving me the lead role and himself taking the supporting one. On another occasion I was welcomed to a large gathering in Accra, capital of Ghana by a senior English professional as 'the Paki who flew over from the US'. So I was amused when the same individual was hilariously put right the next afternoon by a Senegalese colleague for misquoting Chaucer. This colleague made me and all the Africans present feel hugely proud that day, since they were concerned by the racist reception I had just experienced. More recently, a senior professional I was working with in the UK jokingly referred to me as a 'fucking Muslim' when I ordered us a bottle of sparkling water to drink after a long day's work instead of going for something stronger. I immediately saw the funny side of his comment, and its double irony, and in an odd way his uttering it revealed a sense of confidence in me as a colleague. But I also realised that however funny it might be, it just isn't the sort of comment that is acceptable and that as a privileged white man, he might never have experienced an equivalent in his life.

At work I empathised with Asians, Arabs and Africans (actually, with any 'others' who felt excluded for any reason) when they complained about rough cultural treatment. My clients in Zimbabwe would lament over arrogant consultants who would come from 'Mud Island', their own racist code for Britain. Our project adviser used to take me to the Harare Club for lunch and tell me about the goings-on in

President Robert Mugabe's cabinet, to prepare me for to how to play upcoming meetings, which we would then work through expertly. Years later when based in Mumbai, a legendary Indian colleague from Kolkata, known for his animated office theatre, would oscillate between embracing me as his Bengali brother when he liked what I said to dismissing me as a 'cufflink-wearing, brogue-shoed British bastard' when he didn't. Underlying his humour there was a serious point being made about how I sat either side of the East/West, colonial/anti-colonial divide, with consummate ease. Adjusting to a life of being a Western Muslim had given me the tools to find a way in.

The events of 9/11 hit us on one of the few weeks when I found myself in London, having just flown in the night before from a trip to Pakistan. I was at the office in Charing Cross, when colleagues suddenly stopped working and stood speechless watching the events unfold on the TV. These were incredible scenes, as though we were watching a disaster movie. It was difficult to comprehend that civilian aeroplanes were really flying into the World Trade Center, sturdy twin buildings that I had seen at close quarters and admired for their stature and unusual grace. I was so shocked that I was unable to think about the consequences of what was happening; I had to give it time to sink in as I watched, powerless to do anything about it.

An hour into watching the scenes unfold, and after seeing countless replays of the trade center collision, I began to think that this was going to be a drawn-out saga for the West, and bad news for Muslims. When friends and relatives postulated that the difficulties would soon pass, I claimed confidently that we were in the early stages of one hundred years of turmoil that began with the Iranian revolution in 1979. I felt this was how long it would take for generally Western-enforced democracy experiments in the Middle East to run their course and fail, and be replaced by home-grown political movements which would lead to stable and representative government. Whether I will be proved right or wrong, adopting a long-term perspective has helped to reconcile me to a future of difficulty: living with a constant pattern of being pushed into defending or justifying my faith and frequent travel-related suspicion, nuisances and restrictions.

One of my Bangladeshi aunties in Bromley lost her brother that day, on duty as a waiter in the Windows of the World restaurant, high up in one of the twin towers. He left a heavily pregnant wife; she wasn't told of her husband's death until she gave birth a few days later. Tragic as it was, I knew that such losses would gain little sympathy with Western society at large and that Muslims would soon have to start explaining why 9/11 had happened. Having lived in America myself, I could feel how the attack shook its sincere and trusting people. The event put the country into a state of shock, unused as it was to terrorism on its shores. I recall once pointing out an unattended plastic bag to a police officer on the viewing deck of the Empire State Building and being numbed by his ignoring my advice to look into it. In the mid-1990s, at Washington's Dulles International

Airport, you could accompany passengers all the way to the boarding gate for an international flight. At John F. Kennedy Airport in New York, the gates for El Al, Air India and Pakistan International Airlines were adjacent to each other in the same terminal building. Having grown up with Irish Republican terrorism in the UK, I found the US to be lackadaisical about security, negligent and naïve. When 9/11 hit, it was an almighty blow to the nation, affected the country's emotions deeply, and thousands of innocents suffered, or lost their lives or loved ones.

Dealing with the public tragedy of the terrorist attacks required a tactful approach, and many Muslims were getting it badly wrong. Terrorism and its connection to Islam was to become a frequent subject of conversation. I avoided providing political analysis on the matter and steered clear of chiming in with simplistic theories to explain the attacks and links to or not to Islam. These might have been valid topics to unpack, but this wasn't the right time to do so. A common theory doing the rounds was that 9/11 was precipitated by years of ill-conceived US foreign policy in the Middle East. This was a poorly disguised 'you had it coming' thesis, not necessarily helpful, not empathetic to the worries of US citizens following the attacks, and it was a masked way to criticise America without doing it bluntly. It was clearly the case that the US stance towards Iran, Iraq, Palestine, Israel, Egypt, Saudi Arabia, Pakistan and Afghanistan had many flaws and had caused huge grievances against the US in these countries, along with some hatred as well. But 9/11 was the result of a planned set of attacks devised by evil terrorists with an intent to kill thousands of innocent people in a symbolic attack on the heart of America's democratic institutions. Why such evil people did this requires a fuller explanation that few, if any, properly understand even today. Too often, Muslims I listened to found it easy to simply lay the blame on the US. This was partly because some wanted to avoid reaching any conclusion that would lay the blame upon Muslims themselves. It was like playing victim. Others claimed the attack was a Zionist conspiracy to undermine Islam, undertaken by Israel, claiming that no Jews were at work in the twin towers that day as they had been warned to stay away. These disparate views revealed the gulf between Islam as a religion of responsibility, peace and fairness and some of the vindictive, emotional and petty-minded ways in which many Muslims were thinking.

We were under the spotlight, and we were in for a rough ride, and people weren't getting it.

During the horror of the 9/11 attacks by Islamist terrorists, I experienced a seismic quake of my own with the final realisation that my marriage was all but over. After ten years of swallowing the cultural potion that marital union had to be a happy and lifelong Islamic experience, events had forced me to consider that I was going to be better off alone. On 8/11, the day before the US attacks, I was in Pakistan at the end of a harrowing personal trip, ironically just a few kilometres away from Osama bin Laden's later hideout spot. I arrived at London Heathrow off an Emirates flight from Lahore the next morning, shell-shocked from the drama that would change my life, to then sit in our office to watch events that would change everybody's world forever.

With respect to travel, life got worse too. For the two years that followed 9/11, I was confronted with an escalation in cross-border interrogations, as it was during this period that I was advising on internet and telecom reforms in Oman, Bahrain, Ethiopia and Saudi Arabia. My timing, as seemed to be the case in these years, could not have been worse. The frequency of my being stopped at airports and railway stations elsewhere increased too. From 2005, when my name was inserted on the Department of Homeland Security's 'no-fly list' by those overzealous Texan officials, I had become subject to additional questioning when entering the US, as well as extra scrutiny from the intelligence agencies of countries which cooperated with the US. After the London attacks on 7/7/2005, the heightened state of suspicion against Muslims affected how I felt about being on public transport. I stopped carrying a backpack and took to using a briefcase instead, feeling that other commuters might get concerned if they saw a young Muslim man boarding a train with a bag strapped to his back. This was an overreaction on my part, my mind playing games with me as to what people around me were thinking.

I was in New York the day of the London attacks. My American hosts insisted I take a few hours off to recover from the shock of the news before returning to a team meeting. The gesture reinforced how much 9/11 had affected them and how they felt for other victims of terrorism in the West. But whilst a lot of people and media in the West felt solidarity with each other over being the victims of terrorism, there was generally less regard for those affected by terror in countries such as Pakistan, Iraq, Afghanistan or Kenya. This disparity between how much the press, or people in general, showed concern over terrorism in the West versus in the Middle East, Africa or Asia was a source of disappointment for Muslims, and explains some of the emotional reactions over 9/11 where Muslims looked to blame the US. 2019's horrific attack on innocent Muslims offering Friday prayers at a mosque in Christchurch, New Zealand, went some way to changing Westerners' understanding that they are not alone in being victims of terrorism, but arguably this too happened because the attack took place on Western soil.

The post-9/11 years weren't my best ones. I was struggling to keep myself together, as someone in my mid-thirties who had never before experienced the emotions of even breaking up a relationship, yet now stared into divorce, frowned upon in conservative Muslim circles and seen in Bengali society as nothing short of a life failure. As is often the case, the stigma was perhaps greater in my thoughts, more than anywhere else, since my wider family clan was unexpectedly supportive and loving in these difficult times. But emotionally I had been torn to shreds like dry papyrus, parched and damaged at the ends, losing appetite and body weight, lacking energy and presence. It wasn't the right time for me to be facing indiscriminate scrutiny on a regular basis. I was fragile, touchy and extra sensitive, and this resulted in Islamophobia playing on my mind even more than it might otherwise have done.

Before the twin towers attacks, I had started getting more engaged in Muslim community affairs in an attempt to do what I could do close some of the gaps. My motivation was not purely social. I was also looking to get involved in fresh activities that were going to help me move on in my personal life. I had no desire to pour myself into my work as a distraction. In addition to launching an intense programme to master Arabic, I approached a Muslim school in London to help them with plans to build an IT centre and library. The school's original planning application had been submitted a fortnight before 9/11 and rejected for not articulating a sufficiently convincing case for building in the green belt. I hadn't thought deeply at that stage about my views regarding faith-based schools, but my subsequent involvement gave me an opportunity to do so.

A local councillor seemed to have caused a kerfuffle over the matter of the school's planning application by publishing a letter in the local paper which was read by some as implying that the school was planning to build a 'terrorist training centre'. Nothing could be further from the reality, but after the US attacks the matter became a hot political issue in this generally low-key outer London borough. The school didn't have experience in handling press scrutiny, became nervous and panicky, and withdrew into a shell to shield itself from community exposure. Things were made worse when a teacher was caught on the telephone by a local reporter one evening and, seemingly taken off guard, gave an unprepared interview. I and a few others formed a small committee for redoing the planning application and, deciding to take the bull by its horns, embarked on a charm offensive with the local Tory party to try and build some trust. That month, on a whim, the principal and I attended the local Party Annual General Meeting. We had not been invited, but since it was an open meeting, we were welcomed upon arrival by a somewhat surprised-looking set of organisers at the door to the local village hall. The attendees, mainly wealthy white folk who had lived in the leafy neighbourhood for years, were understandably startled to see a smartly dressed Asian man walk in, accompanied by a bearded Indian wearing a sherwani and skull cap. We were easily sighted in our surroundings, two lambs who'd for some reason volunteered to come to a slaughter at the hands of one of the most right-wing communities in the South East. But in keeping with the very best of English courtesy, we were warmly welcomed and made to feel comfortable. When a member asked about the 'proposed minaret' in town, I was politely invited to come to the front and address the meeting attendees, and revelled in the somewhat hostile atmosphere that ensued.

'Sir, you are from the school, aren't you?' hesitated the meeting Chairman, peering over the rows from his stage-top seat and finding me in the crowd.

'Indeed so,' I confirmed in a purposely confident tone, spoken with the clear elocution of a public-school-educated Oxford graduate.

I clambered up onto the hollow, echoey stage somewhat noisily and proceeded to answer questions about the school's plans. The queries were polite but controversial, giving me a wonderful opportunity to state that the school had no plans to turn itself into a mosque, and nor did it plan to build a minaret or sound the call to prayer from loudspeakers. The Tory party faithful listened with great interest. I won them over in a few minutes, no doubt helped by my practised delivery, dark blue suit and familiar English mannerisms.

'We would like to invite all of you as our special guests at the school's Open Day to be held in three weeks' time,' I announced, coming up with the idea whilst on stage.

By the time we left the hall, we were being congratulated by many attendees for having the courage to come to the AGM. It was one of those many moments, rather like the passing jogger who once saved me from being beaten up by skinheads when I was at school, when I am overwhelmed by the sheer open-mindedness that people in Britain often demonstrate. But I also knew that one evening's charm would not last long if the school didn't follow up with specific actions. When we opened the classrooms to local residents soon afterwards, the gesture was well received, though the local press did not choose to cover the occasion. Over the next few years, I felt that the school was not able to take enough steps to integrate successfully with the local community. For example, the school maintained what I thought was an unnecessary Arab dress code for boys, as this made it hard for them to be treated normally when outside the school compound. The dress code was also quite impractical when the children played football during break times.

I am not sure that the school wanted to integrate beyond a minimum level either. Herein lay a problem for me. In theory, I could conceive of the benefits of teaching about faith in a school, but in practise I struggled to see how this could work if the school's overall approach to offering a wide range of subjects and its commitment to community engagement wasn't more mainstream. This view reflected my own life journey, which is one of reaching compatibility between being a person of faith and a fully adjusted member of a secular and multicultural society. Whilst I did not agree with the school's lack of integration, I could understand why the management was so coy about it. The school was run by an honest, moral and straightforward management team, but one that in my view lacked experience in the UK of running such an institution, as well as the confidence to reach out beyond the Muslim community too. Almost five years later, a hard-fought legal, political and PR campaign to get approval for the extension prevailed, and once funds were raised the building was up and running soon after. With this job done, I exited gradually from my committee activities in support of the application.

I didn't exit because I disagreed with faith-based schools. We financially support and occasionally visit a Muslim faith school in Surat, India, set up by my wife's paternal ancestors before they migrated to South Africa in the 1890s. However, the school is secular in its outlook, welcomes a mix of Hindu, Christian and (largely) Muslim students and offers quality education to poor and middle-income children in an area where there is a lack of affordable alternatives. Whilst I am supportive of faith-based schools, I prefer them to be integrated into the mainstream curriculum, to not be faith-exclusive but have a wide variety of studentship, a rich subject mix and rooted links to the local community. I haven't always found that to be the case, especially when presented an opportunity to see some Muslim faith schools in the UK at close quarters.

Along with Jamal, a friend from SOAS, I journeyed into making a series of TV programmes focused on discovering interesting places to eat for Muslims. We recorded episodes in Turkish, Syrian, Indian, Lebanese and Iranian restaurants. The idea was to encourage home-bound Muslims to integrate more. Jamal realised that restaurants would be a great theme, given Asians' love for food and their reticence to eat out over fear of consuming non-halal meat. When my turn came to present, I would comment on the history and culture of the cuisine, peppering my despatch with observations about the country's people and geography. I explained, for example, that the Turks love kebab because they were once Western Chinese nomads who conquered Central Asia and Mesopotamia on horseback, eating more livestock than vegetables since they were constantly on the move.

I also took on the Chair role at Muslim Youth Helpline, a charity providing a voluntary helpline for young British Muslims in distress. Not unlike the origins of Facebook, the helpline was first created by two pioneering Oxford University students who had started taking calls in a student room at their college, from which the overwhelming volume of calls rose to a point where they needed to move to a dedicated facility. The team was soon fielding several thousand calls per year and became a critical, last-resort service to many Muslims in distress, known for providing a caring, non-judgemental listening service to people who needed a safe space. The most common issues that came up were bullying and racism at school, fears over confessing about homosexuality to the family, discrimination at work and in a few cases, radicalisation. We built cooperative relationships with the Metropolitan Police, the Home Office and 10 Downing Street, and we sponsored social and community projects. We created a partnership with the Prince of Wales Trust for mentoring Muslim prisoners for rehabilitation into society, being the only agency that cared to send every Muslim prisoner in Britain an Eid card. Bit by bit, I was recapturing the person I had been before descending into my personal traumas of the past few years, but this time wiser and more able to understand my Islamic duties in their proper context.

Workwise however, I was going nowhere. In late 2002, my firm sold its consulting practise to a major IT company, and this instantly placed my thriving career into a temporary coma. I was to learn much as a strategist working at senior levels, but all the company really wanted me to do was sell technology solutions. Two people were instrumental in my leaving. The first was Giovanni, a flamboyant and wise Italian colleague and confidante with whom I worked for months on a project in Milan. Quite the showman, 'Papa' as we would call him, would lecture the team that Machiavelli was essential reading before a complex negotiation, until the day I humbled him by quoting back an extract from the great political essayist during a conference call. Giovanni had his payback soon after at Fiumicino Airport in Rome, when I asked him for feedback on my support for his team in Italy. He read correctly that this was a vain request for praise, and responded in his pronounced Italian accent:

'Mo-am-ed. You are a man of faith. In my belief as in yours, you 'ave an obligation to use the talents given to you by God. You might be doing comparatively well,' he said, pointing his finger into my chest, 'but you are relaxing, and you are wasting your God-given talent. This, my friend, is a mortal sin.'

Having uttered these words and poked me a few more times in the chest for good measure, the silver-haired Roman turned on his heels with a swish of his stylish rain-coat and waltzed off.

The second person to convince me to change my career was to change my life for good. Little did I know it but I was about to meet her soon.

Eleven

The Wisdom of the Shoe Shiner

Having completed a four-day exploration of Syria's Mediter-ranean coastline, including its 'secret' Russian military base locally known by all as 'Putin's chemical factory', I cross the border into northern Lebanon at Arida, yet another quiet outpost on roads less travelled. Unlike the lofty mountain crossing at Kessab, this one is down at sea level, with the pale yellow walls of the tiny Lebanese immigration building being slapped constantly by a Mediterranean tide. Once through, my Tortosan* taxi driver speeds me into the city of Tripoli, another ancient city but this one with a centre full of buildings under construction, abandoned structures, cranes and site fences which together have removed the soul of the metropolis. As a teenager, watching newscasts with Abba about the Lebanese civil war, I had always thought Tripoli referred to the capital city of Libya which bears the same name. Little did I realise until years later

---

* From Tartus, the Syrian coastal city approximately fifty kilometres north of the Leb-anon border point of Arida.

that this walled settlement, riddled with the marks of bullet holes from gunfire in the 1970s and 1980s, was Lebanon's second city, following the iconic and unmistakable Beirut. Tripoli's central square, known as Sahat at Tell, is overlooked by a slim clock tower built in colonial times and thronged on all sides by the magnificent Mercedes Benz taxis which epitomise my romantic notion of travelling around the Middle East. Decades old, bashed and bruised, their doors still close with a reassuring Teutonic thud. As usual I go out from my hotel without guidebook or camera, having memorised the major street directions. I am armed only with my now dog-eared copy of Robert Fisk's harrowing account of the Lebanese civil war, *Pity the Nation* (1990).

At least I got into Lebanon this time around. For on another occasion, I was turned away at the barren yet heavily militarised Syrian-Lebanese border post of Masnaa, some eighty kilometres east of Beirut and sixty kilometres west of Damascus. The Lebanese border officials could not eliminate the possibility that I was not someone else on their database who bore my name, spelt Mohammed Chaudhry, and who was on a terror suspect watch list. This was despite the other individual being born in 1964 (I was born two years' later) and being of Pakistani origin (I am British). Apologetic to the extreme, the officials pleaded with me that they needed two forms of ID that confirmed I was not this other person, and that one of these had to be Father's name. I filled in my father's name on the form, but the person had for whatever reason not given theirs. And so, with the data fields not aligning, the officials could not pass the threshold of confidence to let me through. I found the whole process rather random, since the officials didn't even request proof of my father's name (not that I could have produced it on the spot anyway). Failing to negotiate a way through and with the sun beginning to dip, I requested our chauffeur to turn our schmaltzy Volvo around and drive to Jordan instead for a night on the Dead Sea. Like so many others I have encountered, this was one of those border-crossing experiences where the process didn't stand up to scrutiny.

Sitting in a Tripoli mosque for evening prayers, I cannot concentrate. Standing in line and performing the physical movements of salaah* with precision just as Maulvi Sahib taught me, I am preoccupied, half-listening to the imam and half-focused on other thoughts. Whilst my prayer might appear sincere and pious to an observer, I am actually thinking about how diversity in Lebanon contrasts with Britain, since here identity is profiled so that it becomes a key to division and social segmentation. Just as a long beard seems to represent being a Shia, a cross on a necklace or hanging from the rear-view mirror of the car reflects being a Christian, and draping a Rafiq Hariri poster in your shop confirms that you must be a Sunni. Pressing my forehead into the mosque's elegant blue carpeting, I hear the imam recite the call to sit up, and then to go again into the humble act of sujud.†

---

* Arabic word for prayer

† prostration

'Allahu akbar . . . Allahu akbar.'

I wonder what London would be like if it was fragmented by sectarian division as Beirut has been, or parts of Syria are today. I imagine Wood Green a Turkish enclave, Brick Lane a Sylheti guerrilla zone, Southall controlled by Sikh separatists who also commandeer access to the strategic Heathrow airstrip, Wembley and Willesden patrolled by a Gujarati-African alliance that straddles the arterial North Circular Road, and Zionist extremists encamped in St John's Wood with a strategic vantage point for launching missiles from Primrose Hill. Across the Thames, on the south side of the river, the Greenwich Observatory is the base from which British Nationalists fire rockets into Mile End, an area now inhabited by Bangladeshi refugees protected by the Brick Lane militia. And amid all the strife, life goes on as usual in Putney, Wandsworth and Parson's Green. Nonsensical thoughts in the context of modern-day British politics, but my weird imaginings help me empathise with the people of the Middle East who have seen a once peaceful region disintegrate piece by piece into a patchwork quilt of irreconcilable ethnic divisions.

'Allahu akbar. Allahu akbar . . .' The imam leads us into prostration again.

Coming into adulthood, I learnt to celebrate my difference from others, and through that to value the richness of Britain's diverse society. But the world is changing rapidly now, reverting to the identity politics I grew up with in the 1970s and 80s. Being a Muslim today in the West comes saddled with a burden to 'answer' for common misperceptions about Islam and the actions of extremist Muslims. The questions are becoming less tolerant and more prejudiced, such that whatever well-intended and balanced response is offered, it doesn't really matter. 'Why do Muslims fast?' has turned into 'Isn't it unhealthy to be forced not to eat or drink for so many hours?' 'Is Islam truly a religion of peace?' has become 'Why do so many Muslims support terrorism?' And 'Why do women wear hijab?' into 'How can you claim Islam respects women if a woman is forced to wear a veil in public, not allowed to drive and not regarded as a reliable witness?' In each case, the context, facts and explanations necessary take time to research and explain, require patience, balance, good knowledge and a large dose of honesty to close the gap of understanding. Starting out with an objective to justify or defend the faith, rather than explain it openly, results in defensiveness and confusion, just as I displayed in my early days at Oxford.

We are on the way to creating grey areas in our societies, where questioning any Muslim for the deeds of other Muslims is deemed acceptable This doesn't just apply to Muslims, but to many minority communities in many countries. One day, even in our most democratic communities, I fear that societies at large may decide that it is in the national interest. We have seen calls for singling out of Muslims from President Trump during his Presidential campaign, and directly after he came to power with the Executive Order related to protecting the US from terrorism,* which singled

---

* Executive Order number 13768

out a number of Muslim countries for special treatment over the future granting of US travel visas, an order now overturned by President Biden. I wonder how the world will look at my children when they are grown up.

Where difference and harmony can be features of a well-integrated and plural society, Lebanon frustrates me by scoring high on one dimension, difference, but aspiring low on the other, harmony. My first few hours of observing how many people openly display their religious identity in Tripoli reminds me of how Sylhetis often choose to emphasise their differences from other Bengalis. During childhood, these behaviours made me angry, I think because Amma was only half-Sylheti and for this reason singled out by relatives from time to time as being a 'foreigner'. She was of course Bangladeshi but, in any case, I found this behaviour towards her quite exclusive. Lebanon doesn't make me angry in this respect, since there isn't a strong personal connection for me here that would parallel what I felt in Sylhet. But my thoughts about Sylhet, triggered by what I have seen here, distract me from prayer.

'As salaamu alaikum wa rahmatullah, as salaamu alaikum wa rahmatullah.' The imam completes the prayer with the customary recital of greeting to guardian angels.

The next morning, I arrange a servees* from Sahat at Tell, a trusty 1980s Mercedes Benz 200 driven by an older man with a creased and interesting face. As the servees fills up to its four-passenger load for longer journeys and we prepare

---

* A concept for a shared taxi found all over Lebanon and also occasionally in Syria and Jordan.

to set off, the driver double-checks the tyre pressure and makes sure the boot is properly locked. All the passengers are men, including a Lebanese soldier in casual uniform and beret who looks like he is taking a trip home to visit his family. The men chit-chat, making small talk to pass the time. Staying out of the conversation, a semblance of tranquillity draws over me; the peace I have come to associate with the anticipation of imminent departure. The road up to Bcharré, home of writer Khalil Gibran, is steep and narrow. The cliff-side carriageway starts out from the lofty townships clustered above Tripoli's city centre and weaves its way into the spectacular Mount Lebanon Range, leaving below us the lush greenery of the beautiful Qadisha Valley. As we ascend into the mountains, we pass through a series of small, organised-looking communities. It becomes cooler and cloudier as we climb. Dressed in shorts, I feel a chill on my bare legs as I nestle into the back seat and photograph the driver, the intensity of whose countenance I have developed a fascination for. Unlike the denominational diversity of religious buildings in coastal Tripoli, up in the mountains I notice a prevalence of churches. At almost every bend along the winding mountain road, there is a Christian monument: a shrine, a memorial or a solitary, brave-looking cross. As we pass through more hamlets and settlements on the way up to Bcharré, an increasing number of streets and buildings are draped in Lebanese flags which bear a red cross at each corner, as well as posters of notable Maronite Christian politicians standing for local elections.

The higher we go, the more I begin to realise that I have left a more multicultural part of Lebanon and entered a tucked-away Maronite Christian stronghold in the mountains. There is nothing of the musty smells and hustle and bustle of Tripoli here. The walls of the homes are high, their gates imposing and gardens neat, and the streets spotlessly clean. The height of the walls is accentuated by the narrowness of the streets, and the feeling of being shut out reminds me of childhood walks around the narrow residential alleys of Sylhet. It was around the 5th century AD that the Maronite Christian community, originally from France, made the lofty valleys of this mountain range their stronghold. In my ignorance I hadn't realised that there are no non-Christians dwelling up here at all. Had I realised this, I might have made the Bcharré trip a day trip only. As we take bend after windy bend, I keep wondering in anticipation of when we will turn a corner and be able to see the town of Bcharré itself.

'Where is the mosque in Bcharré? What time are the Friday prayers?' I ask the driver, his face so admirably composed.

'There are no mosques here,' he tuts, wagging his finger at me. 'If you want to pray, you must return to Tripoli, down below.'

A distinct chill comes over me as the driver casts a glance across to me, taking his eyes off the road for a brief moment. Now just the two of us in the car, our ascent has quickened with the lightened load. I have to the front seat after we stopped at Ehden and the glove compartment now keeps snapping open onto my bare knees, making me feel under-dressed in my shorts. As the climate cools, my sense of being exposed is exacerbated by the expectation that I will meet some hostility here. All of a sudden, I feel silly and touristy up here in the mountains, ignorant of local custom, and wishing I had changed into jeans while waiting to depart Tripoli. Inside the glove box is a stash of documents, a holder that presumably has a pistol in it, plus an apple as emergency nourishment in case of a breakdown. Just like the place, the driver too seems ready for any eventuality. I lean back into my seat, relishing the prospect of another twist to this fascinating journey. Still marvelling at the sturdiness of the Mercedes, I admire the upholstery of the cushion, thirty years old but firm as new.

St Saba Church, perched on the edge of a sheer drop to the valley floor, comes into view as we turn yet another sharp corner. The soft contours of its huge, sandstone-coloured dome announce that at last we have reached Bcharré. The driver points out the Khalil Gibran museum on our right as we drive through town, asking me proudly if I know of him. Bcharré is the Qadisha region's principal cultural, religious and political centre and, at 1500-metre elevation from the valley directly below, it is a place of staggering beauty as well as a strategic location. As though in village fete season, the streets are draped with countless fluttering flags bearing the cross. A series of churches sit along the main street, as well as devotional statues, crosses and figurines adorning almost every doorway and entrance to the town's shops, cafés and homes. There are no Rafiq

Hariri pictures up here; no memories of the Sunni Muslim Prime Minister who was slain just eight months ago. Instead I see hundreds of pictures of Samir and Satrida Geagea, the brother and sister who are leaders of the Lebanese Forces, a Maronite Christian political party which began life in the mid-1970s as a militia in the civil war. The Lebanese flags on their posters bear a prominent red crucifix, just like the ones I saw as we ascended.

The Chbat Hotel is an austere place, appropriate for a stay of quiet reflection and appreciation of this region's awe-inspiring beauty. It is a short and steep climb up from the main town. Immediately upon arrival Walid, the owner, asks at what time I would like hot water since they only turn it on when it is required; and he explains matter-of-factly that breakfast is served between 7 a.m. and 9 a.m. When I ask where the mosque is, the mountain atmosphere grows distinctly cooler.

My room is truly minimalist, not the designer minimalism I am accustomed to in boutique hotels in other places, but the austere sort I would associate with the dormitory of an English boarding school. The sheets are sparkling white and the blankets a cold, military grey. The bathroom is 1970s vintage, but functional and clean with bare and thin towels and a mirror of clouded glass. A medicine cabinet is concealed behind it, empty and spotless except for a scar left behind by a cigarette burn on its plastic shelf. The small singe mark is an offensive scab, a ringed blemish created no doubt by a previous errant guest smoking guiltily in the bathroom, out of sight. Back in the room, I can hardly see out of the narrow slit of a window, which is just above head height. Unsure whether I will last two nights here in the stifled, cell-like atmosphere of my chambers, I decide not to unpack my bags but to head straight into town. I do some printing at the town's sole internet café and then settle for dinner at Makhlouf Elie, a hospitable-seeming restaurant of three tables along the main street.

Bashir, the owner, is friendly. There are several folks in the tiny restaurant and they all take an obvious interest in me: an old, bespectacled man having a pizza, an even older man who doubles as waiter and customer, switching constantly between the two roles, and a mother with a small child who attracts everyone's doting attention. They chat together, greeting others who come in and out and occasionally glancing at me. Engaging me in conversation only at the end of the meal, Bashir does all the talking while the others sit and watch attentively, as though he is the appointed spokesperson for dealing with outsiders. Despite his warmth and genuine sincerity, for the first time in this entire trip I feel decidedly out of place up here in the mountains.

At the till, Bashir asks my name. I make something up and reply in a muffled voice. I don't think uttering the word 'Mohammad' in front of members of this mountain-top community is a good idea, especially this late on a Thursday night. After one more nargileh, it is almost one o'clock in the morning and I find myself faced with a long, deserted and hilly walk back up to the Chbat. I crunch along the gravel road in near silence and darkness, burdened with

thoughts and accompanied by the echoing sounds of bark-
ing dogs rising from the valley floor. Unlike during my late
walk in Tripoli last night, this time I have no option to flag
down a local taxi.

The next morning, after a chilly night as the sole guest in
a spartan mountain-top hotel, driver Georges has turned up
at the hotel in a sky-blue Mercedes. He announces himself
with a baritone and hearty 'bonjour', the de rigueur greeting
for Bcharré folk as they remain fiercely proud of their distant French origins. Moments after bidding farewell to the
hotel staff, we are on our way across the Mount Lebanon
Range to Baalbek.

'Kull ashkhas fi'l alam min Allah, ant' Muslim, wa ana
Misayihin, bas nhne kull min Allah, wa nhne kull mn-rjeh
la Allah,' Georges declares as we set off, saying in Arabic
words to the effect of 'All the men in the world are creatures
of God, you a Muslim, and me a Christian, but we are all
from God, and to God we will all return.'

His statement roughly means that all of the world's
people are created by God, you Muslim and I Christian, we
are all from God and we will all return to him. Not too soon
I hope, as Georges negotiates the first of countless hairpin
bends on this spectacular drive along the ridge of the
mountains. Georges has a stately figure, tall and large, with
a deep, trombone-like voice and a ruddy face. He looks
dapper dressed in dark blue shirt and matching trousers,
his white face permanently blushed with the corpuscles of
blood cells almost bursting through his chubby skin. He
tells me he has been a 'chauffeur' for sixty-five years and has

lived in Bcharré his whole life along with his wife, children and grandchildren. A double take at him suggests he must then have been driving when he was a toddler and, sure enough, a few minutes later he tells me he is seventy-three.

I photograph him as we chat, and after a couple of heavy days in Tripoli and Bcharré, I let go of my tensions, settle into the comfy leather seat of the Mercedes and enjoy the man's gregarious and hearty company. Perhaps inspired a little by me also, Georges continues with inspirational statements about our shared existence. Finding this to be a good opportunity for practising some passionate Arabic speech-making myself, I chime in. Enthused by the staggering scenery, I mix in recitations of oft-rehearsed tracts of the Quran to give myself as much of a shot at continuous Arabic oratory as possible.

'Lakum deenukum wa liya deen,'* I quote the famous exhortation from the Quran to coexist with others of different beliefs, and we both burst out in laughter, rather like Ahmet and I used to do so during those days in Kazakhstan, looking for common words which would unite us, as we drove about in the icy streets of Almaty.

Despite touching potentially adversarial topics, our discussion remains safely rooted in a tamed celebration of shared monotheism, and the friendly tone of our banter goes a long way to restoring my mood after a day of attrition up in the mountains. Speaking in Arabic, our dialogue is facilitated in a way not available to those seeking multi-faith understand-

---

* 'You unto your belief, and me unto mine'.

ing outside this region. To Georges, a faithful Christian and to me, a faithful Muslim, 'Allah' means God, 'bismillah' means in the name of God, and 'Allahu akbar' means God is great. Such terms here in Lebanon do not carry the baggage of being 'Muslim' chants as they do almost everywhere else. Around the world today, a favoured sign off for Islamist suicide bombers is to chant 'Allahu akbar' before they blow themselves up. As a result, these words are now exclusively associated with Islamic terrorism with the result that saying 'God is great' is demonised in the West. Conversations such as the one with Georges serve to reinforce how much of a fallacy is the exclusive association between Arabic and Islam, and how such association fuels suspicion of Arabs (and Arabic) in the West.

As I look out of the Mercedes window and observe how we are descending from mountainous Maronite territory to hot and sticky Shia-populated plain, I scrabble for a foundation, parallel examples, from which to build empathy with Lebanon's fractious geography. I consider Pakistan and India's partition of 1947, hastily conceived by the British months before their final departure. Whilst I realise this was an entirely different case to Lebanon, I note the common feature that both Lebanon and Pakistan were states carved out of greater ones by departing colonial masters. In loose terms, both were done to provide an element of security to a religious minority which would otherwise be swamped in a larger state; Maronite Christians were the minority to be protected by the creation of Lebanon out of Greater Syria, and Muslims by the creation of Pakistan by partitioning British India into an eastern wing for Muslims (East Pakistan) and a western wing (West Pakistan). I wonder what the motivations of Jinnah, Nehru and the other anti-colonial leaders under the British Raj really were, and about how they might have differed from those of the leaders in Cham. I surmise the key difference is that whilst the creation of Pakistan was driven by the colonials themselves over decades of struggle, the creation of Lebanon was determined largely in Paris and done in the interests of a far smaller minority, tens of thousands of Maronites compared to the tens of millions of Muslims in British India. But rather than splintering as Pakistan and Bangladesh did, Lebanon has continued to struggle towards reaching a lasting form of political union or equilibrium. In this respect, Lebanon has arguably been a more sustained failure than the united Pakistan was ever allowed to be. Pakistan's principal (but by no means only) design fault, the concept of East and West, was ironed out, but Lebanon's design fault, the concept of balancing equal minorities continues to stymie it even in peacetime. Similar factionalism is now fracturing Syria too.

'We were taught to respect the Quran above all, but also to fear it and avoid it unless clean. We were not encouraged to touch or approach it without being in a proper state to do so,' I explain, talking to a disarmingly bold and confident shoe shiner on Rue Hamra in Beirut.

In his fifties I would guess, the shoe shiner has a full head of silvery dark hair, cropped and naturally arranged. I cannot resist looking into his eyes, strong and direct, honest and happy. Here is a man whose confident demeanour epitomises this incredible city's bold attitude to life, resistant to any notion of defeat or decline.

'For us, growing up in different parts of the world, much of the teachings of Islam have been a step removed,' I lament to the shoe shiner, as he puts some extra elbow grease into getting a shiny buff on my leather Camel boots.

My conversation with the shoe shiner underlines how access to elements of the religion is so dependent on understanding the Arabic language. Islam's principal religious text, the Quran, is at its most authentic in Arabic since this is the language in which it was revealed to the Prophet and the form in which it was originally committed to paper. As it is accepted as the authentic word of God, memorisation in Arabic is oftentimes, as in my childhood, emphasised more than understanding it in translation. Whilst the primary sources are all available in English and other languages, since the Quran is believed to be the revealed word of God, Muslims who do not understand it can experience an element of detachment, even incapacity, when they have to resort to consulting translations. After the initial years of disliking reading the Quran in Arabic without understanding it, gradually I came to appreciate that only in the original Arabic did the Quran's true beauty reveal itself: its poetry, its lyricism and its symmetry.

As an Arab and one who has never left Lebanon, these are challenges the shoe shiner is blissfully unaware of. Similarly, when I started Arabic classes, the stern Bilal rebuked me for being able to read Quran yet not understand it. He stopped short of calling me an idiot that day, but I certainly felt like one when I saw the look of horror on his face after I read a few lines from the Quran quite fluently in Arabic, but then couldn't tell him what any of it meant.

'Quran means "the reading" not "the storing",' he chuckles warmly, his eyes penetrating, his conviction unerring and strong, plucking a miniature copy of the Quran out of his pocket, unzipping it open, and quoting me a few more lines.

My mind wanders as the shoe shiner reads, his rendition of the Quran matter-of-fact as though reading from a text-book, and not refreshingly unmelodic. Our street-side conversation distracts me into thinking about how social hierarchy in some Muslim societies at times gets in the way of our developing a direct relationship with Allah. In my childhood, the social grading that I saw in Indian, Pakistani and Bengali communities extended to how religion was practised, and this had an impact on my feelings of a lack of real closeness to God. The insistence that children pray at the back of the mosque, or the conviction in some Paki-stani-run mosques in London that Urdu was a purer lan-guage than Bengali for conversing about religion, were just two examples of this. The bigoted claim about Urdu being a purer language for Islamic discourse emanated from how it was written in an Arabic-looking script* since the language had evolved from Hindustani specifically to become a

---

* Urdu is written in a script derived from Persian, which uses letters similar to Arabic. Urdu is grammatically, however, almost identical to modern-day Hindi, with both languages being derivatives of 'Hindustani', a common language spoken by many Hindus and Muslims in India during the time of the Mughals.

dialect for Muslims in Greater India. On the other hand, Bengali was the regional language of Bengal, and spoken not only by Muslims but by Hindus as well. Another example of hierarchy in how Islam was practised was that when it came to touching feet to show respect, I would never see my relatives touching the feet of our servants even when they were older. These and other manifestations of hierarchy had the impact of making me feel less capable, less empowered and less entitled to reach God than others.

'Reach out to God.'

This was Maulvi Sahib's advice to me when we discussed my mental preparations for an upcoming trip to Hajj.

'Make your connection with Him personal, make it real. Talk to Him directly and not through what it says in Hajj guides or through others' advice.' These words of wisdom remain with me to this day.

But then too many Muslims keep introducing a middleman. The mysterious role of the 'pir' was a version of such mediation I experienced during my childhood, and like many social and business structures, it came with the trappings of influence, control and manipulation. Pirs are saintly characters or soothsayers believed by their followers to be endowed with mystical powers. They are found commonly across India, Pakistan and Bangladesh and in other parts of the Muslim world where they are known by other titles, and of course pirs have their equivalents in all other faiths and civilisations too. Pirs are believed to have vested in them special powers and privileged access to God. Because of this, in the eyes of their followers, or 'murids', I used to find that they were revered as though their being a channel to God made them just a little godlike themselves. Pirs are men, always men it seems, of a status through whom interlocution in matters of divine inspiration can be sought. Murids go to huge lengths to serve and support their pirs, spending vast sums of money, travelling long distances and even giving up their jobs and their family allegiances. The pirs I have met have been fascinating characters. Most had strong Sufi qualities of mysticism, love and piety, and almost all were capable of showing great care and devotion to their disciples and for the Prophet. But how their mediatory role can be manipulated, once institutionalised with significant social, political and financial power, troubles me.

When in Dhaka every summer during childhood, we would pay annual visits to visit a relative known to most as Bara Bhai* in the locality of Bailey Road. Bara Bhai was one of Dhaka's most revered pirs, and the son of one of Kolkata's respected saints from the early- to mid-20th-century, known as Dadaji. A few years ago, armed with intriguing instructions to look for it behind a local cinema hall, I traced Dadaji's house tucked away in a narrow street close to the bustling Howrah Station in Kolkata. There was a simple man guarding over the tomb and tending to the flowers and plants that adorn it, and he told me that to this day dozens flock to the mausoleum to offer their respects. Amma would take us to Bara Bhai's palatial home once every few weeks during those long, hot summers, sitting

---

* Literally 'eldest brother'

with him discussing issues, problems and aspirations. Abba would drop us and pick us up after; he never commented on the trips but it was noticeable that he never came into the house himself.

A quiet but warm man and a cricket obsessive, Bara Bhai was surrounded by murids who would perform servile rituals in his presence. They would touch his feet, kiss his hands or kneel on the floor before him when they spoke to him. Performing full salaam honours was an absolute must, and Amma was distinctly nervous as to how I would behave on future visits to Bailey Road once I had undertaken my disgracful salaam revolt in Sylhet. Whilst I had affection for the man himself and saw qualities of wisdom and vision in him, I felt uncomfortable visiting Bara Bhai's home and experiencing the obsequious way people around him behaved in his presence. The behaviour of the coterie of disciples felt alien and my frustrations at this were on a par with my dislike of other cultural practices such as salaam. I could not reconcile the institutionalisation of the pir with my understanding of Islamic principles. I recognised that some of us have greater spirituality than others and that some people can be a valuable source of guidance and wisdom. I recognised that such people should be worthy of being treated with a special form of attention and respect. Consequently, and over time I grew into this, accepting that such 'genuine' pirs could indeed play an important role, almost as a mentor or guide, in spiritual and religious matters. But I could not understand how a pir's powers could be hereditary, disliked the servile ritual that had developed around them, and absolutely despised the habit of some pirs to sustain around themselves a network of high level contacts, followers and spiritual dependants who served to fortify their role, even finance them, and extend people's need for their intermediation.

Pirs have been part of the social landscape in the Indian subcontinent for many generations, dating back to the Mughals of the 16th century, and continuing traditions of Hindu soothsayers from before and somehow mixing this with the mystic traditions of Sufis from Turkey. Dynastic in succession, most pirs have handed down their status to their sons from generation to generation. Some follow quite open-minded routes to spiritual connection, paying attention to learning from other faiths and many have Hindu, Sikh and Buddhist followers as well as Muslims. Many pirs amass powerful social connections and considerable wealth, like the one who now lives in a posh locality of Dhaka in a castle-like mansion with haunting-looking Gothic-style windows and doors, and an impregnable and towering front gate. Of the several pirs I have seen, most have skilfully combined whatever spiritual connectedness they have with their worldly powers, with some doing so to formidable effect for their avid followers. Some pirs in village areas of Bangladesh are influential to the extent that they can convene groups of people in a way that politicians have to be careful about.

Like leaders in many walks of life, pirs are people whose real personality can become shrouded behind a cloak of ritual perpetuated by their closest followers. Murids would bring bottles of water for pirs to blow prayers on, from which they would drink for weeks afterwards or store in special places so that the surroundings would become blessed or protected from evil. Even years after Bara Bhai's death, disciples would bring vessels of drink or oil to his grand mausoleum, leaving them to be blessed by his departed soul before returning to collect them later. Many in my community swear by such rituals today, whereas I find such activities to be an antithesis to our basic beliefs that Islam is a religion of true surrender only to God, and that when a soul has departed, his place of burial bears no special powers. It is this type of activity that in a wider sense contributes to lending illegitimate power to many local religious leaders, drives blind behaviour amongst the ignorant and feeds non-Muslims' confusion over what the religion truly stands for.

Some Pakistani friends in London once insisted I visit their pir at his Hampstead Garden Suburb home for an evening of meditation. As we walked in, the couple warned me never to turn my back to the pir while in his presence, and that if I did he might curse me. The man himself may not actually be so bad, I thought, but it was the aura being created around him by his disciples which was the real issue. It seemed to me that my friends, both senior professionals, had fallen under the spell of that aura themselves despite all their worldly education and awareness.

Alongside pirs, during childhood I also experienced stories of jinns, never quite sure how much to believe in them. Jinns were explained to me to be like kindred spirits, good or evil, and capable of summoning special powers to do unimaginable things. They would often take human form, but would usually live alone. I was intrigued to learn that jinns have no shadow, and that this is how you can tell if you are in their presence. My paternal uncles in Sylhet used to tell me how they knew a helpful jinn in Sonarpur, who would bring them medicines only available in pharmacies in faraway Dhaka or sweets from a particular store in Bombay, leaving packages outside the door within minutes of their asking for it. Another told me once how he and his friends one night saw an eight-foot tall jinn walking towards them in an alley in Sylhet, and about how one should never pray deep inside a mosque at night as the jinns pray then and that if they are disturbed, they will literally throw you to the back of the prayer hall. Defying common scientific wisdom and way outside the boundaries of any empirical evidence, I didn't believe these stories. In fact I thought it was claptrap; tales from uncles who thought they could make a fool out of a young and impressionable 'Ingleesh' nephew who was visiting Bangladesh and was good for a bit of ridicule.

But then one night when driving in Dhaka, I experienced the presence of a jinn myself, the spirit of a young, deceased woman. I was seventeen years old and in Bangladesh for the holidays. The family clan were at our home, attending a dinner party. It was already late and Khala and my cousin Tina, the same girl who as a woman many years later was to move to Saudi Arabia, had to go home. I drove them, having just learnt to drive. Once outside their home, I let the Datsun's engine tick over as I waited for the two ladies to unlock the gates to Khala's house and go in. Job done, I eased off the handbrake and headed home. Looking carefully to the left and right and enjoying the easy movement of the clutch between gear changes, I approached the junction with Road No. 9, the busy route through Banani that is used frequently by commuters looking for a shortcut. The tall betel trees that line the road were swaying gently. All of a sudden I felt as though someone was watching me. As I took the turn, there was a laugh from the back seat. A young woman, about my age. I was puzzled, certain that I had seen Tina and Khala get out of the car and go inside their house.

'Perhaps Tina's still in the car, playing a trick on me?' I wondered, confused, as I knew that my cousin wasn't the type to play such pranks.

The girl laughed again, mocking me, only it didn't sound like my fourteen-year-old cousin; the voice was older, more mature. I glanced at the rear-view mirror and saw the statuesque profile of a young woman sitting in the centre of the back seat, looking straight ahead. I could not see her face, only a black silhouette in stark contrast to the silent headlights of a truck way behind us. It was quiet all around, the Banani roads deserted and silent.

'Tina? Eh, Tina?' I laughed out nervously, knowing it wasn't her. 'Tumi naki? Is it you?'

Instinctively I looked into the rear-view mirror again, and this time I could see from her profile that the girl had long, flowing hair. She sat tall and upright, her head almost touching the rear of the car's low roofline. Her stillness showed her to have strength and confidence, yet at the same time her voice was flirty and playful. The cool of the evening air turned to a chill inside the car, as I scrabbled around for ideas as to what this might be. My confusion turned rapidly to fear.

'Bismillah-ir-Rahman-ir-Raheem,"* I said out aloud, gripping harder on the Datsun's spindly steering wheel.

Continuing to keep the car moving, I needed to confirm whether it is a real person or some sort of apparition. Gasping for air and oblivious for a moment of where I was, distracting thoughts began to pass through my mind. Taking a sharp intake of breath, and gripping the steering wheel extra hard to make sure the car wouldn't swerve, I decided to look round. The back of the car was empty. As I stared at the emptiness of the back seat, all I could make out were the white lines of stitching on the seat cushion as they contrasted with the blackness of the car's interior. The foot wells were dark, like deep, bottomless pools. I checked them to make sure that nobody was hiding down there, playing a practical joke. I was alone, and trembling. I felt my heart pumping inside my shirt, beating hard from the realisation that I was in the presence of something unreal, a spirit or a jinn. Perhaps it was the distressed soul of a dead woman looking for a connection of some sort.

I felt vulnerable, touchable. Of all my fears, the greatest was that she would reach forward and make contact with my body, brushing the hairs on the back of my tense neck

---

* Arabic for 'In the name of God, the Beneficent, the Merciful'.

with what I imagined would be her slender, bony fingers. I tried to scream, but no sound came out. My legs were stuck, as though in cement; my voice muted. My heart beat harder, throbbing in my eardrums. I squeezed the steering wheel harder, my knuckles sticking up in profile above the dark, sweeping line of the Datsun's plastic dashboard, my fingers moist and their tips pulsing with circulation. I waved my knees restlessly from side to side and said prayers, my recitation jumbled in a frenzy of Arabic and English.

'La-ilaaha illallah, LA-ILAAHA ILLALLAH,'* I called out desperately as we hurtled down Kemal Ataturk Avenue, the speed of the car edging up towards forty miles per hour.

All along she laughed, ridiculing me, baiting me to do something silly, to go to her, to join her. I sensed her desire to transform this momentary connection into something more meaningful and lasting. Like an attractive girl egging a guy on, it was like she was watching me, provoking me. But physical contact would forge a connection: she a spirit and me a living being, and so I focused on the road and on finishing the short journey. I could feel the heat of her gaze on the back of my neck. I imagined her fingertips stroking the hair on the back of my head, bristling through my curls and scratching my scalp with her nails. I felt helpless and heavy, my knees and ankles knotty at the joints, my stomach tight against the top of my jeans. I wanted to tuck my legs together but I had to keep driving. I was conscious that the top buttons of my shirt were undone. I was defenceless.

---

* Arabic for 'There is no God but God, There is no God but God'; a central plank of all Muslims' belief and often recited in times of need.

I drove at higher and higher speed, on a sure path to disaster. My senses convinced me that I had the car under full control, but at the same time I knew that the extra velocity was taking me no further away from my back-seat tormentor. I slowed down, gradually guiding the car back to thirty miles per hour as we approached Airport Road. I tightened my grip on the wheel again and, taking a deep breath and in a show of strength, glanced round once more. I twisted my torso from the waist up this time, giving me a better angle to look behind but also relieving my back and shoulders from the danger of being touched by those bony fingertips. There was nobody there. I looked forwards again. At the usually busy crossroads there were no vehicles approaching, and I hurried across without coming to the mandatory stop. Once over, only the railway line stood between me and home. The car's narrow tyres trundled across the shiny steel rails; my determination to remain calm was disintegrating into a desperate scramble to reach home as we approached the finishing line. The headlight beam of the Datsun dipped momentarily as the car angled off the shallow slope from the tracks and back onto the tarmac. As I passed the local mosque and turned right into 5th Street, barely three hundred metres from home, I remembered that Fufu's first-floor apartment was just on the corner. Swiftly I turned the car into her driveway, turned off the engine and ran upstairs.

As I return to the real world from my reveries, I realise that the shoe shiner has long since finished his work. He has lit up a cigarette, which he puffs on with some need, having worked hard on my boots and earned himself a break. I take one more look at him and engage with that confident gaze, shake his hand and pay him a few dollars extra and move on. This is my last afternoon in Beirut, and it's fitting that one of the final people I meet here is one whose attitude epitomises the character of this city.

Despite it being outpaced by the cut and thrust of Beirut, the Westernising aspirations of Istanbul or the small-town feistiness of Latakia, I harbour a special affection for Damascus because this is where I fastened myself to the task of mastering Arabic. It was in the eternal city that I put behind me years of frustration emanating from how my parents, Maulvi Sahib and my wider family community had, out of ignorance not malice, seeded misplaced notions of Arabic and its relationship with Islam. Damascus delivered me from the burden of decades of misconception. It was here that I experienced how close Christians and Muslims really are when you strip away the cultural differences of language, race and food. This is where I first saw Christians praying in Arabic, and where I witnessed Muslims calling the faithful to prayer in the style that Christians used in the Byzantine period, and where I saw Christians and Muslims worshipping under the same roof. Damascus was like long-awaited therapy.

It was during a tour of the monastery of St Sergius in Maa'loula, a town some sixty kilometres northeast of Damascus, that our Christian guide recited the Lord's Prayer first in Aramaic, and then in her native Arabic. In Arabic the verses sounded similar to Surah Fat'ha, the opening verse of the Quran and the one recited by every Muslim in every prayer, and once translated back into English, it all made perfect sense to me. Of course, I realised, when Arab Christians call god, they say 'Allah' just as Georges did during the drive to the Bekaa Valley in Lebanon, driving us down from those chilly mountains. Plainly obvious, you might think, but again it made a difference when I felt the difference myself by spending time in the Christian and Jewish quarters of Aleppo and old Damascus.

'So how did they become Christians in Syria?' one of my friends asked me back in London.

'Erm, Jesus happened to have been born about a hundred miles from there,' I replied to her sarcastically, restraining myself from adding that Christ wasn't an Englishman born in Westminster Abbey.

Understandably she wasn't pleased with my facetiousness, and I should really have held back from giving her a sarcastic response. But her reaction confirmed how in the minds of so many (Christians or Muslims) the locus of Christianity is firmly in the West, leaving the Middle East and the Arabic language to be bundled conveniently with Islam. And so to thousands of Muslims, uttering phrases or giving names in Arabic is one of the most visible ways in which they differentiate themselves from non-Muslims. Many use Arabic for impact, employing phrases and words even when they don't know what they mean. One of my favourite dinner-party tricks is to read to guests from a Bible bought from a Coptic Cairo bookstore. The script looks and sounds like something from Quran, and when I read it, virtually no non-Arabic-speaking guest will believe it is the Bible. Most insist it is Quran and some are almost angry with me when I say it is the Bible, as though I am saying something unacceptable and heinous. The exercise serves to illustrate a point, which is that the belief gap between Muslims and Christians is small, especially when we remove cultural and linguistic differences. Language has become another of the erroneous barriers that puts distance between our communities. Being in the town of Maa'loula not only reminded me of my own conditioning, misconceptions and weaknesses in this respect, but to an extent helped complete the healing of this wound too.

Steeped in over forty centuries of urban history, Old Damascus is a four-thousand-year-old city of some five square kilometres, set within stone walls erected during the Roman period, adorned with a splendour inside them that is unmistakably Ottoman. In its grandeur, taking in the breadth and depth of this city's antiquity makes Istanbul's own Grand Bazaar seem like a modern shopping mall. Mark Twain once wrote that Damascus is so old that all of world history that's ever been recorded would have had the despatches sent here. Labyrinthine alleys, cobbled paths and narrow, winding streets connect its landmarks in hundreds of different ways. Rather like its history, the old city's colour scheme is layered too. The dominant colour is the light brown of the sand-coloured masonry which complements Damascus' dusty, arid air, this being a settlement that has lain in the middle of this flat, hot plain overlooked by mountains since well before the time of Mohammad or

Christ. Refreshing contrast is provided by the lush and fragrant green of the creepers overhead that offer a canopy, and the bougainvillea with its pink and crimson blush which trespasses everywhere, following no rules or guidelines for where it grows. In this respect Damascus is in contrast to Syria's principal northern city, Aleppo. That too is an ancient settlement, of a similar vintage, but dominated by a central and magnificent enclosed fort, with interesting markets and settlements around it. Damascus' Old City is far larger and more elaborate than Aleppo's fort area, and once inside the city walls, it conveys the feeling of full-fledged city as opposed to fortified building.

Damascus' architectural, political and historic masterpiece is the magnificent Umayyad Mosque, rivalling Granada's Alhambra for finesse, Istanbul's Blue Mosque for scale and Agra's Taj Mahal for emotion. In normal times before today's civil war, at night the blinding beams of halogen lamps would illuminate its marble minarets in dazzling white relief against the night sky. Insomniac birds and confused bats would flutter under the lights, failing to find a place to settle. The whirr of their wings made a hundred echoing sounds, each of which bounces around the Umayyad's marbled courtyard to make a haunting chorus. I have always marvelled at the Umayyad, although I feel sadness at seeing any place that has been altered from use by one faith to that for another. Santa Sofia in Istanbul went from being a church to a mosque. The Mezquita in Cordoba went the other way, where the brutal masonry alterations that inserted rough-edged stone columns in place of thin pillars are part of a hasty Christian makeover which marked the end of Muslim rule in Spain. The Gothic architecture violates the Mezquita's innermost sanctity, something which apparently the visiting Ferdinand, leader of the Spanish reconquest, berated the local Cordoban mayor for allowing to happen. How it brought tears to my eyes when first I saw it. The Spanish Police all but arrested me when I began a small prayer at the mihrab,* having been advised to do so by the imam of Madrid's main mosque. As I insisted I should be left alone to complete a quiet prayer, two Spanish policemen pulled me back onto my heels and began to drag me away, offering no explanation as to what authority they had to prevent me from praying in a public place of worship.

The Umayyad's diminutive dome, stained-glass windows and turret-like tower at one corner reveal how it has followed a more gradual evolution than the abrupt defacement experienced by the Mezquita. Originally a holy site for the Aramaeans, it was then a temple celebrating the Roman god Jupiter and finally a basilica dedicated to John the Baptist, whose tomb is still there, right inside the mosque. Muslims pay their respects here too, since to them John is a significant figure, the Prophet Yahya in Arabic. When the Muslims took Damascus in AD 636 the basilica was initially shared, with the Muslims praying in its eastern wing and the Christians in the western part.

Whereas in all other mosques I have visited, the call to prayer, referred to in Arabic as the 'adhan', is delivered by a

---

* A niche or decorative panel inside a mosque which designates the direction of qiblah.

solitary muezzin, at the Umayyad it is sung by a chorus of six men. This carries forward a Byzantine tradition for calling the faithful used in the Christian era. On my last visit, I somewhat cockily approached the Umayyad's chief muezzin to ask him to permit me to join in the adhan.

I crave the ability to recite a melodious adhan, a performance that will confine to history years of sheepish efforts of chanting in the corners of relatives' living rooms, trousers rolled up and palms behind ears, wondering all along if I can possibly risk stretching out the next syllable for a few more seconds. Not exactly endowed with talent in this department, the muezzin laughed me out of the room after asking me to give it my best shot by reciting a couple of lines in his office.

'What did you eat for breakfast, brother?' was his unexpected question as I prepared to leave the room.

'Fowl, bread, coffee and watermelon.'

'Battaikh! Watermelon!' he laughed loudly, instructing me that the muezzin must never interfere with the texture of his throat before duty, and that watermelon is the worst culprit.

With a solemn-eyed 'I am sorry, I cannot help you', he patted me gently on the shoulder, smiled cheekily, and sent me on my way. As I traipsed off, shoulders slumped, the muezzin must have taken pity as he called me back, handed me a used-looking cassette tape and told me to revise the lessons in it and return the next day. With nowhere discreet to practise a loud recital of adhan without attracting suspicion, I stood by a traffic-filled main road, my exhortations neatly drowned out by vehicle noise.

Old Damascus is a high-walled maze of narrow alleys and gullies, darting off in a confusing multitude of directions. A casual visitor walking around the old city, I seldom make it directly to a specific destination. It doesn't really matter. Sylhet's claustrophobic alleyways make me want to escape but Damascus encourages me to explore its deepest recesses, rather like Istanbul during that Bosphorus boat ride when I attended that wedding. Every crooked path and alley has a series of left and right turns which in some way resembles another set somewhere else. I can never see more than a few metres ahead and each short straight begs investigation as to what might be around the next corner, baiting me to unfurl its mysteries. The narrow paths limit my perspective and confuse my sense of direction, but their intrigue feeds my curiosity while their safety leaves me with no fear about proceeding. With the streets changing their atmosphere every few metres, my most determined logistical plans fall away until I gradually discard the rationality of having a destination, and the functionality of having a route. As soon as I see a mosque, I want to know where the next church is, and when I spot a man drinking from an Ottoman-era water tap, I wonder how far it will be to the next one. Damascus' anatomy resembles the complexities of my own heart and mind, and the city's temptations to reach inwards are instantly therapeutic. As I explore its mysteries, so does the city and its thousand adhans casually unravel my own. Damascus' ability to reach inwards is subtle, caring and strangely therapeutic.

Awaiting the onset of evening prayer, the call of the Umayyad muezzin reverberates through the building's cloisters. The voice radiates across the city and adjacent buildings bounce the sound waves back, lending the adhan the mysterious qualities of a rippling echo.

'Allahu-akbar, allahu-akbar
Allahu-akbar, allahu-akbar
Ash-hadoo allah ilaha illallah
Ash-hadoo allah ilaha illallah . . .'

The syllables of each word are joined together seamlessly, leaving the muezzin's mouth like a flowing stream full of sonic rises and falls, peaks and troughs. Today's adhan is an operatic performance, a superlative form of the florid chant which most muezzins deliver so lyrically, tuned to perfection through daily repetition. For these moments the adhan is Damascus' epicentre, and for the first time in weeks, prayer lifts me up from the captivity of worldly thoughts. As it soaks through this city of mazes, the muezzin's voice ushers my mind into its own alleys and cul-de-sacs, reaching sensitively into its shadowy corners. Heart and soul are laid bare like an artefact ready to be explored, rearranged and carefully restored.

I can see and touch the walls of Sylhet now, and wind down the windows of the Sunbeam Arrow as we edge along Chinbrook Road, watching the boys spit at Amma and me.

---

* Each line is recited twice: 'God is great, God is great, I witness that there is only one God and no god except God, I witness that Mohammad is his messenger'.

There is no desire to confront the veils and curtains any more, the feelings of exclusion are dissolving, and the memories are chapters neatly filed away as passages of personal history. Now I am pushing at open doors elsewhere, exploring the sights and scents within. I think of the men on the front bench at the Hazaripur mosque in Sylhet and of myself, my angers and frustrations. I wonder when I will be able to see beyond our labyrinthine worlds and emulate what Socrates referred to in his final words:

'I am wiser than this person; for it is likely that neither of us knows anything good and beautiful, but he thinks he knows something not knowing, while I, as one who does not know, do not think that I do. Therefore I went away from him being a little wiser in just this respect, that what I do not know I do not think that I know.'[*]

Bizarrely, the last time I prayed at the Umayyad during a Ramadan visit to Syria, a German television documentary film crew was recording the proceedings in the mosque. The imam spoke freely and fluently and traversed many subjects, focusing on the principle of the fast and concluding with a plea for Allah to relieve all who suffer on the earth, singling out special mention for the people of Iraq, Palestine and Kashmir. He inhaled one final breath to complete his address.

'We pray for the health of our President, Bashar al Assad.'

Unlike Lebanon where pictures of Sunni, Hizbullah and Christian leaders vie for every available square inch of wall

---

[*] From Plato's *Apology*, in which he quotes and defends Socrates after the latter's trial in 399 BC.

space, for decades in Syria there has been no such competition for iconic imagery. This is reserved for the President, Bashar al Assad, and his late father, Hafez. Ever since Hafez became President in 1971, the people of this country have been looking at the faces of one or other of the Assad clan. An enormous bust of Hafez, some two metres high and immortalised in gold like the Pharaohs of Egypt, sits shining and lonely at the entrance to the Military Museum near the historic Hejaz Railway Station. His face, calm and composed, looks on ominously from the station, a place I associated with the World War I escapades of T. E. Lawrence, as he plotted with Arab factions the overthrow of the Ottomans and their German allies to remove them from the Levant. The imagery of leadership in Syria is so ubiquitous that it permeates everything, inspiring some and irritating others. But like all things so widespread, the images are largely ignored and the statues are destined to one day be discarded and forgotten.

Lost in thoughts of closing cultural gaps and completing my own journey, this politicised utterance by the imam of the Umayyad brought me back to earth with a crash, not expecting to hear the President's name uttered in prayers of remembrance in the mosque. As I consider these Damascene experiences today, in light of the current civil war and the challenges it has brought to the Assad regime, some of my observations about Syria ring true – that this is one of those Middle Eastern countries where an iconic culture and a deep-rooted network of informants and intelligence are an integral part of the set-up that legitimises and jealously protects those in power.

My love for this enchanting city came partly from the vivacity of its people, despite the presence of crony leaders who have served these same people decades of great disservice. One of the people that epitomised my affection for Damascus was Ahmad Moualla, the Syrian modern artist who agreed to meet me one afternoon. When I call to ask if there might be an opportunity to . . .

'Now?' he says in Arabic, after some short words of customary welcome.

'Sure, it doesn't have to be right now, anytime in the ne—. . .'

'Now? Are you ready now?'

'Sure, yes.'

Standing in the doorway of his apartment, Ahmad Moualla greets the taxi driver who brings me here as warmly as he greets me. The hüzün that burdens other intellectuals is evidently irrelevant to this one. This man's face is lined with creases and marked by exhaustion, but nothing can conceal an overwhelming sense of energy and contentment. Moualla is one of Syria's foremost artists and his work adorns galleries and posters all over this country and many others.* Most of his work is created in a studio in the dusty suburb of Qudsiyya, about twenty kilometres north of Damascus. Dressed in a messy Arab tunic and sandals, he offers me a choice of coffee or cigarettes. When I tell him I am fasting, he says he isn't and lights up another smoke.

---

* https://www.artsy.net/artist/ahmad-moualla

Having called him at the behest of a friend in London, standing before him now, I am unsure as to what I am supposed to do or say. I hesitate. I wonder why I have come here to bother this busy man at all and how soon I can return to Damascus, to the safety of the traveller's anonymity. Ahmad shows me the output of a new project, 'Daleel Watani' or 'A Guide to Citizenship'. It is a collection of photographs of plaster and clay images evoking the book's four themes on citizenship. One of the pictures shows a grey clay figure with a disfigured face, and a square gap where his heart should be. Blackness is coming out of his empty mouth, like vomit, and despite the removal of his heart, the figure is at pains to offer a hollow, ironic smile. It reminds me of a shocking Salvador Dali statue, spewing blood, in his museum at Figueres in Catalonia, which almost made me physically sick when looking at it. From Figueres my mind jumps to the Dali in the lobby of the Quality Inn in Tripoli, the city with its heart replaced by the faceless void of the trade-fair complex. The vulnerability and innocence of Ahmad's smiling clay figure resonates with that of the Aroma barista in Damascus, and of all the other people in this world without voice. As we leaf through the book, I am still lacking confidence, hoping that the rest of our discussion might be concluded in another few minutes. Just then, he stops.

'Let us talk.'

'Oh, no. What on earth am I going to talk about now?' I panic. 'I can't conduct such a conversation in Arabic.'

He gestures towards a chair, signalling that I should sit

down. He looks at me, his large eyes fired with belief. I stare back at him and he waits patiently.

'Huzun,' I stammer, not knowing what on earth I am doing.

'Huzun?'

'Huzun.' The seconds are running out and I need to articulate something sensible.

I begin hesitantly with a dribble of words about a story in Istanbul, to Lebanon, of decline and of hüzün. He likes 'hazin', as it is in Arabic, and we elaborate on it, building a theme from an incoherent and stuttering start. Ahmad suggests that Beirut is an exception to hüzün because its people are wealthier; live more in the world of material things than elsewhere in Lebanon. As we speak I settle, and within a few moments we are in flowing discussion, the gaps in my Arabic and his English now being filled by whatever words from whichever languages we can find between us. In a mini-performance of dialogue without borders, we let go of the boundaries offered by form and syntax, and for the next hour and a half, we argue, look at paintings and review photographs in a language which is as strange a melange as it is untethered to any source. I leave smiling, telling him that I've seen the painting he did for my friend in London which hangs on her wall.

'Yes, that one was "Nescafé with pastels",' he laughs.

My afternoon with Moualla sums up the romantic notion I will always hold of Damascus, the warm-hearted and civilised city with a sense of not only its own but of the whole world's history, the fragrance and colours of its windy and mysterious pathways and the innocence of its warm and welcoming people.

Moualla also inspired me to spend more of my life resisting the symbolism and hierarchy that I have seen in the world, and to search for the realities that lie beneath. I have experienced feared pirs, revered saints, knuckle-fisted political leaders, family patriarchs, elders who expect servile behaviour and arrogant headmasters who see children as their subjects and classrooms as their fiefdom. As I listen to the muezzin at the Umayyad, I am distracted yet again. I return to the mosque in Hazaripur and to the prayers of my father. Here was a man with a status on par with the local elders and entitled to a seat on the front row, yet Abba was a man who would pray anonymously, dressed in trousers and a shirt, and more often than not stand in line amongst a mob of noisy and fidgety teenagers somewhere near the back. He would pray quietly and leave, and when he donated to the mosque fund, by and large he would do it quietly. His prayer was as unceremonious as it was genuine.

Twelve

Trusted Adviser

Approaching forty, I felt more than ever before the need to find my true partner in life. I needed an anchor and someone I could love and who loved me without questions, someone I had been looking for ever since leaving home all those years ago. Rehana and I were introduced by mutual friends who set us up on a 'blind date'. A young lawyer, Rehana had been working in the UK for a few years, having moved there from Brisbane, Australia. She helped me uncover the path to my unfulfilled potential, something I felt I had lost track of over the past few years. In Rehana's opinion, rather like Giovanni's, I was wasting my talent. She urged me to reclaim the path I had taken before, and as well as helping me refocus, Rehana helped me relax. Barely a year after we met, we were married, had had our first child and spent several months living in South Africa where I was closing a major deal. We had perhaps too much to deal with so quickly after marriage, and struggled with the tidal wave of change at first. But over time, we started to bring out the best in each other.

I left my job to join one of the world's leading mobile tele-communications operators, and we moved to Egypt where I took up a senior role in the company's operations there. Cairo was the start of an adventure which would see us move continuously eastwards for the next decade. On the first afternoon after we arrived, when a taxi driver threw our luggage onto the open-air roof rack of his black and yellow Fiat and told us to forget about a car seat for baby Ehsan, we laughed out loud that this was going to be a roller-coaster ride. We started off at a hotel originally built as a palace for Napoleon Bonaparte, dined on luxury yachts on the Nile and drove across the romantic desert behind the pyramids of Giza every morning to bypass traffic and get to work on time. At every chance, we would climb into our four-wheel drive and explore. We would go to the Sinai desert, south to El Gouna and Hurghada, or west to the remarkable oasis of Fayoum. A Ghanaian friend in London, almost a brother to me, had let me know me that Kwame Nkrumah's son lived in Cairo. He knew of my fascination with President Nkrumah, the founder of Ghana and one of Africa's first post-colonial leaders.

'Gamal is his name. And he works for Cairo's leading newspaper. Look him up if you get the chance.'

Months after we moved to Cairo, one evening a journalist I was sitting next to at a dinner told me she knew Gamal and that he was her colleague at *Al-Ahram* newspaper. Minutes later she connected me to him on her mobile. We talked, met up a week later and became good friends.

During our stay in Cairo, we would spend time at Gamal's mansion, a lavish but now-tired looking villa on the edge of the Nile River, gifted to his late father President Kwame Nkrumah by President Nasser of Egypt on the occasion of Nkrumah's wedding to a Coptic Christian. While the young Ehsan would roam around the deserted mansion, Gamal, Rehana and I would look over photographs of the two late heads of state in discussions about the Non-Aligned Movement.*

When we moved to the land of the Pharaohs, there was an overhanging fear that President Hosni Mubarak's regime was approaching the end, after almost three decades. Despite (or perhaps because of) the euphoria of a visit to Cairo University from the newly elected President Barack Obama, the heat placed on the regime from local democracy groups had started turning up. In a desperate attempt to guard against an uprising, the government started putting pressure on telecommunications operators to allow them free access to the networks. Responsible for external affairs, I bore the burden of this, facing off senior military officials who were concerned about terrorists hacking the mobile networks or civil groups mobilising mass protests. Nervy meetings would take place in government buildings. Understanding the Arabs well, I could almost smell the officials' fears of the political turmoil they wanted to somehow avoid. Barely a year later, thousands of protestors were converging in Tahrir Square, the same spot where I had been

---

* The Non-Aligned Movement (NAM) is a group of states that are not formally aligned with or against any major power bloc, founded in 1956 by Josip Broz Tito of Yugoslavia, Jawaharlal Nehru of India, Sukarno of Indonesia, Gamal Abdul Nasser of Egypt and Kwame Nkrumah of Ghana.

questioned by the Egyptian intelligence authorities a few years before. We watched on TV from our flat in Marylebone, with me excitedly calling my friends in Egypt to say I wish I could be with them.

For in the end, President Mubarak's demise was hastened not by arms and ammunitions but by the messages enabled over the communications network, principally Facebook, that mobilised tens of thousands of people. Rehana and I had wept when we left Cairo for the final time, so much had we enjoyed our time there. There is a saying among the Cairene that once you taste the water of the Nile, you can never leave it behind. The joke is that once you taste the water of the Nile, you will die right there. We had fallen in love with the vivacity of the city and with the people of Egypt.

Just over a year after moving back to London, I rejoined my old firm and we moved to India. There was a lot going on with the development of mobile and internet there, and I was hungry to be part of the action. We had loved being in Egypt, and with a young family, we were still mobile and keen to see more of the developing world. Since starting my career, I had always wanted to work in the subcontinent, having spent months at a time in Bangladesh. Professionally, India was the main draw in the region, as it was a compelling growth market desperately in need of experienced advisers who could make a difference. It was fascinating to experience living in such a multicultural country as someone who speaks several of her languages, bears a local skin complexion and yet has the rather different perspective of a foreigner. As Muslims, we found India difficult at times, given many Indians' hatred of neighbouring Pakistan being conflated with animosity towards Muslims, general disdain towards other neighbouring Muslim nations (such as Bangladesh), and a sometimes misplaced notion that Indian Muslims were treated in completely the same way as Hindus. Legally and constitutionally this appears to be the case, but I remain unconvinced that under Prime Minister Modi secular India continues to deliver the same privileges of equality to religious minorities as it has to the Hindu majority. The defensiveness some Indians feel over the treatment of Muslims is something I have seen ever since my Oxford Majlis days, when there would be heated debates between a few of us over India's treatment of minorities. Although Bangladesh (with the Chakmas) and Pakistan (with Bengalis, Hindus and Balochis) have transgressed against minorities, I haven't seen such resistance to criticism from Bangladeshis or Pakistanis when it comes to calling out their activities over the treatment of minorities. It is almost as though India has given itself too heavy a burden of expectation, given that it is the largest and most established democracy in the region and a self-professed secular state (whereas Pakistan is an Islamic Republic).

The Indian disdain pertaining to Pakistan mirrored my earlier experience of spending time visiting and working on projects in Pakistan too, where there was a unifying dislike for India on a wide scale, and within that a complex animosity towards Indian Muslims as well. As a Bangladeshi, I found this mutual chauvinism between Indians and Pakistanis to be self-obsessed. It was of course open to political manipulation by leaders too, that so many have exploited, especially before important elections. 'Crush India' badges worn by kids in Pakistan, and Pakistan-hate posters at my local gym in Mumbai, epitomised this general mutual dislike. What irritated me most about this was the de-humanising element of such propaganda, as it meant that ordinary people in India and Pakistan were prevented from forming connections across borders to celebrate so many shared elements of culture, history, language and ways of living. Peace wasn't a priority agenda item in my view, as politicians on both sides were probably happier with having a level of controlled enmity as a useful asset. I never experienced personal animosity in India from clients or colleagues, but as time went on and especially when Prime Minister Narendra Modi* came to power, I feared that matters for Indian Muslims would get worse.

During our stay in India, Amma's sudden death came to pass in London in early 2013. Instinctively I had skipped a family holiday over that Christmas to go to the UK to see her, as she hadn't been keeping well, and was thankful that I did, given that I would have been in Australia otherwise, over 20 hours' flight away. A week before she died, I could feel it approaching, and so I put the word out to Rehana to rush over if she could. She and Ehsan flew right away and Jamal picked them up weary-eyed at the airport and whisked them to the hospital where I was on duty receiving streams of visitors day and night, praying, reading Quran in

---

* Modi is alleged to have been aware of massacres of Muslims in Gujarat in 2002 at the time that he was Chief Minister of the State, though he has denied any involvement.

the waiting room, chatting and catching up with relatives not seen in years. A few days later we buried my mother at the cemetery in Luton, thirty kilometres north of London, in the same graveyard where my father was buried twenty-one years before her.

We interred Amma on that short, windswept January evening, just a few hours after she had died and in a Muslim style 'open coffin', where you leave a metre of clear space above the body, created by fitting wooden slats across the grave so that the soil can be dropped in above that. Both my parents were now gone, the one who had over the years drilled the goodness and regular practise of Islam into us, and the other who had shown us how to wear our wisdom quietly and lightly. My last few years with Amma had been more harmonious than earlier ones where we had clashed from time to time, during those years when I carried guilt over not spending as much time looking after her as my sister did. In recent years I had become clearer about the differences between living my life and choosing where to live, and that no matter what I did in these matters, it could still be compatible with caring for my mother.

Barely a fortnight after Amma's death and once we were back in Mumbai, Rehana was involved in a major car accident where our driver suffered a fit while at the wheel, drove for one minute in a frenzied daze at high speeds through the narrow streets of Bandra where we lived, ran down two innocent people who later died and piled into a traffic junction at high speed. Rehana miraculously survived albeit with serious injuries, the driver was beaten on the streets before his arrest and a year later was jailed for homicide, and we remained the subject of intense press and TV scrutiny for days until the matter settled down. Our lives were turned upside down as a result, and it took us years to get past this, including at the start, finding ways to deal with the emotional shock of how other innocent people had lost their lives and had their families forever impacted. As our India adventure and another testing chapter of life drew towards a close, we were expecting our second child. This time, with Amma gone and my London career options looking less appealing than what my firm planned for me to do in Asia, we decided to have the baby in Brisbane, where Rehana's family is based and take matters from there. We named him Zaki, an Arabic name meaning intelligent, and the middle name Ali, in remembrance of my father who also had the same middle name.

To recover from the emotional exhaustion of that last, difficult year in India, I took a few months off work, and during this time I got a call from the Minister of Communications in Myanmar who asked me to help his country prepare their first ever sector master plan. Otherwise known as Burma, Myanmar was preparing for a transition to civilian government after decades of military rule since independence from the British in 1948. Over the course of a few months when I'd fly in the Myanmar for two weeks at a time, usually dressed in official Burmese longyee,* I worked with a committed team in the capital Nai Pyi Taw,

---

* Traditional Burmese dress for men, and very similar to the 'lungi' worn in Bangladesh.

balancing my understanding of technology, economics and politics to help finalise the plan in preparation for Myanmar's first parliamentary election.

Largely ignorant of Indonesia and its politics until moving there, when I settled into the megacity of Jakarta to begin a two-year stint with my firm's South East Asia practice, I began to appreciate that this vast country is one of the most liberal and open-minded Muslim countries I have seen. With a population of over 250 million, most of whom are not connected to the internet, I became involved in the nation-building challenge of driving Indonesia's modernisation agenda. With my family by now fully based in Australia, I took on the role in Jakarta on a commuting basis, making it back to Brisbane once every two or three weekends for a few days, before getting on another flight out again. This was from a personal perspective yet more hardship for us as a family, with all of us weathering the pain of family isolation in rather different ways. For me, I suffered prolonged periods of loneliness at times, whiling away evenings in my flat in Jakarta, aimlessly watching TV or working out in the gym, an unfair burden of responsibility on Rehana to look after the family's needs on a day to day basis without much support, and unfulfilled weekends for Ehsan who couldn't bear to see me leave the house on a Sunday night to fly back up to Asia.

There is an easy-going way in which Islam is practised in Indonesia, and Muslim identity doesn't appear to be as conflicting a topic as it is in the West. Steeped in local community beliefs and traditions, and with people who are respectful and modest in demeanour, Indonesia is similar to how Bangladesh was a few years ago. As in Bangladesh, many Indonesians take non-Arab names, such as Agung, Lucy or Robert. Most dress in shirts and trousers and relatively few men keep beards. Seldom are Indonesians seen in Arab tunics, shalwar kameez or Palestinian design black-and-white cheque scarves. Yet the vast majority are observant of Islam; in my office, there was space for wudhu* and prayer on every floor. Dozens of colleagues anonymously trickled in and out of prayer rooms all day before returning to conference calls, slide presentations or client meetings. Whilst many Indonesians take their beliefs and daily rituals with seriousness, they appear comfortable in interpreting the faith through the context of existing culture and tradition. This flexibility is central to the pluralism of my faith.

If you were to take a piece of string, a long piece of string, to a globe and connect London to Cairo, to Mumbai and then to Jakarta, stretching the line forward would land you in Australia, which is precisely where we have landed. Marrying the Aussie I met years ago in London, neither of us had an inkling back then or even a few years' ago that settling in Australia might be on the cards. How events unfolded in the months after Rehana's accident in Mumbai changed all that.

Moving to Australia presented me with a new challenge. Here is a country that desires to embrace new generation technologies to transform from being a mineral-exporting, China-dependent economy to one that earns a more

---

* ablution

esteemed place in the broader, emerging Asian economic system. This is how I define the national challenge from an economic perspective, and part of my job is to have the debate with clients to balance out different perspectives about what this nation wants to be. Australia needs more digital capabilities to enrich how it adds value through the talent and creativity of its people and through technology and innovation, to create greater inclusion of people in remote, rural and indigenous communities and to be less dependent on the value of extraction from the earth. Today, the nation's politics reveal a schizophrenia about Asia, seeing her both as a new marketplace as well as a threat to national security and a source of too much immigration. The struggle emanates from perceiving there is a trade-off between being adjacent to Asia and being a Western country allied to the US and UK. In my mind, there is no trade-off. Australia should both live the Asian dream and be the staunch Western ally, and it is uniquely positioned to do both. The key is for the nation to develop the diplomacy skills needed to manage these objectives compatibly, and not be forced to choose between them. I have learned from years in Asia that soft political skills are the most valuable for dealing with major powers or long-term balance. Most Asian nations deal with each other thus, whereas Australia is often blunt or needlessly confrontational in foreign dealings. There is complacency in Australia too, since the economy didn't face a single quarter of negative growth for over twenty years, until COVID-19.

My journey into Australia as a Western Muslim has thrown up a now familiar challenge for my career, which is that of establishing myself in a new market. In Australia this has been more difficult than expected, more because I am a foreigner without local history and less because I am a Muslim or a person of colour. Integration into Australia's corporate and government world as a trusted adviser benefits from having a shared history, and it may take a few more years before I reach that point. In 2019 we moved to Melbourne, so that I can be closer to clients, our children can grow up in one of Australia's most multicultural environments, and Rehana can settle into a career, something she has not had continuity with over the past decade. Having worked in eighty-five countries, I stay involved with global projects too, to keep my hard-earned worldwide base of experience up to date.

How I manage my sons' cultural upbringing takes me back to my own experience as a child. Our children, like my wife and I did during our respective childhoods, attend a school that exposes them to a wide range of subjects, a multicultural class and a variety of learning environments in school, outdoors and in camps. Both our sons attend a faith-based school. Not a Muslim school but an Anglican one. We chose this school not because it was faith-based but because we felt it was secular and open-minded and driven by a curiosity to learn. School will not satisfy all of our boys' needs for wider exposure, not least because we live in a fortunate country where exposure to poverty, disease, urban congestion and social hardship is limited.

Hence personal connection to the world is important to us. We take our children to visit their maternal grandparents often (in Brisbane) but we also make regular trips to a diverse range of places such as the UK, India, Indonesia and Bangladesh, some of which have important family roots for them too. We encourage debate about cross-cultural topics. For religious instruction, we encourage but do not force our children to observe Islamic rituals such as prayer or fasting. We pray at home several times a day, and the children are left to join in of their own choice. Messing around during prayer is still fully tolerated since they are at a young age.* We do not encourage our children to fast since they are too young, though our elder son fasted once or twice in the Ramadan that just passed.

From some perspectives, Australian Muslims appear to be under the spotlight a little more than their counterparts in other Western countries. Muslims certainly are a newer brand of immigrant compared to the US or the UK. Many like to think that Australia's story of Muslim immigration parallels that of the UK minus fifty odd years, although I think this is too much of a simple generalisation. Where the UK's Muslims (such as my parents and to some extent us) integrated into the host nation before the rise of Islamism, most Australian Muslims are doing so after 9/11. This event fundamentally changed the nature of Muslim integration, accelerating the need to do so but at the same time making it harder to accomplish. Australia's Muslims are therefore sometimes exposed to a higher degree of suspicion and

---

* The movements involved in Muslim prayer (such as bowing down on the ground) present significant opportunity for young children to mess about.

have more to do to become as accepted as their counter-parts elsewhere.

At the time when I grew up in Britain in the 1970s and 80s, most English people were ignorant of the specific beliefs and cultural backgrounds of Muslims. Whether we immigrants were Muslim or Hindu mattered little when compared to the fact that we were non-white. My Hindu, Sikh and Muslim friends were all 'Pakis' in the eyes of English racists. We were connected by racism and shared cultures first, and hardly at all by faith. My parents could more easily mix with Hindu Indians, since they shared language and food cultures, than with Muslim Egyptians. Before the rise of Islamic Fundamentalism, there were few specific suspicions associated with Muslims in the UK. Any such stigma didn't scale up till well into the 1990s. The only exception was the odd, oblique historical reference to 'thieving Arabs' or 'Barbaric Muslims' (literally meaning bearded) handed down from centuries-old Crusader folk-lore. At the time of mass immigration into Britain and other European states, such as France, Belgium, Germany and Spain, the host nations were accustomed to the idea of former colonial nationals migrating to their shores. Indians, Pakistanis, Bangladeshis and West Indians galore flocked to Britain, Africans and Arabs to France, Africans to Belgium, Turks to Germany and Latin Americans to Spain. Whether they welcomed it or not, Europe's host peoples knew that assimilating immigrants went with the territory of having colonised many nations in their gloried past. Whilst the US never had a colonial collection the size of Britain's, it too knew that it was a post-war target for mass migration and had a welcoming culture for accepting economic migrants.

Australia is altogether different. Muslims are integrating here in an era of global suspicion of the faith, and many Australians are less aware of Islam than host populations in other Western countries. Consequently, there is under-standable unease about Muslim immigration at times, and about the differences between the Muslim religion and the culture of immigrants from Muslim countries.

'We don't want their food here,' was the response from the CEO of a major Australian dairy when asked what he thought of halal food in local supermarkets.

This CEO explained that he didn't want to see Middle Eastern meat imported here, as opposed to understanding halal is a term that describes a specific method for prepar-ing meat, in this case applied to Australian animals reared on Australian farms.

Australians' views of Islam are also influenced by what they hear about the faith from events unfolding across the world, and with the Middle East in turmoil, much of such news is negative. Every week in the Australian media there are stories of uprisings, suicide bombings, terror attacks and incidents across the Middle East and the Western world and in neighbouring Asian countries. The news is at times con-nected to Australia too, where Australians might be involved in jihadist groups, or where there are attacks involving Australian soldiers in action in territories such as Iraq and Afghanistan. Australian unease with Islam is often piqued by prominent politicians and the media.

The 2019 attacks in Christchurch across the 'ditch' in neighbouring New Zealand served as a signal that Muslims are also victims of terrorism. Around Australia this, as well as other events such as the killing of George Floyd under the knee of a police officer in Minneapolis, have surfaced debate about cross-cultural tolerance, diversity in cultural backgrounds and, most importantly here, the status of and respect for Aboriginal people in Australia. I don't think these issues are being debated enough yet – with the diversity topic in Australia continuing to be rooted in gender and LGBTI discussion. Whilst I fully support addressing gender and LGBTI topics, I think that in Australia it's time we got more diverse about diversity.

It is now over forty years since the 1979 Iranian revolution, and so we are almost halfway through the century that I predicted is needed for political systems in the Muslim world to reform from being authoritarian and unrepresentative regimes to inclusive, secular and progressive societies guided by stable and representative leadership. Such desired outcomes in Muslim countries won't come easily. Progress will be delayed by ill-informed, foreign-induced democracy experiments and propping up of dictatorships, and selfish motives to protect agendas such as security of energy supplies. Even once these impediments are addressed, it may take decades of internal turmoil before nations emerge with stable and transparent government systems.

Whilst the Muslim world is more in need of new thinking and knowledge than ever, the supply of new thinking is still scarce. After a golden age between around AD 800 to 1492, the Muslim world in the past few hundred years has produced relatively little by way of new scholarship or canons of thought on how to develop society – politically, economically or scientifically. Many Muslims reminisce about their ancestors' scholarship as being the source of great inventions and discoveries. They are usually referring to the work of thinkers such as Ibn Khaldun, Ibn Rushd and Ibn Sina (known in the West as Avicenni), noted for their amazing achievements in diverse fields, such as chemistry, mathematics, medicine and philosophy. But the motivation behind such posturing is generally fuelled by a rose-tinted nostalgia about Islamic history and a cultural jealousy towards the West. As a global community we lack a deeper recognition that the Islamic world desperately needs critical thinking today to keep progressing.

'What we need today are critical thinkers who force Muslims to think and not feel-good narratives that create comfort bubbles and inhibit thought. It is only through reading and engaging in philosophical discourses will the intellectual level of the Muslim community rise.'*

In my border crossings, I have seen three levels where the challenge for Islamic scholarship must be addressed. The first would be to improve how young Muslims in Western countries are taught about Islam, so that they are not presented with falsities around matters which are Islamic (where cultural practice, such as touching feet, is passed on

---

* Professor Muqtedar Khan of the University of Delaware in the Huffington Post, May 2015.

as being Islamic practice) and falsities about what is Western (due to cultural jealousy of the West). As I mentioned
briefly earlier, when I was a child, a religious scholar once
instructed my sister and me that man going to the moon
was untrue, some sort of *Capricorn One** type fiction to fool
us about how advanced America is. The scholar was equat-
ing space travel with being a 'Western' invention and therefore a Christian one not compatible with Islam. His explanation was laced with religious guilt induction, exhorting
us to reject lunar missions as fake as if our credibility as
Muslims depended on it. Quite the brainwashing for young
teenaged children. Fortunately, I didn't believe him even in the
moment.

'Do you think space travel is made up too, like when
rockets take off with astronauts in them?' I asked.

'That part is true,' came the considered response.

When he responded that he believed this to be true, I felt
the scholar did so since he'd otherwise need to convince us
that watching a rocket take off from Cape Canaveral was a
complete fantasy, something which we simply wouldn't
believe.

I complained to Amma that we were being brainwashed,
and she agreed. We faced much of this as children. Looking
at the instruction offered to my own children, I believe that
teaching has moved on significantly and that there is less of
the brainwashing today than when we were children. I

---

* *Capricorn One* was a 1977 movie about how the US government made up fake news
to show astronauts had landed on Mars once it had failed to launch the real manned
craft for the mission.

would expect that many, though by no means all, religious teachers who provide instruction to Muslim children are more open-minded and knowledgeable today about accepting Western progress as their progress too.

There is another part to being taught better too, which is to address the conflation of Islam with Arabic. I don't believe this has changed considerably since when we were taught how to read the Quran and pray in Arabic years ago. Today, young Muslim children (especially those who are not from Arabic-speaking families) are still memorising prayers off by heart in Arabic without much understanding of their meaning, and are not necessarily being made aware of the differences between faith as a concept and Arabic as a preferred medium for much of the faith.

My second observation is that Muslim communities must encourage Islamic teaching in schools to be more multidisciplinary, so that religious studies undertaken by young Muslims can set them up to advance in fields beyond purely doctrinal ones. Subjects such as politics, economics, finance, history, mathematics and science, to name a few, should be as important to the curriculum for Islamic schools as teaching Quran or Sunnah. Too many 'madrassahs', that is Islamic schools, whether in Muslim countries or in the West, focus on traditional teaching of the Quran and Sunnah (the teachings of the Prophet) and have limited or no focus on subjects from other faculties. In fact, many madrassahs (and parents who send their children to them) discourage the pursuit of other subjects as being a distraction from religion.

Reforming this would result in Muslims receiving a more balanced education for adjusting to Western life, and also enable them to advance in more fields. Many schools of thought, such as Wahhabism, see breadth as a distraction and focus narrowly on applying religious strictures literally. Aside from stifling intellectual curiosity, Wahhabi-style thinking is forcing young Muslims into a binary worldview, where you are either with Islam or with the West. My experience of advising the Islamic school in London indicated that there was a challenge in the UK, with some schools at risk of not being encouraged sufficiently to give priority to a wider range of subjects. Graduates from such schools emerge often not equipped to take their learning and apply it into a wide range of vocational fields beyond religious jobs in mosques or teaching in Muslim schools.

Wahhabi-inspired narrow-mindedness contradicts the spirit of classical Islamic thought, much of which was multidisciplinary and developed in cosmopolitan cities such as Baghdad, Cairo, Cordoba and Florence. Thought in these cities was also culturally collaborative, involving Muslim intellectuals working closely with Christians and Jews. In this age of unrepresentative governments in much of the Muslim world, political influences are headed in the opposite direction, with some political parties' targets being to influence the thinking of the mass population.

At least at tertiary level institutions both in Western countries as well as in Muslim countries, there is some progress. Aligarh Muslim University in India, Government

College in Pakistan and BUET* in Bangladesh are examples of multidisciplinary and high-quality secular universities aimed at students who are principally Muslim. Aligarh was established in 1875 as a Mohammedan college by Sir Syed Ahmed Khan in northern India. It was fashioned on Oxbridge and since becoming a university in 1920, has educated Indian Muslims in a wide range of subjects beyond religious studies and produced many graduates who excelled in diverse fields, such as politics, law, science and the military. Aligarh's notable alumni illustrate the breadth of subject coverage, and include Saeed Jaffrey and Naseeruddin Shah (actors), Khwaja Nizamuddin and Liaquat Ali Khan (politicians) and M. A. K. Pataudi (Indian Test cricket captain).† In recent years, Aligarh was ranked 2nd amongst India's law schools and 8th in medical schools,‡ showing that it is still highly relevant as a Muslim university producing qualified professionals in diverse fields.

There are many respected Islamic studies institutes across the Muslim world, including Cairo University and Al Azhar University in Cairo, plus numerous universities in places such as Morocco, Saudi Arabia, Turkey, Malaysia, Jordan and Palestine, with deep coverage of topics, such as finance, jurisprudence and law, economics, politics and history where academics and practitioners from these institutions are taking their societies forward with important contributions to industry as well as society.

---

* Bangladesh University of Engineering and Technology

† My great uncle General M. A. G. Osmani studied Geography at Aligarh graduating in 1938. Mohammed Ali Jinnah, founder of Pakistan, was a graduate of Aligarh.

‡ *India Today*, 2017

Lasting uplift in how Islamic studies contribute to global civilisation may ironically come from the West though, since it is in numerous Western centres of thought that many ground-breaking Muslim thinkers reside. The scholarship of Islamic thinkers in the West is, bit by bit, eclipsing the traditionalist thinking that emanated from countries such as Saudi Arabia and India in the past two hundred years. To name a few universities in the UK – Birmingham, Leeds, Oxford, Cambridge and Edinburgh – these offer established Islamic Studies-related courses with a tradition of intellectual rigour which is in line with the wider reputation of these universities. In North America, McGill University in Montreal, and Georgetown, University of California in Los Angeles, Boston College, Emory and University of Texas at Austin offer well-recognised Islamic Studies courses. However, the total number of postgraduates produced by these North American universities numbered less than thirty just a few years ago,* so it does appear that we are in the early stages of the emergence of a recognised Western-educated cadre of Islamic thinkers who will help shape better adjustment of Islam in the West.

Many Islamic institutions in Asia and the Middle East are less used to the type of open, unadulterated intellectual enquiry we see in places such as Oxford, Harvard or University of California, Berkeley. Some institutions in the Muslim world, such as in Qatar, are making serious efforts to establish such cultures of thinking themselves. In another

---

* According to various US university course reviews, the top 10 US universities for Islamic studies produced some 20 graduates in 2015.

sixty years, it is therefore possible that Islam will have reformed itself with a major following in the East, but with its intellectual momentum generated by scholars in the Western tradition. Today there are few Muslim scholars or intellectuals who are regarded as contributing significantly to a specific field. There are few inventions, standards or patents which emanate from the research work of Muslims or Islamic institutes, although there are numerous Muslims in Western countries who provide inspiring leadership in other fields including politics, journalism, the law, economics, medicine, culture and other creative industries.

My third point is related to the development of better secular, non-religious education in Muslim countries, especially primary and secondary education, that will in the long term do much to ease the adjustment between Islam and the West. This is a bigger topic than that of my border crossings or journey as a Western Muslim but is the type of contextual development that over the next sixty years gives us all a better chance of having a more adjusted world where Islamic and Western civilisations are far more intertwined and collaborative.

Thirteen

Return to Origin

Barely wider than our shiny white Toyota Corolla, the slithery track that winds into Sonarpur from the Sherpur–Sylhet trunk road goes on for an eternity. The village is only three kilometres from the oblique and sloped turning that comes off the highway, but the narrowness of the road, the flatness of the land around us and the absence of an urban skyline makes the distances appear logarithmically longer. After years of waiting, I am on my way to the village where my father's family has its origins and where Abba himself grew up. At first my uncles were thunderstruck by the idea that their nephew wished to spend a night in Sonarpur, but today I am happy that both Mumtaz and Jamal Chachas have decided to accompany me. As we trundle along over the bumps, I recall from years ago the meeting of UK-based Sonarpur villagers that my father once organised in East London's Brick Lane.* I had just left university and started

---

* A focal point for London's Bangladeshi community.

work and, doing nothing much that day, had decided to give Abba some company. The purpose of the meeting was to raise funds from punters to put down a tarmac covering on the three-kilometre grit track that connected our village to the main trunk road. We collected pledges for over £40,000 in less than an hour.

'What does the young man do, Shahee Bhai?' one of the former villagers asked, putting his arm around my shoulder, as we walked out of the meeting and into the late afternoon glare of an English summer's day.

'He works at a "company",' Abba smiled back.

I had rather hoped my father might explain how prestigious my place of work was, or that I had graduated with a Master's degree from Cambridge, and prior to that a Bachelor's degree from Oxford. But this would not have been his style.

'Oh. A company!' the old man muttered. 'You must be proud. Good on you.'

We cut through the bustling hutment of Burungabazar, on the road that that meeting in Brick Lane years ago had raised precious funds for. Our car scrapes past goods held out by staring hawkers and past narrow shopfronts displaying dusty plastic toys, fresh fruit and essential medicines, touchable through our open windows. Then, abruptly, the market sounds give way to a vast landscape of silent paddy fields and parched river inlets, their soil cracked after months of dry winter sun. We stop so that I can take a picture of a rickshaw wobbling its way down an uneven track. Children stop and giggle as I focus my camera; what is European artistic to me appears Bangladeshi ordinary to them.

'Vote for Makbul. Makbul Bhai is our friend,' reads a slogan that has been spray-painted in neat Bengali lettering onto the side of a power transistor cabin, this being one of the more recent villages to have been wired up under Bangladesh's rural electrification programme. The poster of Makbul strangely casts my mind back to the pictures of Maronite Christian politicians hanging off telegraph lines on the climb up into Bcharré.

'Tufael, look, all this belonged to your family once,' remarks Mumtaz Chacha wistfully with a generous wave of his arm through a ninety-degree arc, a hint of melancholy in his scratchy voice.

Of the eight siblings in my father's line, Mumtaz Chacha is the one immediately younger to Abba. In their youth, it was these two pioneering young brothers, Mumtaz and my father, who left the family nest to go out and earn a living to support the younger ones. Their actions back then were acts of immense courage, venturing out as they did from a cosseted village life which had sustained the family for generations. Bar the occasional overseas trip, Mumtaz stayed his whole life in Bangladesh, to build a monumental career as a jute planter and producer, rising to the lofty post of General Manager of the world's largest jute mill employing some 100,000 people. Now a bearded and wise-looking old man of dignity and grace, I recall a picture of him from the mid-1960s, dressed in a fancy white suit and shades, and holding a tennis racket. For my father, who barely spoke any English at the time but had decided to leave the country altogether and go to London, travelling by a mixture of aircraft and ship, leaving Sonarpur behind must have been a little daunting. Knowing his penchant for adventure and the desperation many young men had to just get out and be free, I am not too sure the migration would have phased him too much.

For all the years of hardship they would have endured after leaving the family fold, the emotions Sonarpur evokes in my uncle Mumtaz's heart today must be complex, combining the nostalgia of grand times, the hüzün of the family's decline and the sacrifice of hard labour earning money to support his family. Born in a generation where we are unaccustomed to the culture of financing the upbringing of brothers, sisters and cousins, Abba's (and his brothers') are experiences that I cannot properly empathise with. Looking across the swathes of paddy field that once belonged to my grandfather, I choose not to reply to Mumtaz Chacha's rose-tinted sentiments about the once gloried ownership of this beautiful and fertile land. Now is not the moment to confront the family's history. I savour the moment for when finally I will get to see Sonarpur, soon now.

'Tonight will be the first time a member of the Chowdhury family has spent a night there in almost fifty years,'* Chacha announces.

When the Chowdhurys left behind their life of lorded mastery in Sonarpur, they sold their land and palatial

---

* Apart from when some relatives fled here to take refuge for a few nights from the atrocities carried out by the Pakistan army during the 1971 civil war.

home, leaving no place to stay. The only option of returning to the village would be to sleep in the home of a former subject, which for most Chowdhurys had always meant much humiliation.

'Chacha, I want to wake up in Sonarpur, to see it in the morning mist. Just like Abba would have done when he was a kid. To see this mist, I have to wake up there after a night's sleep. I have to undo my mosquito net, open up the curtains and look out of a window,' I had remarked to my uncles last week when explaining why I had to stay one night.

Now, as I notice the sadness in my elder uncle's eyes, I realise the deeper symbolic nature of what we are doing. My visit to the village will pass by as a flight of curiosity and soon I will be back in London, but to my uncles this is an act of bravery, borne of a willingness to face their past and the humiliation of their departure.

'I am sorry you are having to do this,' I confess, examining the wiriness of my uncle's long, white beard. 'It is all because of me.'

'No. It is time to do this now. Let us enjoy it,' he replies, patting my knee.

We can neither see nor hear the main road we left behind fifteen minutes ago and my phone shows a solitary bar of radio signal. Cut off from the rest of civilisation, for the next twenty-four hours I will be in a different world.

'Where do you live?' one of the men asks as I wait on the veranda of the home of a 'Londoni', who is back from Stoke Newington for the holidays with his son and new daughter-in-law.

A short man, he looks up at me through quick, agile eyes whose dark pupils contrast with his light skin and electric blue polo shirt. He looks a sprightly character, probably in his early sixties. I survey his hands and cannot help but stare at his extraordinarily large and bulbous fingernails.

'I live in the UK. In London,' I reply.

'London. Is London the UK? Manchester is the UK,' he remarks rather oddly.

A couple of villagers look on. One of them is toothless and with dark, sun-blackened skin.

'They are both cities within the UK. London and Manchester,' I answer, not wishing to confront the man over his confusion about British geography.

'Manchester is the capital of the UK,' he announces, with a hint of pride.

I ask him which is his house in the village.

'I don't live here. I am just visiting my brother.'

'Oh, where do you live?'

'Manchester.'

'Ah,' I continue. 'How long have you lived in Manchester?'

'Since 1965.'

'What did you do there?' I guess he is retired, wondering how it is possible for him to have lived there for fifty years and still think it is England's capital. But then again my context is entirely misplaced. Many of these folks exist on a plain where world events, general knowledge and consumption of Western culture isn't their focus. Theirs is a single-minded existence to earn and save money, and send it home.

'I worked in a factory,' he explains, gesticulating with his fascinating bulb-fingered hands, which I guess must have become misshapen from manual labour, operating the particular Manchester machine tool that he would have worked on.

'I used to play with your Redwan Chacha, may God rest his soul. This is Ganga,' he continues. 'He and your father used to play together when they were kids.'

Ganga is a tall, wiry man and must be about the same age as my father would have been today. He has been looking on, his teeth shining in contrast to his chargrilled, tight skin. As we shake hands he whips off his woolly Nike cap to reveal a short crop of bristly white hair, sticking up and pointing to the sky above.

He points to a corner of Sonarpur, a settlement covering some dozen square kilometres, mostly flat, open paddy field and dotted with a few clusters of densely populated settlement. The area is connected together by trodden-down pathways, muddy when it rains, stagnant ponds and watering holes, numerous mosques and a single tarmac track which can be used by cars and trucks.

'That, over there, ju . . . just there,' Harun, one of the villagers, points to a short pontoon in the distance that straddles a narrow waterway. 'Your f . . . father used to jump off there when he was a ch . . . ch . . . child going to school.'

'Mati taan dise re! The soil pulled him here! It tugged at his heart, and here he is,' pronounces Ganga gleefully to the other villagers who sit with me on the veranda at Imtiaz Ali's house later in the evening.

I haven't felt better about Sylhet ever, than I do today. Here in the village, away from the closed feeling of the town, Sylhet feels free and open. There is a subtle chill in the Sonarpur air tonight. There is no electricity this evening. Out of the darkness I can see the banana leaves swaying quietly as we sit on the outer of the two verandas of Imtiaz's house, this one reserved for use by guests. Imtiaz Ali lives in Mile End, London and his father used to be my grandfather's cook. Imtiaz himself was my father's attendant during his short career as a forester in Mymensingh before Abba moved to the UK, and he followed Abba in the 1960s once he had arranged a job and the necessary immigration papers. The Ali house is regarded as the grandest in the village, occupying two acres including a vast pond in front. It sits on the site which used to be the Chowdhury home and retains the original layout. With dilemmas as to where to put me for the night, evidently after much consultation the village murubbi have determined it would be fitting for me to stay here.

Helpfully, it is one of the few houses in Sonarpur with a modern flushing toilet, though I am sure they couldn't have known about my desperate experiences with hole-in-the-ground toilet visits during childhood trips to Sylhet. As it happens, my hosts have gone to meticulous lengths to ensure my comfort, including buying new bedding and evidently employing someone to spend hours scrubbing that toilet clean. Its cracked blue porcelain bowl sparkles. A gas lantern, or 'lemton' in the vernacular, hanging from the ceiling sways gently in the breeze, hissing as it throws out a

blue-white light across the veranda, cutting the dewy darkness that envelopes us. Ganga sits close to it and his expressive face is lit up, accentuating the contours of his sharp
nose and full lips. The shadow thrown on the wall behind
him is only slightly darker than his face. He and about
thirty other villagers stare at me, waiting. A number of the
men either side of him have a muffler tied around their
heads to keep the cold air away from their ears. They look
bizarre, as though they have tied their heads to their bodies
to stop them from falling off. Out on the veranda we can see
the moonlit sky and the branches of tall palm trees moving
in unison with the evening breeze.

'Oi oi, mati hasao tan dise,'* agrees another of the villagers
in 'khati' village Sylheti.

'It is going to take an effort to engage them in conversation,' I think, wondering what the options are to stimulate
and include them quickly.

'So how do you spend your days and evenings?' I ask
generally, engaging eye contact with as many as I can.

I inject a heightened sense of energy into my voice and it
has the desired impact, since several speak out all at once,
only to fall silent again to avoid interrupting the others.

'Why don't you start?' I ask one of the younger-looking
guys, a rickshaw puller who explains how his day consists of
beginning work at seven and finishing at around dusk.

We perform the usual calculation, and the answer interestingly yields that here in the village the rickshaw wallah's

---

* Sylheti for 'Yes, yes, the earth really has pulled at him.'

income is typically about a third less than in town, and so on a good day he earns the equivalent of about two dollars.

'I lived in Jeddah for a year, and worked there, till I got found out and deported,' says another, grabbing his moment to address everyone with something interesting. 'I spent five days in jail and then was sent back home.'

'Wallahi.* How was it, in jail? Were they bad to you?'

'No,' he beams, looking to his left and right as he continues. 'They were great! They treat you really well, give you nice clothes to wear, and the food is fantastic.'

A few chortles ring around the villagers, now gathering into a bigger crowd on Imtiaz's veranda. The lit end of a cigarette glows sharply in the darkness, the burning tobacco almost audibly roasting its way through its white casing, the ruddiness of the butt end deepening as the smoker inhales. The conversation starts to flow and finally the gates between us begin to open up. The villagers speak with a lyrical lilt and the smoker joins in, now flicking his ash away casually as he shares his own story. Many say they are too old to work and cannot do anything now, others use the opportunity to vent their frustrations or to voice their needs for assistance, sensing that I may be a potential source of support.

As the voices pipe up, some out of the darkness since they are out of reach of the gaslight that burns in the middle of the veranda, I think about how our lives are so different yet, but for my father moving from here to Britain, could have been so similar. I just have to look at Mumtaz or Jamal

---

* Roughly equivalent to saying 'My God!'

Chacha to see that, given how different they are to me, or to my father. I see curiosity in the villagers' eyes, probably because they too are wondering the same.

'I am a tin worker and I fell off a roof last year and cracked my ribs.' As he starts to lift up his shirt, Ganga reaches across and stops him, while his mates snigger blokeishly at the imagined clumsiness of this unfortunate accident.

'So now I cannot do heavy work any more. I would be so grateful if you could . . .'

'No.' Firmly Ganga cuts him off mid-sentence, giving him a disapproving look. 'Not now. Not here.'

The village imam has come and sat on one of the benches right across from me. Dressed in a long tunic and Arab headdress, he greets me politely in Arabic.

'Kifak ya habibi? We'in taskun?' I ask him in Arabic dialect, meaning 'How are you my friend? Where do you live?'

'Ana Mahmoud Ali,' my name is Mahmoud Ali, he replies.

Mahmoud hasn't understood my question but interestingly he realises it, telling me later as we walk under the moonlight that it is a shame how clerics like himself cannot speak Arabic. I relate to him the story of how Mustafa Kemal, later Ataturk of Turkey, visited a madrassah near Ankara once and was disappointed to find the teachers could not speak Arabic. I also share with him my own journey of how I have been learning Arabic, emphasising that I focused on conversational and modern Arabic not just Quranic, because I wanted to understand the language. Mahmoud Ali wants me to visit him tomorrow at the madrassah and look at their syllabus. I feel unqualified to do so, since even with a bit of Arabic language under my belt, I am not really qualified to be looking at syllabi, my knowledge of religion and its teachings being so shallow.

The men here are used to sitting through evenings doing nothing except chatting, clapping on mosquitoes, smoking and waiting for the electricity to come back. Their shoulders are more relaxed than when they first arrived tonight, and several have removed their sandals and are stretching their feet and rotating them at the ankles. Others yawn, relaxing and unwinding. One man slouches, flossing his teeth with the broken end of a matchstick. Most of these men are barely literate, only a handful have a mobile phone, and most do not have a TV set in their thatched, muggy homes. Of the three hundred homes in this settlement, only two have a news-paper delivered. I have no idea what time it is, and don't want to look at my watch in case it prompts people to think it is time to leave. I scan the forearms around me in the half-darkness and spot only one wristwatch, but it is too far away for me to see what hour the dial is showing.

'When my father died over twenty years ago in 1991, I missed him a lot . . . Well, for around a year or so it affected me. I was twenty-four,' I pause to swallow. 'Recently I have been remembering him a lot. I wanted to come and see his birthplace. And to see you.'

'Mati tanche reeee! Ekh taan dise! Ooohh the soil pulled him all right! One mighty tug!' says Ganga, showing the gap in his front teeth as he smiles in satisfaction at his pronouncements.

The rest hum in agreement. They emanate a kind of rural wisdom, as though they have seen all this before: the story of the ones who depart and the few who return. There is silence on the veranda.

'Doesn't anybody watch TV then, in the evenings?' I ask.

'TV? TV? My stomach is TV! If I can fill it, I have TV!' Ganga replies gregariously, and bursts into another hearty, self-congratulatory laugh.

We join him, loudly and in unison, awakening the village vegetation which is unaccustomed to such late night revelry. He repeats the line, rolling about on the bench like a wobbling egg as he laughs. With muffler wrapped around his ears, Nike top and worn out lungi, Ganga really looks the picture of a confused and entertaining comedian. Interestingly nobody raises an objection to TV on religious grounds, as one of my uncles did on another trip to Sylhet. Sonarpur does appear more liberal than the stifling atmosphere of Sylhet town.

'We . . . we . . . usually sleep by ni . . . ni . . . nine, and get up at five,' stammers Harun.

'OK, so would you like me to tell you about my days then? Something about my world?'

'Yes, tell us.' They are warming up now, and chattering amongst themselves a bit.

'Hold on, let's see now,' I reach into my knapsack, flip open my laptop and press on the keyboard, wanting to create some theatre, just like I do with my clients. Impatiently, I wait for the machine to come back to life, tapping my fingers on the machine. Pavlovian conditioning from years of running presentations and workshops, I cannot resist the opportunity to perform to the crowd.

'I am going to show you photographs of places I have been to this year. Do you like looking at photographs?'

The enthusiasm to see them is unbridled, uncomplicated by the attitude common in Sylhet town where many take a more conservative stance on photography, artwork and television. Contrary to the stiffer behaviour I have seen in the community at Hazaripur, here the folk seem more relaxed and liberal. There is laughter and speculation as I load up the programme and people wonder what on earth the computer contains.

We gradually work our way through a slideshow of images, covering destinations across Europe, the Middle East and Asia. We start with my New Year trip to Bangladesh, then Madrid and Seville, various places in Italy and Switzerland and several other locations. When they ask me what I do for a living, I say that I work for a 'company', a comment met with heavy moans of approval and pride. I advise them to look out for me on BBC News, talking about this, that or the other, saying that I have been on it quite a few times recently. A few of my audience adjust their seating positions to gain a better view of the computer screen, which throws out a brightness onto the dark veranda.

'It's Rome. Capital of Italy. Like Ar-rum in the Quran. Where the Prophet sent the letter to.'

Only one or two have heard of Rome, and my reference to the Quran doesn't help since nobody seems to appreciate the link with the Romans. They love the picture of the Bedouin of Wadi Rum in Jordan, and are intrigued as I explain how these nomadic desert folk are even poorer than most in this village, since they don't have housing, electricity or sewage and need to travel several kilometres to collect water.

'This one is Madinah, the dome of the Prophet's Mosque.'

'How did you get it? I thought you are not allowed,' one of the guys asks.

'I sneaked it,' I respond cheekily and they laugh.

'Maybe they'd have jailed you too if they caught you!'

'What else do you have inside your computer? Is your house in there?' asks one of the men. He appears confused as to the physics concerning the limits of what my computer can perform. But the crowd's ease with interacting with the digital technology is apparent, and they are consumed by the content and not bothered about the gadget.

'Yes, and an aeroplane too!'

Everyone else laughs while my questioner looks about, puzzled. It's well past nine, the Sonarpur bedtime. But nobody seems restless to move on.

'Are you getting bored? Isn't it time for you to go off to sleep?'

'No, no.' The response is unanimous and genuine. 'We want more. Take us with you in your computer, and we will see the world too.'

'Yes, I will take you with me and show you to the others,

just like you see them now,' taking implicit permission for some photographs tomorrow morning.

I decide to show them the shoe shiner from Rue Hamra in Beirut.

'Oh look, here is a man from Beirut, which is the capital of Lebanon.'

The men look on, waiting for me to explain more.

'He is a shoe shiner and works on the street.' My voice trembles as I wander into some photographic interpretation, not quite sure how this will pan out.

'What do you see?'

Initially there is silence.

'He has life. Attitude! You can see it in his eyes,' claims Ganga out loud, hitting the spot with his quick observations.

Wonderful. I love these men. They are unfettered by the limitations of their education or by the narrow outlook encouraged by village life and its lack of exposure to the outside world. I explain how the shoe shiner carries a Quran in his shirt pocket and plucks it out regularly to read from it. Mahmoud Ali, the village imam and I steal a quick glance at each other. We both smile knowingly. I look forward to spending time with him tomorrow.

We carry on going through the pictures. Hyenas cry out in the distance, squealing like little children hungry for milk. I miss my father now, holding back the tears as I press on with my presentation, accelerating as I pass through the final pictures. My hours and minutes here in the village are precious, reliving the times my father spent here. I know these moments will end as soon as I leave tomorrow, as abruptly as my time with my father did all those years ago when he died suddenly in a London hospital. Hardly did I get a chance to know him once I was a grown man.

'So this is my life.'

I explain more about my life today as we go through a final few pictures at a faster pace. Sensing the crowd's curiosity about my personal situation, I talk about how I married a few years ago and have two young sons, that we have in the past decade lived in London, Johannesburg, Cairo and Mumbai and now have moved east with bases in Jakarta and Brisbane, and that I still have a job which keeps me in an almost constant mode of travel. The revelation that I have two sons is duly acknowledged by the village faithful with patriarchal coughs and murmurs of satisfaction, noting that the Chowdhury name now proudly reassociated with this community will live on beyond me.

Finally we look at a picture of the wall that separates Israel from the occupied Palestinian territories. Its cold, grey cement and rough texture epitomises for me the harrowing and humiliating daily lives of the Palestinians. This, interestingly, is a story that they seem to know all about.

'I travel to these places because I want to be able to tell people at home what it is like,' I explain. 'It was very depressing when I went to Jerusalem and saw how the Palestinians are living now.'

'How is life for the Muslims in England?' It is the young man who defeated me in a quick game of carrom earlier today.

'Life is good. You can live and work in peace. There is

freedom and justice. If you earn money, nobody will take it away from you.'

'Are you allowed to pray freely?' he continues, leaning in.

'Sure, I pray anytime I want. I have been travelling the world for almost twenty-five years and can account for every one of the five daily prayers, may God forgive me, and only missed three days of fasts in a thousand.'

'Why did you miss the three?' he asks, concerned.

'Come on, give me a break, I was sick!'

Faces stare, eyes popping in and out of pools of light.

The men look on, some nodding out of politeness whilst others are engaged in understanding that the wider context touches all of us. They want to know more. Their silhouettes and faces belie a mixture of intrigue at this world outside theirs, and pride that one of their sons has traversed some of its many borders. I have only just arrived in Sonarpur, but in an instant these people look upon me as one of their own. Whilst it was barely sixty kilometres to travel here from Sylhet, the short drive this afternoon somehow represented the decades long journey I have taken across many border crossings in my life so far. As a child, I was rejected by both the Bangladeshi and the British sides of my life and at times struggled to feel a complete part of either. How I have been welcomed in Sonarpur today is a measure of how I have progressed in that journey as a Western Muslim, fully adjusted in the West and now fully accepted in the East. Perhaps more than ever before on this topic, I feel satisfied. I settle down into bed, carefully tucking in the mosquito net around the mattress edges and making sure it isn't too tight, as a stretched net can let a mosquito push its way in through the gaps. I snuggle in under the super clean quilt the villagers must have gone out and purchased before my arrival, and prepare for a chilly single night's sleep in the village.

'They say you are like your father,' the driver explains as we set off back to Dhaka the next morning. 'They said he too would come to the village, sit with everyone and chat about nothing in particular. They want you to come back.'

Acknowledgements

My story refers to many people and places which have influenced my life. For respect and privacy, I have masked many people and place names in the book. I refer to real names below.

My mother and father shaped the person I am today. My efforts in this book to appreciate how they raised me are a dedication to their memory. Please forgive me for all the times I argued and clashed with you. Despite all the indications to the contrary, they remained fiercely determined to ensure I knew my Bengali roots and Muslim beliefs and to give me a first-class English education. In this way, they opened up my perspectives to live a multicultured life. May Allah rest them both in peace and forgive them their faults. Rehana, my amazing wife, has without intermission supported this project. Her belief in me has on many occasions been the difference between my giving up and carrying on, not just with the book but with many other things too, and over the years she has suffered as much as or more than me as we have balanced the challenges of living itinerant lives around the world. My two incredible sons, Ehsan and Zaki, too young to fully appreciate the book, have enthused about its release and youthfully willed me on through the process to publication. Three of my journalist friends in India, Deepak Ajwani, Peter Griffin and Indrajit Gupta, brought me into the Forbes family and then introduced me to literary agent Mita Kapur of Siyahi, a hugely resourceful professional who at once loved my manuscript but also saw a path to profile and publish it. Mita led me to Charlotte Seymour at Andrew Nurnberg and Associates in London, the most detail-oriented and tenacious of agents. I thank my teammates at work and clients who have taken interest in the book's progress and supported me to publication, and my friends at Renata Limited and Pubali Bank Limited for their generous corporate support.

I thank my publisher Unbound and the team there led by Katy Guest, Georgia Odd, Anna Simpson and Emily Sweet, who put a great deal of energy into the publication, crowdfunding campaign and design. The Unbound team gave this book a chance: several others in the industry had asked the question 'Is he a member of Al Qaeda?' in considering the merits of taking on the story and selling it. The irony was not lost on us! I will remain forever grateful to the late Robert Fisk of the *Independent*, who provided timely inspiration and corrections through his commentary on my travels through various parts of the Middle East and who, due to his sudden and unfortunate demise in 2020, will not see the book in published form. Several others have reviewed sections or the entire script, shared invaluable perspectives and considerations or otherwise significantly influenced my thinking at important points of my journey including (but in no way restricted to) Ahmad Moualla, Andrew Blacknell, Andrew Feinstein, Dr Anwar Seedat, Aye Mon Nyein, David Marshall, Ekow Nelson, Elly Livingstone, Francis Plowden, Gabriele Taylor, Gamal Nkrumah, Gianfranco Giannella, Ghinwa Mamari, Gowher Rizvi, Gulnar Hasnain, Haroon Hassan, Inge Hansen, J. Gabriel Palma, Jameel Khan, Jim Egan, John Iberson, John Sender, Jon Gower, Kabir Yaqub, Kaiser Kabir, Khaleel Siddiqui, Kim Gillespie, Leo Martin, Matthew Levitt, Mike Dyson, Mohammed Imran, Mridul Chowdhury, Nigel Bowles, Dr Rana Mehta, Rebecca Cox, Reem al Botmeh, Revathi Shenoy, Rosemary Radcliffe, Rim al Attrache, Sabera Chowdhury and Samad Ali-Abdullah, Sara Hossain, Shahabuddin Hossain Munir (may God rest him in peace), Shakil Shaikh, Shenaz Seedat, Simone Sultana and Syed Akhtar Mahmood. I am grateful to the many others who have guided my journey, some of whom are referred to in the book.

Unbound is the world's first crowdfunding publisher, established in 2011.

We believe that wonderful things can happen when you clear a path for people who share a passion. That's why we've built a platform that brings together readers and authors to crowdfund books they believe in – and give fresh ideas that don't fit the traditional mould the chance they deserve.

This book is in your hands because readers made it possible. Everyone who pledged their support is listed below. Join them by visiting unbound.com and supporting a book today.

A.M.M. A'abad

Riyad Abbasakoor

Amr Abdallah

Sam Abusah

Sumeet Agarkar

For Ahdiya, Yusraa &
    Younus

Faraz Ahmad

Akeela Ahmed

Ameen Ahmed

Milad Ahmed

Ryan Ahmed

Vaseem Ahmed

Mobasser Ahsan

Arosh Ali

Shahzad Ali

Samad Ali-Abdullah

Hany Aly

Yusuf Ameer

Shafqat Anwar

Leoni Ardita

Omar Ashour

Emily Bamford

Andrew Beale

Amol Bhat
Ahmad Bhinder
Andy Blacknell
Andrea Boccotti
Celestine Bond
Harrison Bongiorno
Miles Bredin
Andy Brereton
Thea Caminada
Martin Carroll
Ian Carson
Ahmed Cassim
Mohamed Cassim
John Chan
Deepa Chaudhuri
Salatin Chawdhury
AbdulMumin Choudhury
Matiur Choudhury
Sulaiman Choudhury
Azhar Chowdhury
Barik Chowdhury
Ehsan Mohammad
    Chowdhury
Haneef Chowdhury
Mobin Chowdhury
Mohammed Chowdhury
Mohammod Chowdhury
Sadequa Khan Chowdhury
Sadiya Chowdhury
Shahneela Chowdhury

Shahzeea Chowdhury
Zaki Ali Chowdhury
Ziaul Chowdhury
Khawla Chowdhury Haque
Jill Clark
Mark Cockburn
Sten Coeur
Jo Conlon
Hayden Cooper
Ross Cormack
Janet Cox
James Crabtree
Aadila Dada
Rick Daly
Alastair Davidson
Eileen Davidson
Colman Deegan
Amela Delic
Sander den Hartog
Faizul Doola
Muhammad Doola
Farooq Dudhia
Fintan Michael Dudleston
Ravi Dugal
Snigdha Dutt
Jim Egan
Sherif El-Said
Atha Elahi
Mohamed Elharras
Romi Elsass

Shehmila Farooki

Brendan Francis

Robin Francis

Richard Francis-Sakai

Catherine Gardner-Elahi

Florence Gaudry-Perkins

Pamir Gelenbe

Subarno Ghosh

Kim Gillespie

Richard Gleed

Emma Glencross

Prasad Gokhale

Lawrence Goldstone

John Gooday

Jon Gower

Katy Guest

Yogita Gupta

Farzana Hakim

Philippe Hamam

Sharn Hannan

Inge Hansen

Asif Sami Haque

Rezaul Haque

Simon Haslam

Gulnar Hasnain

Haroon Hassan

Riaz Hassan

Anne Hayden

Layla Hazmi-Gomez

Sue Horlin

Robert Horndasch

Masud Hossain

Shammi Huda

Farzana Hussain

Syed N Hussain

Mona Hussein

Ikhsan

Salahdin Imam

Bassem Itani

Ravi Ivaturi

Ram Narayan Iyer

Vivek Jhamb

Anthony Jones

David Jordan

Ankur Kamalia

Neeraj Katariya

Hilary Kemp

Rishi Keskar

Jameel Khan

Reduan Khan

Monnujan Khanam

Ibrahim Husain Khatri

Fahmid Khondaker

Avneesh Khosla

Abu Kibria

Dan Kieran

Jonathan Kingan

Jennifer Klemm

Matthew Kuperholz

Jeffry Kusnadi

Yashin Latif

Allen Lee

Peter Kuek Kong Lee

Ferdy Leemput

Matthew Levitt

Imran Liaquat

Elly Livingstone

Rob MacAndrew

Siobhan Mackenzie

Farhad Mahbub

Syed Akhtar Mahmood

Osama Manzar

Peter Mastos

Mike McGrath

Doug McKenzie

Vivek Menon

Imon Miah

John Mitchinson

Tariq Modood

Moyukh Monsoor

Faizal Moosa

Michael Morgan-Curran

Matthias Muehlbauer

Soumen Mukerji

All Mulk

Myo Myint

Sivakumar N V

Steven Nagy

Carlo Navato

Ekow Nelson

Gerard Newman

Tenzin Norbhu

Mochammad Kiky Noviar

Marcus Nyholm

Zaahid Pandie

Justin Papps

Andrew Parker

Parvez & Anni

Alastair Pearson

Francis Plowden

Justin Pollard

Laura Pollard

Farhan Qazi

Abul Rahman

Fatima Rahman

Jubaidur Rahman

Mashid Rahman

Vivek Rao

Razin and Rivana

Paul Reilly

Shaheen Reza

Mike Robbins

Jason Romney

Sadhli Roomy

Sabera

Mehran Sami

Dipa Sarkar

Haytham Sawalhy

Anwar Seedat

Rehana Seedat

Shenaz Seedat

Shireeen Seedat

Yasmeen Seedat

Iwan Setiawan

Richard Shackcloth

Ben Shepherd

Sirajul Islam Shopan

Firdaus A Siddik

M-Khaleel Siddiqi
(Molvisb)

Rahima Siddique

GP Singh

Satjit Singh

Tully Smith

Dennis Smyth

Wendy Staden

Jonathan Stagg

Roary Stasko

Martin Stokie

John Studley

Mustafa Suleyman

Heri Supriadi

Aparnaa Suresh

Nick Swain

Ali Tahir

Mark Tan

Siewhoon Tan

Tanjina Tanni

Zaki Thompson

Jeremy Thorpe

Mike Turner

Syed A H Uddin

Zarrar Usmani

Paul Van der Aa

Vincent van Veen

Madhu Varshitt

Stephanie Volk

Masood Vorajee

Lisa Wagner

Chrisna Wardhana

Canan Weir

Andrew Wellington

Cameron Whittfield

Sacha Kurt Winzenried

Xinyuan Yao

Muhammed Yaqub

Nicole Yeong

Richard Young

Dina Zakkas

Asif Zaman

Nadeya Zaman

Nadia Zaman

Hadeya Dina Zaman &
Timothy Foster

Joe Ziskin

A Note on the Author

Mohammad Chowdhury was one of the first British-born Bangladeshis to study at Oxford, where he read Politics, Philosophy and Economics, following which he completed a Master's in Economics at Cambridge and, later on, executive training at Harvard Business School. Having worked in over eighty countries advising ministers and CEOs, Chowdhury is now a senior partner at a global consulting firm in its practice across Asia and Australia. He is recognised as a leading emerging markets technology expert by the BBC, the *Financial Times* and Forbes.

@mtchowdhury